The Taste of American Place

A Reader on Regional and Ethnic Foods

The Taste of American Place

A Reader on Regional and Ethnic Foods

Edited by
BARBARA G. SHORTRIDGE
and
JAMES R. SHORTRIDGE

ROWMAN & LITTLEFIELD PUBLISHERS, INC.
Lanham • Boulder • New York • Oxford

ROWMAN & LITTLEFIELD PUBLISHERS, INC.

Published in the United States of America
by Rowman & Littlefield Publishers, Inc.
A wholly owned subsidary of The Rowman & Littlefield Publishing Group, Inc.
4501 Forbes Boulevard, Suite 200, Lanham, Maryland 20706
www.rowmanlittlefield.com

PO Box 317
Oxford
OX2 9RU, UK

British Library Cataloguing in Publication Information Available

Library of Congress Cataloging-in-Publication Data

The taste of American place : a reader on regional and ethnic foods /
edited by Barbara G. Shortridge and James R. Shortridge.
p. cm.
Includes bibliographical references and index.
ISBN 0-8476-8506-3 (cloth : alk. paper). — ISBN 0-8476-8507-1
(pbk. : alk. paper)
1. Cookery, American. 2. Cookery, International 3. Food
consumption—United States. I. Shortridge, Barbara Gimla, 1943–
II. Shortridge, James R., 1944– .
TX715.T2127 1998
641.5973—dc21
97-52006
CIP

ISBN 0-8476-8506-3 (cloth : alk. paper)
ISBN 0-8476-8507-1 (pbk. : alk. paper)

Printed in the United States of America

♾ ™ The paper used in this publication meets the minimum requirements of
American National Standard for Information Sciences—Permanence of Paper
for Printed Library Materials, ANSI Z39.48—1984.

To our mothers and grandmothers,
who taught us to appreciate good home cooking.

Anna, Bertha, Clara, Harriette, Nelle, and Tekla

Contents

Section Two—Ethnic Foods

Section Three—Eating Out

Illustrations

Introduction

Food and American Culture

Barbara G. Shortridge and James R. Shortridge

Food is a sensitive indicator of identity and change in American culture. Everyone eats, of course, and the overall wealth and diversity of peoples in the United States have generated an unprecedented variety of food-stuffs from which to select. Each time we reach for even a snack, we are making a conscious decision that serves to define us. Is that choice determined by where we live within the United States? Yes, in part. Is it based on our ethnic background and that of others in our community? Yes, to some degree. As much as the advertisements for franchise restaurants and processed foods would like us to believe that we have a homogeneous national cuisine, we do not. Our diet is richly varied and constantly in flux.

We present in this volume a set of readings that express the diversity of eating habits across the United States. Social and economic issues are apparent in nearly every selection, but our focus is on current regional and ethnic patterns. Place matters, we argue; location is a variable that rivals class, gender, and race in its significance for understanding the postmodern world. As geographers we want to know what New Yorkers, Angelinos, and rural Kansans eat, and then why they select this particular fare. Intriguingly, such variations not only persist in this age of mass marketing, but actually seem to be growing in distinction and appeal. Geographers also integrate information on food habits with other aspects of cultural variation to create a more complete profile of the people who live in a given area. Such interests are not limited to one academic discipline, of course, and many of the essays that follow are written by anthropologists, folklorists, and sociologists. We based our selections on readability as well as subject content, and hope that you enjoy what we have chosen.

1

The first part of this introduction is intended primarily for the student, and the second for the instructor, but cross-reading is encouraged. The essays themselves are divided into three sections: regional foods, ethnic foods, and eating out. A bibliography of publications about food and American culture completes the book.

To the Student

Surveys show that people in certain regions of this country eat more lamb than beef. Residents of other places spread jam on their breads far more frequently than is the national norm, while people in still other locales consume more rice than potatoes. Discovery of such variation is fun for its own sake and can help to enrich travel experiences. The enjoyment is deepened by reflection on the causes of these behaviors. Each case is unique, of course, but the overall pattern involves an interplay of physical geography, culture history, and more. Let us provide some illustrations. Perhaps you live in a strawberry-growing area where pick-your-own patches are abundant. You are likely to be accustomed to eating fresh red berries warmed by the sun, and maybe the food provider for your family also puts a few quarts in the freezer as a wintertime reminder of their sweetness. These berries are an example of proximity guiding some of our food choices. Even with modern means of transportation, a location near a specialized agricultural producing area remains an important determinant of what is consumed. If you live near the ocean, you eat more fish. If you live on the Plains, you probably have tasted buffalo meat.

Environmental conditions, especially climatic ones, affect food choice in other ways, too. More carbohydrates in the form of potatoes, pasta, and bread are needed to maintain body energy during the long, cold winters of North Dakota than during the mild ones of Southern California. People in arid parts of the United States need more liquid per day than those in humid climes.

Ethnic heritage is a second important consideration in food choice. Perhaps you live in an area settled four generations ago by Scandinavians. Although you personally may have no relatives who came from Norway, and Norwegian Americans may no longer be the dominant cultural stock locally, nevertheless it is likely that you still have had to contend with jokes about lefse and lutefisk. Maybe you've even had the courage to consume these foods at a local ethnic festival or holiday celebration. Many foods that have come to be symbolic of regions today are holdovers from a time of widespread immigrant settlement. These dishes are varied, ranging from main courses such as pasties in the

Upper Peninsula of Michigan to snack items such as soft pretzels in Philadelphia. Often, however, this ancestral food is a dessert, the part of a meal most associated with special occasions and one of the easiest parts to replicate when recipes are handed down from generation to generation.

Now consider a different kind of ethnic experience. Perhaps your best friend in high school was of Vietnamese background. You were invited into her home for spring rolls and other delicacies, and, having been exposed to this food at an impressionable age, you continue to seek it out as an adult. Moreover, your Vietnamese American friend likely will reciprocate the experience and maintain her taste for the tacos, refried beans, and tamales that were served when she visited your home. Food interchange can occur with people of any age, but adoptions tend to be most rapid for teenagers. Young people often bring new food items and ideas home to their family unit and the process of experimentation and adoption continues from there.

Restaurants provide another vehicle for enlarging our range of food choices. Some of the best eating establishments in the Kansas City area are barbecue specialists, for example, with ribs that taste like heaven to their devotees. These businesses originated in the city's African American community, and once served only this clientele. Somehow, though (partly through the writings of Calvin Trillin in *The New Yorker* magazine), news of their quality began to spread. Now, when people from other parts of the country come to visit, they want to experience this regionally famous food, too. Kansas City barbecue is a good example of a food that has escaped from an ethnic association to become part of the general culture. Pizza, chili, and vegetable stir-fry are others. Many people now consider such dishes to be genuinely "American," and some purists agree. The experts point out that significant differences almost invariably exist between the current form of these foods and what they were in their ethnic past.

Patterns of personal food consumption are anything but static, and this is another part of the reason social scientists find them interesting and revealing. Consider how easily change can happen in your own life. You can experiment in public by ordering a new item off a restaurant menu. In the privacy of your home, you can add unfamiliar ingredients to familiar soups or casseroles or put together an Ethiopian dinner from a new recipe book. By temporarily changing diets in such ways and trying out varied tastes, new dishes eventually come into our personal foods inventory. Modern Americans have no lifelong commitment to a cuisine comparable to that which may bind us to a given religion or language.

Jon May recently has observed a nice example of food fashion in England (1996). Conspicuous consumption of exotic dishes is being used there as a way for young professional people to claim social status. The process involves knowing right and wrong ways to prepare, consume, and order various items; the difference between authentic and inauthentic ingredients; and which ethnic cuisine is about to become fashionable. Such behavior is common enough in England to have produced an epithet for its adherents—"foodies"—and it exists in the United States as well. The Stephen Frenkel reading on the espresso coffee movement explores this issue.

Beyond their direct involvement in social movements, foods also can be good markers for several important, but somewhat nebulous, general trends in society, ways for researchers to document change. We used patterns of rice consumption to chart the spread of the counterculture movement across the nation in the 1960s and 1970s, for example (see the Shortridge and Shortridge reading). Today, people are writing about a more general back-to-the-land movement, an attempt to reconnect with nature. Several obvious indicators for this involve food: numbers of home vegetable gardens, sales in farmers' markets, and rates of consumption for fresh and locally grown produce. Sales of horticultural products through time also might prove useful in this regard, as would data on the proliferation of retail nurseries, the number of gardening columns in newspapers, and the appearance of experts to help those who have never gardened before. As geographers we would especially like to know where home gardening has always been the custom and where it has expanded rapidly. With such information we could develop ideas about which aspects of place seem to lead to an embracing of grow-it-yourself ideals. Unfortunately, no one, to our knowledge, has compiled or worked with such data. In fact, we wanted to include a section on home gardening in this book, but could not because of a shortage of relevant analytical materials.

Lack of Food Studies

It has always amazed us how little work has been done on food by social science- and humanities-oriented scholars. The billions of words written by cookbook authors, by food writers in the popular press, and in personal accounts or family histories are not to be ignored, of course, but these sources rarely are well documented or contain much analysis. A clue to understanding this absence of solid research studies, perhaps, is the similar lack of attention to popular or vernacular music, sport, and housing. These subjects all lie at the core of everyday life, and, as such, may have seemed too mundane to be worthy of attention by some intellectuals. Accordingly, we have in the libraries many studies on bank architecture but few on horse stables, many on chef-prepared gourmet food but few on corned beef and cabbage.

All the blame for the scarcity of good studies on food should not be laid at the feet of intellectuals. Another issue, somewhat surprisingly, is a scarcity of data. Imagine first an idealized set of information: food diaries from the entire American population of everything eaten for a year, everyone's grocery receipts or a store-by-store compilation of products purchased during a specific time period, restaurant menus and receipts, and a listing of every home cook's repertoire of dishes prepared for ordinary eating and for special occasions. Accompanying this would be statistical data on socio-economic and locational variables for purposes of correlation and a promise to repeat the inventory at regular five-year intervals in order to track trends.

Such data do not exist; neither does anything that even approaches them. This is ironic in a way, for the federal government long has collected equivalent information on food production through their detailed censuses of agriculture. We know down to the county where the tomatoes in this country are grown, but have only a vague idea of where they are eaten. Some government data have been published on food distribution systems, but rarely with information on destinations (we explore an exception to this generality in Shortridge and Shortridge 1989).

Direct, government-compiled information on food consumption is not totally absent. The U.S. Department of Agriculture has conducted a national food consumption survey in 1936, 1942, 1948, and then roughly every ten years beginning with 1955. Based on a complex sampling procedure, their most recent report for 1987–88 received responses from 6,000 households across the country regarding the use of particular foodstuffs during a three-day period. The answers were converted to nutritional equivalents for analysis, and used officially to assess consumption behavior and dietary status for school-lunch programs and similar projects. These national surveys are tantalizing, but most scholars agree that their sample size is not large enough to reveal important social and economic variations, and that their coarse, four-part division of the United States masks key regional patterns as well.

Given the absence of a detailed national census, what are the alternatives for a data-minded food scholar? The best potential sources for countrywide information are individual food-processing companies, marketing associations (such as Sunkist or the National Pork Producers Council), and large supermarket chains. All of these groups maintain details on the distribution and sales of their products, but, so far, we have not heard of any of it being released to outsiders for analysis.

Instead of letting a lack of detailed national data inhibit research at this nascent stage of cultural food studies, we suggest that students concentrate instead on the eating habits of a particular group of people. Many of the readings in this book involve data-collection techniques that can be replicated in other locales and demonstrate how local materials can be linked to larger issues in American culture. Another need is for individual projects that focus on the personal and the subjective. Conduct interviews; look at reflections of food in American films, fiction, and paintings; explore nontraditional sources of information. Experience the place; observe the landscape; and start asking people what they ate today, where they procured this food, who they ate it with, and what they were doing while eating. It does not take long to create a regional or ethnic portrait in this way.

Food As a Symbol of Identity

Research on the cultural aspects of food has increased markedly during the 1980s and 1990s. A growing interest in American vernacular issues, in combination with greater sophistication in thinking about cultural meaning, has prompted activity by small groups of people within anthropology, folklore, geography, history, and sociology. Most of their work stresses the symbolic nature of food. Some of it concentrates on issues of celebration, such as how plum pudding adds meaning to Christmas gatherings; some of it considers the evolution of food associations, such as why cereal and orange juice have come to represent breakfast. Issues of age, class, gender, and race represent a third focus, while still another (our emphasis in this book) is regional and ethnic diversity. These concerns all are highly interconnected, of course, so much so that overarching themes are difficult to discern at times. For the study of food and place, however, a unifying issue is a concept called cultural identity. This idea—how people go about constructing a meaning and context for themselves in the rapidly changing world of the late twentieth century—is developed in the paragraphs below and weaves its way through many of the following readings. Food, it is clear, plays an important and growing role in the process.

Regional Identity

To begin thinking about the relationship between place and identity, consider for a moment the collective meaning of Disney World, Dodge City, Gettysburg, the Golden Gate Bridge, the Grand Canyon, Hollywood, the Statue of Liberty, and the White House. These places have become popular stops for vacationing Americans (as well as foreign visitors) not so much by virtue of their own physical characteristics, but because they serve as symbols for the country as a whole. Such locales have been much studied in this regard, and deservedly so. They are important repositories of positive feelings about ourselves and of who we are as a nation. A parallel process operates at smaller scales, with individuals seeking firmer attachments to their home regions and cities. We all want (and perhaps need) things in our community to brag about, to participate in, and to cheer for. In the past, when people had deeper ties to place through the residence of several generations in individual towns and a more locally based general mentality, special symbols of belonging at this scale perhaps were not necessary. Today, though, they are.

Many studies show that Americans have paid for their mobile, fast-paced lifestyles with growing feelings of angst and anomie. We miss having a sense of community and region to provide an anchor of identity. One upshot of this need is a renewed commitment to experiencing things close to home. We call this phenomenon neolocalism, and see it manifested through such diverse expressions as reenactments of historical events, purchases of books on state history, interest in community political contests, patronage of microbreweries, and, of course, consumption of regional foods. "Locally grown produce" has become the culinary buzz phrase of the 1990s, and the enthusiasm extends to foodstuffs manufactured in the vicinity (for example, potato chips, honey, and popcorn), to food festivals, and to special restaurant items. The ultimate occurs when a particular food assumes the role of an icon for a place, as have baked beans for Boston, cheese for Wisconsin, and gumbo for southern Louisiana.

We recently began a project on the Midwestern states that may serve as one possible model for neolocalist food study. The region was selected partly as a challenge, since people repeatedly had told us either that "there's nothing distinctive about Midwest eating" or that "it's just Jell-O and casseroles." Through a mailed questionnaire we asked respondents to prepare a hypothetical menu for out-of-state guests, a meal that was typical and representative of their part of the state. A reading of the more than eight hundred answers as they arrived soon made it clear that a typical Midwestern meal indeed exists. It consists of beef (roast or grilled steak), with potatoes (mashed with gravy or baked), corn on the cob, green beans, and apple pie. Although we have yet to do a detailed analysis and mapping, several intriguing regional variations also stand out, including a turkey preference area in Minnesota; a large pork-chop zone in central Illinois, Iowa, and eastern Nebraska; a tendency for cakes to replace pies in the western Plains states; and, yes, even a Jell-O and casserole belt in the Dakotas.

Ethnic Identity

Cultural pluralism or melting pot? The conversations about which is the most plausible description for ethnic mixing in the United States have been ongoing now for over two centuries. Since these two views represent such antithetical stances, the real processes probably lie somewhere in between, and no one model is likely to encompass all interactions. An interesting recent trend, for example, is a renewed desire for ethnic affiliation driven by the same sense of alienation in modern American life that has sparked neolocalism.

Food offers an appropriate way to approach the complicated issues of ethnic differentiation in the 1990s because it is a part of culture that simultaneously is easy to retain and to alter. Retention is possible in that people may restrict their eating to homes and other private places so that no one need know the details of their diet. On the other hand, alteration of diets can occur in extremely short periods of time. Food is inexpensive and a nearly perfect vehicle for experimentation. Food also is one of the world's most time-honored ways of sharing. Borrowing one another's foodstuffs is neither assimilation nor pluralism, but a measure of the acceptance of diversity.

Look at what is happening in metropolitan ethnic restaurants today. In addition to a proliferation of cuisines beyond the classic triad of Chinese, Italian, and Mexican, one has the phenomenon known as fusion cooking. Under this concept, the flavors from several countries are combined into larger categories such as Caribbean, Mediterranean, South Asian, or Nuevo Latino. Unexpected combinations exist as well, including Creole-Chinese and Italian-Thai. When cooks carry such taste combinations into their homes, the blendings take on even more nuance. Although some people might argue that this fusion cooking is a sham because one can no longer derive the precise origin for the foods served, others would counter that the sources of most foods are vague and that such mixed cuisine represents not only a new American food, but also a new America in a much broader sense.

To the Instructor

Because everybody makes eating decisions at least three times a day, we guarantee that foodways will prompt spontaneous classroom discussion. What follows are suggestions for student activities that will raise awareness about the subject, lead to specific topics of concern to geographers and other social scientists, and introduce students to several data-gathering techniques. We have arranged the ideas into categories from which instructors may select as appropriate.

Food Awareness

Food Diary

As an early activity to get students started and focused we suggest a look at their own patterns of food consumption. Have each person keep a food diary to be shared with the class at the end of a given period of time (two weeks should be sufficient). Provide simple tally sheets with columns for time, food eaten, setting, and comments. Participants should include formal meals as well as snacks and beverages.

Students will complain about this activity—it takes too much time, they can't remember what they ate, it reveals too much about their private choices, and so forth. Make them do it anyhow because, in the end, they will know a lot more about food consumption and start asking informed questions. Remembering what you had to eat forty-eight hours ago is difficult (similar to remembering the weather) so encourage students to keep up with the task and make entries at least once a day, if not after each time they eat.

The food diary is a good basis for a discussion about current trends in food consumption. Pay particular attention to how many times participants eat outside of the home (or outside of a dormitory situation). Is there any pattern to the meals? Some students have told us that they always know which night to expect pot roast in their families. Do similar regularities carry over to their college years? Does anyone always have fish on Friday or Italian cuisine on weekends? Note the timing of the food events throughout the day. Do these time frames differ from those of the population at large? The context in which food is eaten also can be revealing. Is it typically alone in front of the TV or with a group? Are participants eating while they are doing something else? Finally, see whether gender differences exist in any of the responses.

Mapping of Local Restaurants

A second useful consciousness-raising device is to map public eating establishments. Start first with a campus-based survey using a map from the admissions office or parking service. As a class, plot the cafeterias and vending-machine facilities on this base (or a sketch map derived from it) using student recall or, if necessary, field reconnaissance to check out specific buildings. The exercise will prompt interesting discussions. The question of whether or not the contents of vending machines should be considered food may arise, for example, together with the fundamental one of how to classify campus dining facilities. The distinction between university-affiliated and private or franchise vendors also is important on several campuses these days, an issue that involves aesthetics and freedom of choice along with nutrition. Campus and peripheral areas are carefully zoned at the University of Kansas, for example, making privately owned restaurants rare. In contrast, street vendors park in front of the main row of buildings at the University of Vermont, giving students a wide set of lunchtime options. At project's end, students can observe whether or not certain areas of the campus are underserved with food; perhaps they can share the results of their survey with others as a step toward general campus improvement.

A related activity would be to map eating establishments for an entire city (or part of it depending on size). Again, an early, critical issue is a classification scheme: fast-food versus sit-down service, franchise versus privately owned, ethnic cuisines, and so forth. Depending upon time available, student interest, and the complexity of the urban setting, either a cognitive map created from student recollections or a more traditional rendering based on addresses from the yellow pages of the local telephone book is possible. This topic also could be subdivided and structured as group projects. Mapping such information should lead to a discussion of restaurant "neighborhoods." Are all the white-tablecloth establishments in one part of town? Are the Chinese restaurants together or interspersed among other ethnic businesses? Is the college population well served or is something missing? Where would you go on a date?

If this type of analysis is of interest to students, the project may be extended by a plotting of locations for national food chains. Maps that we have included in Appendix B of this volume for several bagel and coffee franchises can serve as examples of food trade areas, the one for Thai restaurants as an illustration of a newer ethnic cuisine. Data for such studies also are in the yellow pages of telephone directories (see the Roark and the Zelinsky readings), a resource available at many libraries either in traditional collections of printed volumes or in a CD-ROM version such as ProBiz. The same information is accessible through the Internet using the reference section of Yahoo! or other search engines. Remember that a simple counting of taco chain restaurants in each city is not enough to show the relative popularity of this type of food across the nation. A more powerful way of making comparisons is to standardize the number of taco places (dividing their number in an urban area by the total population of that place). Census data from the annually published *Statistical Abstract of the United States* or the

County and City Data Book can be used for determining populations of urban areas or states. For a map of cities the results are best symbolized by drawing circles with sizes proportional to the taco/population ratio of each locale. If you are working instead with statewide restaurant counts, make a choropleth map where each state is marked with colors or shades of gray. Here the mapmaker needs to partition the data set into classes in order to communicate information to the reader. Arrange the standardized data values from high to low and then divide them systematically in three, four, or five groups based on some logical criteria. Two acceptable methods are dividing the set into equal numbers of states per class or dividing the range of values (highest minus lowest) by five (or four or three). Mark the members of each class with the same color.

100 Quickies

To prove to students that food habits vary by region and/or ethnicity, we suggest two versions of a simple quiz known as 100 Quickies (copies are in Appendix A). Have students complete one or both of these questionnaires early in the semester while everyone is still naive about the subject. The first questionnaire is a listing of ethnic and regional foods. It includes, for example, frappe (an East-coast milkshake) and cabrito (a Mexican delicacy of whole roast kid cooked over a mesquite fire). We think the categories are self-explanatory. The second questionnaire is a listing of franchised eating-out establishments, some with very restricted trade areas.

If the first questionnaire were distributed to college students nationwide, the results might be an interesting measure of the assimilation of ethnicities in various parts of the United States. This blending process is ongoing, of course, but it is our experience that you still cannot get a good taco in New England or an authentic Italian meal in most of Texas. A nationwide sample is ambitious, but one way to obtain it is through the participation of classes such as yours. If the instructor for the course will collect responses to our 100 Quickies unusual foods questionnaire and mail all the forms to us at the University of Kansas, Department of Geography, Lawrence, Kansas 66045-2121, we would, in turn, be willing to provide your class with summaries of results from other parts of the country. Students then would have the opportunity to make regional comparisons.

Field Trips

Sending students as participant observers to grocery stores, restaurants, and public food events such as farmers' markets, food festivals, or

county fairs is a good way to heighten sensitivity to food-related presenta-
tions in our society. The activity forces a careful look at places perhaps
visited many times before and teaches the basics of what scholars call
the deconstruction of meaning. The only difficulty we have encountered
with the activity is a quite reasonable suspicion on the part of store managers and other officials to having strange people with clipboards invade
their facilities. Advance arrangements usually can alleviate this problem
and, by arranging for an interview with the manager at the same time,
can perhaps even turn a liability into an asset.

We suggest several lines of inquiry for grocery stores. Have students
compare the amount of shelf space devoted to specific items (for example, beef versus lamb, pork, and poultry) or even to larger categories
such as produce versus bottled soft drinks. Do such ratios reflect the
food consumption patterns of the community? How much of the floor
space actually is allocated to food? Where are the brand-name items
located for a product such as cereal as opposed to the generic or store
labels? If time allows, have students do a study of place-name use on
product labels (see the de Wit reading). Selecting retail stores from differing socio-economic neighborhoods would be especially revealing, of
course, as would a comparison between a standard supermarket and a
natural-foods store.

The opportunities for restaurant comparisons in the United States are
almost limitless because of the variety of our eating-out establishments.
To be different in this line of business often is equated with attracting
customers. Current fads among franchises include food as entertain-
ment, theme designs, and family-oriented establishments (where children are specifically welcomed). Add to these the down-home cafes and
the chef-centered, upscale businesses, and one can begin to see the magnitude of the restaurant universe. The regional popularity of some of
the basic types are illustrated on the maps we have made for
Appendix B.

How can you focus students' attentions during a site visit? Start them
off with the Milbauer reading and his emphasis on commonalities and
differences on menus. Then have them analyze the menus of several
local restaurants looking for regional foods. Paradise, a restaurant in
our city of Lawrence, offers Douglas County pie, for example, and even
franchise restaurants such as Applebee's purposely put such foods on
their menus. Some restaurants readily will give you a menu that can be
brought to the classroom for analysis. Ask. Variation in the presentation
of food is another topic for restaurant research. Is it served in courses;
are the utensils metal or plastic; are waitpersons present?

The list of public-food events is long: ethnic celebrations, county fairs,
farmers' markets, and food festivals as varied as beef days, peach festi-

vals, chili cook-offs, chitterlings suppers, jam tastings, apple-butter festivals and shrimp feeds. With luck, one will be near you at the right time for your class. We were lucky with our first seminar when Alice Waters, the noted Berkeley chef, was in town for a fund-raising event. In conjunction with her visit, a special tasting of fresh and regional foods was held at the normal Saturday-morning farmers' market. Another timely event for us was a Native American powwow held at Haskell Indian Nations University that featured food stalls as one of its components.

Interviews

Interviewing is sometimes intimidating, but we find that its interactive nature quickly overcomes the initial hesitation of students and makes this activity both fun and intellectually rewarding. People like to talk about food and do so readily. Since highly structured questionnaires often stop the flow of information, we recommend saving them for mailed surveys. Instead, have the interviewers concentrate on a few critical questions that will guide the conversation to specific topics of interest. We like to interview in pairs and not to use a recorder or take notes. Notebooks and machines seem to inhibit speech in all but those used to being interviewed often. If we sit down immediately afterwards and write out notes in tandem, we have found that we can recall almost everything (Goldstein 1964 and Western 1992 provide nice discussions about this informal style of interviewing).

A good warm-up activity is to ask an articulate student or faculty colleague who has had considerable exposure to a foreign culture to visit the class and act as an information source for the cuisine of that country. No formal presentation is involved here, just answering questions posed by the students. We have done this for Chinese foodways. First we handed out a relevant section from Jacqueline Newman's *Melting Pot* (1993) to give the students a crash course on this cuisine. The visitor appeared fifteen minutes later and the questioning began. The assignment was to find out about the foods and meal structure in this culture (they ended up asking such things as how many meals a day do you eat, what do you drink with meals, where do your family members sit around the table) and then to address the idea of how authentic is the Chinese food experience as presented in American restaurants. After the informant leaves, the discussion begins. Perhaps the most frequent comment is the classic "we should have asked . . ." The selection of an international colleague when we are dealing with American foodways may seem odd, but we recommend it. First, because the difference between cultures was great, it was relatively easy for beginning interviewers to feel a measure of success. Moreover, ethnic cuisines, including Chinese, are a major part of the American experience.

After an initial interview experience in the classroom, we suggest the following contacts and issues:

Chefs—Do they purposely prepare regional foods? What are the advantages and disadvantages of using local products? What are the differences between cooking at home and at the commercial scale? During an unexpected vehicular breakdown at Tamarack, the new and spectacular showcase for West Virginia folk crafts and foods in Beckley, we were able to have such a conversation with Chef Tom Stoner during his afternoon break. His success with fried green tomato sandwiches suggests that regional cuisine is gaining in popularity.

Residents of nursing homes or participants at group meals hosted by churches and other organizations—What was different about eating in the past? What did they do for grade-school meals when they were youngsters? What was their reaction to such "new" foods as bananas and pizza when they first became available? An extension agent in Ohio has written to us how a question about a regional meal to be served to out-of-state visitors led one such group into a lively discussion about ham and beans, rhubarb pie, and other comfort foods of the past.

Older relatives—What traditional family recipes and holiday customs have been handed down through the generations? Is the pattern for such continuity mostly matrilineal?

Peers—The goal here might not be so much to ask a unique set of questions as to establish a panel (roommates, hometown friends, and so on) to use for interviewing and surveys throughout the semester. E-mail is a good possibility to increase the geographic spread (for example, high-school classmates at other universities) and speed of response. By pooling the replies from each student's panel to a specific set of questions, the sample size for the class as a whole may be raised to a convincing number.

Other Sources of Information

The range of possible sources for food data is large. In addition to interviews, field trips, and the other possibilities already discussed, a wealth of information also is available in cookbooks, in popular magazines, from formal surveys, and elsewhere. Each such source, of course, has its attractions and drawbacks.

Cookbooks

Cookbooks are perhaps the most obvious data source for foodways. They truly are rich in information and potential, but are frustrating too. Their sheer numbers is one issue. We suggest sampling by geographic area, time period, and/or kind of compilation (for example, nonprofit organizations) and point you to the Ireland reading for more information. Seven American institutions have especially famous assemblages: the Louis Szathmary collection at the University of Iowa, the Schlesinger collection at Radcliffe College, and the holdings at the Library of Congress, New York Public Library, Indiana University, New York University, and Johnson and Wales Culinary School in Providence, Rhode Island. Almost all land-grant institutions have good holdings in this area, and so do many public libraries (cookbooks are among their most circulated items).

Students who do not know how to cook can become overwhelmed with the complexity of recipes and specialized terms. We suggest, therefore, beginning with standard or limited categories. Desserts, for example, could be examined for some subset of books (perhaps a sample of recipes from Midwestern Catholic church groups) to find the most common local pies or recipes that may be unique to the region. How many of these desserts call for locally grown fruits? Is there something akin to the seasonal bounty of Michigan blueberries in all states? Another line of inquiry is to follow one preparation method through several cultures and then to compare the variations. For example, many ethnic groups have a food item that is a meal enclosed in a pastry or dough similar to the bierocks described in the Isern reading. Another possibility would be to use a set of quasi-official cookbooks for a particular locale to count the number of times pork or another meat is used in a main-dish or casserole recipe. Many states have such a compilation based on state-fair competitions; others have something published by their university press that is drawn from recipes collected from cooks throughout the state.

So little work has been done with analyzing recipes in cookbooks that it is embarrassing—a rich legacy from mostly female cooks that has been ignored in academic circles. Use this embarrassment to motivate student research. Keep in mind, though, the single biggest problem with this line of inquiry. These cooks have submitted their best recipes to the compiler. "Best" typically means "unusual," and so rarely will you find instructions for fried chicken or grilled hamburgers despite the almost certain prominence of these two items in the repertoires of most home cooks. The recipes, in other words, more accurately reflect special-occasion meals than what is cooked every day or what is consumed outside the home.

Popular Magazine Archives

If a student wishes to examine food-consumption trends for the past, good sources are popular shelter magazines such as *Better Homes and Gardens, Good Housekeeping,* and *Southern Living.* Select a narrow span of time (perhaps a decade) and try to unravel what was special about cookery during that period. Was it a time of processed-food use where every sauce had a can of Campbell's soup in it? Is it evident that consumers are being manipulated by the food companies (look for product brand names appearing in recipes as discussed in Shapiro 1996)? Ads are as good a source for information here as the articles. Another approach is to track one food category through a longer period of time or by region. Do meatloaf recipes come and go? How often are regional or ethnic affiliations discussed in connection with recipes and/or articles? Have recipes for standard items such as pecan pie or cornbread in the South changed over the years?

Tourist Guides

As noted earlier, we personally are interested in symbolic foods of regions, items that are closely associated with, say, Chicago or the Appalachians. Potatoes representing Idaho is an obvious example. One way to get at this information is to look at how a state chooses to advertise itself and what visual symbols it uses as enticement. A good source here is a state's official tourist guide that can be ordered easily from addresses found on the Internet or in advertisements at the backs of popular magazines.

We have two sample guides for 1997 in front of us, one to Louisiana and the other to South Dakota. They vary markedly in how they present food as part of a visitor's potential experience. Meat pies and boiled crabs are displayed prominently in the mosaic of photographs on the front and back covers of the Louisiana guide, and numerous other color shots of prepared foods and raw ingredients can be found throughout this volume. In addition, the book contains a listing of fairs and food festivals. A clear implication of Louisiana's slogan "Come As You Are. Leave Different." is that a visitor will eat well and exotically. In contrast to Louisiana, the comparably sized South Dakota guide has many agricultural photographs, but only one of a prepared food. Numerous possibilities exist in this state for image-building dishes, including German breads, buffalo roast, pheasant, and chuckwagon-style informal suppers. That none of these has yet been exploited would be an interesting topic for class discussion.

Food Festivals/Farmers' Markets

Food festivals and farmers' markets, in addition to being good places for students to visit as participant observers, offer useful data for other projects. Geffen and Berglie (1994) have published a compendium of food festivals with brief commentary on each entry. In addition, almost every state has a directory compiled and distributed by the marketing division of their department of agriculture or state tourism agency. We have in front of us, for example, the "Virginia Food Festival Directory 1997." This fold-out brochure has a month-by-month listing with locations for 125 food festivals. It also includes the telephone number of a contact person for each event. From our experience in Kansas, many of these local festivals will have prepared materials that the organizers will readily mail to you. From such a collection, students can plot locations and individual food offerings, with perhaps a seasonal component to the analysis.

Directories for farmers' markets also are widely available through marketing divisions of state departments of agriculture. Those that we have seen usually provide not only community names but also location within the city, season, days/hours, contact person, and phone number. Some states compile other brochures for pick-your-own establishments, roadside markets, and produce wholesalers, with details as to kind of products available. Students may want to compare produce offerings in farmers' markets with the maps in the U.S. Census's regularly published *Agricultural Atlas of the United States* or in Pillsbury and Florin's *Atlas of American Agriculture: The American Cornucopia* (1996).

Surveys

If working with existing food data becomes boring, new information may be created by surveying a selected group of people about their food habits. The design, administration, and analysis of a mail, phone, or e-mail questionnaire is an educational experience with lifelong utility for students. Help them select a narrow topic and create questions that are designed to answer a specific research issue. To make the research valid make sure they ask exactly the same question of everyone, and aim for a total of at least thirty responses. Biographical data such as age, sex, hometown, rural or urban upbringing, educational background, racial or ethnic affiliation, and family income are useful for helping to make sense of the results, but the last three items are sensitive issues and their presence on a survey form can lead to refusals to participate.

Ideas from the previous pages provide many topics that students may want to explore in a survey. If none of them appeal, here are several more random suggestions to consider: family meal patterns including who is at each meal and where it is eaten; changes in the "regular" schedule on holidays and weekends; typical breakfast menus; frequency and content of snacks; favorite desserts; usual drink to accompany a meal (if coffee or tea, is it amended with sugar?); presence of a household vegetable garden; frequency of grocery shopping; who cooks in the family; most common sources for new recipes or other ideas for food preparation; the standard items always found on the family dining table (for example, salt and pepper shakers); variety of food events in the community (such as Boy Scout chili feeds); and special menus for holidays or family celebrations.

Scrapbook

To look at food from another viewpoint, collect all food-related articles in some print media such as a local newspaper (one that carries news stories from the Associated Press) for a given period of time. Have students analyze the content of these stories to see what journalists bring before the public. The interest here is the contrast between food as an everyday activity taken for granted by many and a journalist's predilection for stories about unusual or atypical happenings. Are any of the articles about common foods and food activities? Is the majority of attention focused on new food items in the marketplace, food safety, obesity and eating disorders, and agricultural disasters?

Food in the Classroom

We close with an obvious but important suggestion—use food in the classroom to bring the group together, to promote sharing, to inform, and to entertain. This can be done at minimal cost; the emphasis should be on sampling instead of pigging out. Tasting several varieties of oranges was a focus for one of our class periods. In another, as a follow-up to a discussion of Southern foods, someone baked a sweet-potato pie and we brought in the traditional snack combination of RC Cola and Moon Pies. If more money is available, the possibilities expand: pasties from Marquette, Michigan; king cake from New Orleans at pre-Lent time; Moravian cookies from Winston-Salem, North Carolina; and steak from Omaha.

Section One

Regional Foods

Common sense would suggest that most strong identifications of foods with particular places would develop from deep historical roots. These dishes would feature locally grown agricultural products, for example, or reflect methods of seasoning or preparation introduced by early settlers and then passed along to more recent residents. Such a narrative indeed is common, but it is by no means the only scenario possible. A gradual blending of ideas from old and new settlers to create new and publicly recognized dishes is easily imagined, as is an overnight invention by a particular individual. The readings in this section reflect all of these pathways. What unites them is the way each food has come to promote and/or reflect regional pride.

The first two articles are field-based studies that describe traditional foods in widely varying locations: the Upper Peninsula of Michigan and the Great Plains. Yvonne and William Lockwood first tell us about pasties, crescent-shaped turnovers filled with a stew-like mixture of meat, potatoes, onions, and either rutabagas or carrots. Pasties came to the UP in the nineteenth century with Cornish miners and spread to other working peoples because of their practicality as a portable lunch. They rose to the status of place icon in the 1950s as a way for local residents simultaneously to honor their hard-working past and to distinguish themselves from a growing tourist culture. Rocky Mountain oysters (i.e. calf testicles), the subject of Jim Hoy's essay, have a working-class history similar to pasties, but they have yet to achieve the status of general regional symbol. Though commonly served in the homes and lodge halls of the Great Plains and intermontane West, they rarely appear on restaurant menus or supermarket shelves.

Loco moco, a mixture of rice, hamburger patty, and fried egg topped with gravy, is a Hawaiian example of a food hybrid that has achieved statewide fame. Jim Kelly describes how it combines not only ingredients from different spheres, but also the slower, Asian style of eating (it is served in a bowl) with the faster, Western way of preparation. Popularity for loco moco and other dishes that fuse existing traditions is not difficult to understand. More intriguing is Timothy Lloyd's account of Cincinnati-style chili. In this case the inventor was from Macedonia and the ingredients not particularly local. Still, somehow, the product has come to be seen by residents as symbolic of their city. The Cincinnati tradition has been building since the 1920s, but the creation of symbolic foods is an ongoing process as well. Stephen Frenkel's study of the specialized coffee industry in the Pacific Northwest is an excellent case in point.

The last of the place-specific readings, George Lewis's look at the Maine lobster, is a fascinating demonstration and useful reminder that regional icons can be more complex than they seem. To most outsiders the lobster appears to be an ideal symbol for that state—something at once local and tasty. Poor residents who cannot afford such fare disagree, however, as do Mainers who live away from the coast. For these people the lobster is an inappropriate emblem imposed on them by elitist "summer people." The conflict actually heightens the symbolism of the lobster but gives it multiple meanings.

The reading by Cary de Wit and the one by ourselves turn the approach to regional foods slightly. Both focus on linkages among particular lifestyles, foods that symbolize these orientations, and places across the country that either market or consume such foods. Both also are data-driven studies. Our look at rice contrasts a pattern of consumption from the 1950s that was linked to production areas with a newer one that is associated with people who embrace a more relaxed and ecologically responsible way of existence. Cary de Wit, with a simple but innovative survey of food labels in grocery stores, demonstrates how marketing people reflect and reinforce such popular identifications as California with easy-going yet sophisticated food (and life) and Vermont with wholesome simplicity. This section of readings concludes with a methodological suggestion, Lynne Ireland's insights into the potentials for regional study inherent in local, fund-raising cookbooks. Thousands of these compilations exist, some dating back to the 1860s.

1

Pasties in Michigan's Upper Peninsula

Foodways, Interethnic Relations, and Regionalism

Yvonne R. Lockwood and William G. Lockwood

The transformation of an immigrant culture to an ethnic culture is a complex process. Immigrant communities are not (as they were so often treated in the past) detached pieces of the Old Country. Even in the period immediately after arrival, the culture of immigrants has already been changed due to selective processes on emigration and the immediate effects of the journey and the new environment. Acculturation—the focus of attention of most existing studies—is only one aspect of the cultural transformation that takes place. The new cultural configuration of immigrants draws not only from "mainstream" American culture, but from that of other immigrant groups as well. Groups previously arrived from other countries are emulated. Cultural traits of the majority population are imposed and sometimes eagerly accepted. Old customs acquire new functions and meanings. The cultures of a variety of regional and social groups from the same country of origin are amalgamated and standardized. Eventually the culture of the ethnic group diverges significantly from that of the homeland, which, of course, has continued to evolve along its own path. Elsewhere we have discussed this process of ethnogenesis in greater detail.[1]

Ethnogenesis can be demonstrated in virtually any aspect of culture, but nowhere is it more graphically illustrated than in American foodways. In this essay, we will trace the natural history of a single item of prepared food—the pasty (pronounced pass-tee)—in the Upper Penin-

Reprinted by permission from *Creative Ethnicity: Symbols and Strategies of Contemporary Ethnic Life*, edited by Stephen Stern and John A. Cicala (Logan: Utah State University Press, 1991), 3–20.

sula of Michigan to demonstrate the complex development of ethnic cultures. By observing how the pasty, introduced by one ethnic group, was claimed by many ethnic groups and the region as a whole, we will illustrate the complex relationships existing between immigrant, ethnic, and regional identity and culture.

The U.P. (as it is called by Michiganders) is a peninsula separated from the remainder of Michigan by the Straits of Mackinac, Lake Michigan, and Lake Huron. Not until 1957, when the Mackinac Bridge was completed, was direct connection made between the two parts of the state. Previously, one could get to the lower peninsula only by ferry or by traveling the length of Wisconsin and circling back through Chicago. Consequently, the U.P. is a region much more closely related culturally, historically, and demographically to northern Wisconsin and northeastern Minnesota than to the lower peninsula of Michigan. Yoopers (from U.P.ers) have a highly developed regional consciousness. Because the lower peninsula of the state includes the large population centers, the important industries, the major cultural institutions, and the state capital, Yoopers feel neglected by state government and looked down upon by the rest of the population. This situation has given rise to a separatist movement, only half in jest, to establish the U.P. as the fifty-first state of Superior.

Soon after Michigan became a state in 1837, some residents traveled north to investigate the upper peninsula that Congress had included in the state's territory. The reports they brought back triggered the first major mining boom in the United States.[2] From the beginning of the iron and copper industry, Cornish immigrants played a major role.[3] By 1844, two copper mining companies with some twenty Cornish employees were already in operation. Since they had experience with the deep-mining techniques and machinery used in the tin mines of Cornwall, these Cornishmen were valuable to the developing mining industry and set the pattern of mine work in the U.P.[4] By the late nineteenth century, when the origin of European immigration to the United States shifted eastward and southward, the Cornish were already well established in the mines as skilled workers, foremen, bosses, and mining captains. Sons of Cornish immigrants were among the first graduates of the new Michigan College of Mines (now Michigan Technological University) in the 1880s, and many of them took professional positions in the local mining industry. More recently arrived Finns, Italians, Poles, Croats, and Serbs provided the unskilled labor. As mining technology developed, the need for skilled workers lessened. Consequently, the unskilled were promoted very slowly, if at all, which encouraged the entrenchment of the earlier immigrants in a hierarchical position over more recent arrivals.

Just as Cornish influence was felt in methods of mining, the Cornish also established much of the cultural life of the mining communities. The new immigrants looked upon the Cornish as representatives of American culture.[5] They had status and their lifestyle was taken as a model of American life. This situation was typical of cultural relations between members of the New and Old Immigration.[6] Elsewhere the Irish—as the most numerous of the "Old Immigrants"—were often emulated by newly arrived eastern and southern Europeans. In Detroit, for example, some new immigrants "Americanized" their Serbian family names Obradović and Dragić by changing them to O'Bradovich and O'Dragich.[7]

Thus, the earlier immigrants from northwestern Europe often influenced the cultural patterns of later-arriving immigrants from southern and eastern Europe. From the perspective of these "greenhorns" from the other side of Europe, the practices of earlier arrivals, whose immigrant cultures had already been transformed to ethnic cultures, were accepted as the "American Way." These earlier arrivals, after all, were the Americans with whom new immigrants were most apt to have contact. It was likely to be their neighborhoods in which new immigrants settled, and they who were most likely to be the foremen and supervisors in the mills and mines where the immigrants went to work. It is not surprising, then, that the ethnic culture that took shape was profoundly influenced by that of earlier immigrants. Ethnic foodways provide particularly good examples of this process.

The pasty is a turnover with a pie-like crust filled with a variety of food combinations. It is the national dish of Cornwall, and it played an important role in the diet of Cornish-Americans wherever they settled.[8] The pasty was quickly adopted by newer immigrants who worked by their sides and under their direction in the mines of the U.P. It was not just a recipe that was passed from one ethnic group to another, but an entire cultural complex including the occasions for which pasties are prepared, the ways they are prepared and eaten, and some of the folklore associated with them. At the same time, significant alterations and innovations in the pasty took place during the process of diffusion and adoption by non-Cornish.

A principal reason that the Cornish pasty was readily adopted by members of other ethnic groups in the U.P. was its close association with work. Philip Harben, writing on the traditional dishes of Britain, observes:

> The Cornish pasty [is] one of the best examples in the world of what one might call *functional food*. For the Cornish pasty . . . is not merely delicious food, it was designed for a certain quite definite purpose; it was designed to be carried to work and eaten in the hand, to be taken down the mine, to sea, to the fields. You will see a Cornishman munching his tasty pasty

squatting in the narrow tin-mine workings, sitting on the nets in his leaping
fishing boat, leaning against a grassy bank whilst the patient plough-horses
wait.[9]

In Cornwall, the pasty was particularly associated with mining.[10] It is very
well suited to this context: it is easily carried in pails or specially made
sacks, it retains its heat for a long time, it can be eaten with the hands,
and it is a hearty meal-in-one. Little wonder that the Finns, Italians, and
Slavs who saw their Cornish foremen eating pasty soon were demanding
the same of their own wives.

Today, the Cornish are a relatively small component of the U.P.'s population. The largest ethnic group is the Finns. The first Finnish immigrants to the U.P. began to arrive in 1864, well after Cornish
immigration but thirty years prior to the massive Finnish immigration
to the United States that began around the turn of the century.[11] By
1880, foreign-born Finns numbered over one thousand. The first arrivals tended to be skilled workers who were given employment as carpen-
ters, blacksmiths, and skilled yardmen at the mines. Thus, they were well
established and somewhat acculturated by the time of the mass immigration. It was probably from these earlier Finnish arrivals, rather than from
the Cornish themselves, that later Finnish immigrants adopted the
pasty.[12] Some Finns were receptive to pasty because they had similar regional dishes—such as *piiraat* and *kukko*—which resemble pasty. These
are dough-enveloped specialties of meat, fish, vegetables, rice, and so
on, varying in size from individual turnovers to large loafs.[13] How was a
Finn newly arrived in America, seeing a pasty in the lunch pail of a fellow
countryman arrived some twenty years before, to know that this was not
merely a regional variant of food with which he was already familiar?
Thus, we would argue, many Finns came to believe the pasty was a Finnish food. In a similar way, some Italians in the U.P. also regard the pasty
as Italian.

The development of a U.P. regional culture was thereby shaped not
only by mainstream "American" culture, but also by the cultural traditions of ethnic groups in contact with one another. The adoption and
finally the standardization of pasty is the result of its appropriation by
many ethnic groups. The development of a "polka subculture" in the
United States, drawing upon and amalgamating Polish, German, Bohemian, Slovenian, and Croatian traditions, is an example of the same
kind of process occurring nationwide.

Despite the regionalization of the pasty, it is still claimed as the ethnic
heritage of several groups. By and large, Yoopers know the Cornish origin of pasty because of attention to it by mass media. Some even refer
to it as a "Cousin jack mouth organ," Cousin Jack being a popular syn-

onym for Cornishman. On the other hand, its association with Finns cannot be ignored. For example, Raymond Sokolov, former Michigander and free-lance ethnoculinary journalist, writes of the "Finnish flavor" of pasties.[14] Some U.P. Finns themselves regard pasty as a Finnish food. This belief is perpetuated by family tradition, Finnish "ethnic" church suppers, and annual Finnish traditional celebrations, where pasty is a featured Finnish specialty. This Finnish association can be explained historically by the role of Finns in the diffusion of the pasty and by the predominance of Finns in the U.P. Many pasty shops, for example, seem to be owned and staffed by Finns. On the other hand, the family is an important factor in the issue of ethnic attribution: pasty is first and foremost a family tradition. Yoopers make and east pasties according to the recipes and traditions of their mothers and grandmothers. The authors know Michigan Finns who were unaware that other ethnic groups also make and eat pasties. This is also true of in-laws not from the U.P. who assume pasty is Finnish because the spouse's Finnish family serves it.

In the course of its transformation from monoethnic to multiethnic, the pasty has been diversified, then standardized, and, finally, rediversified. In Cornwall today, as in the U.P. at the turn of the century, pasty can be made from a variety of ingredients: rice and leeks, egg and bacon, meat and potatoes, lamb and parsley or venison, fish, apple, and so on. The possible variants are endless, so much so that it is said "the devil never dared cross the Tamar River from Devonshire to Cornwall for fear of the Cornish women's habit of putting anything and everything into a pasty."[15] The content of the pasty, as it developed in the U.P., is a standardization of but one of the many Cornwall variants: a basic mixture of meat, potatoes, onion, rutabagas, and/or carrots. Although some variation still occurs, it cannot deviate far from this particular combination of ingredients and still qualify as pasty. Meat may consist of beef, a beef and pork combination, or even venison when available. Some may add parsley; others omit both carrots and rutabagas. But for U.P. residents today, the U.P. pasty is this meat and root vegetable specialty.

One area of particular controversy is the crust. Crust recipes are usually guarded secrets. In Cornwall, pasty is made with either a puff pastry or a crust similar to that used for American pie. It is the latter that was adopted for the U.P. pasty. The dough, according to Yoopers, should be light and short and hold together, yet not be quite as flaky as pie crust. The secret lies in the proportion of shortening and water to flour and in the type of shortening used. Traditionalists, both Cornish and non-Cornish, claim that suet is the original and best shortening. Others use lard because it is more convenient and, they state, just as good as suet.

With the contemporary emphasis on lighter foods, vegetable shortening is now being used which, claim purists, produces an inferior, tough, and tasteless crust.

Sealing the pasty is another area for variation. According to older Cousin Jacks and Cousin Jennies, a "real" Cornish pasty is sealed by "making a rope," a particular method of tightly closing the dough, usually across the top of the pasty.[16] Today few Yoopers—including those of Cornish background—know this technique. Instead, most make a seal by pinching, folding, or crimping the edge as they would for pie. Those few Yoopers who do use "the Cornish rope" are invariably Cornish-Americans.

Another distinctively Cornish feature is the addition of initials indicating for whom the pasty in intended. These are formed from dough and baked on top of one end, serving to identify pasties made to suit individual likes and dislikes, through the omission or increase of certain ingredients, and to mark uneaten parts of pasties for later consumption. This tradition is observed in some Cornish Yooper families with toothpicks: one, two, or three toothpicks stuck into the crust designate to whom it belongs.

Although pasty ingredients have been standardized, adaptation to the U.P. context has produced variation in pasty construction and consumption and in attitudes and values about pasty. Most Yoopers agree that ingredients should be chopped with a knife, though for convenience many will use ground meat—usually hamburger, ground chuck, or "pasty meat" (a coarsely ground beef, with or without pork, sold in local markets). Some maintain that all ingredients should be mixed so that the flavors blend during baking. Others, especially Cornish, argue that ingredients should be layered (potatoes topped by rutabagas and/or carrots, followed by onions and, finally, meat, salt, pepper, and butter or suet—either of which are optional) so that the meat juices and seasonings percolate down through the vegetables. This latter view is probably the older, and we assume that mixing was first done, again, for the sake of convenience.

Accompaniments and condiments with pasty have become highly variable, with patterns strongly linked to family tradition. Some Yoopers would not enjoy pasty without catsup. Other accompaniments are equally essential for different individuals or families: chowchow pickles, crisp vegetables, tea, buttermilk, beer, tomato juice. These accompaniments are not casual choices. One or several of them is absolutely necessary to complete a satisfactory pasty meal.

Originally pasty was hand food. Its traditional shape, size, and substantial crust attest to its function as a working person's meal intended to be carried in a pocket or lunch pail. Rolled into a circle and folded into the shape of a half-moon approximately seven to nine inches long, the crust enfolds its ingredients and is sealed across the top or along the lower edge. The traditional way to east pasty is to begin at the end, holding it parallel with the body so the juices keep the filling moist. However, more and more Yoopers now eat pasty on plates with forks, a manner which opens the door to still more variation. Once pasty rests on a plate, it lends itself to innovations that some regard as abuse: its crust is broken in the center, releasing its moisture and heat, and it is smothered with butter, gravy, or other substances. Change has also occurred in structure. Although the half-moon shape remains standard, a common family version has evolved known as "pasty pie": pasty ingredients baked in a pie pan with a bottom and top crust and served in wedges on plates. Since the interwar period, pasties have not only been made in this form but also oversized in the traditional shape and cut in half to serve. Both forms are acknowledged as quick innovations, and are reserved for family.

The U.P. pasty remained relatively stable in form and content for many decades; the narrow range of variance that exists usually is associated with particular ethnic groups. For example, rutabagas in pasty are said to be Cornish and carrots Finnish. Pasty accompanied by buttermilk is regarded as a Finnish ("bad") habit, especially by the Cornish. "Chipping" rather than chopping the meat and rutabagas, closing with a "rope," and layering ingredients, are known as Cornish. Although these examples are not exclusive to one ethnic group, they are stereotyped as such, even to the extent that "carrot pasty" is a derisive term for Finnish-style pasty. Acknowledgment of an Italian variation is communicated in the expression "the Cornish originated it; the Finns disseminated it; the Italians improved it." This was heard in the university communities of Hougthon and Marquette, but we were not able to discover there or elsewhere what is considered distinctive about an Italian-style pasty.[17] Only one Yooper, in the western end, recognized his Italian mother-in-law's pasty as different: she adds "a little bit of hot banana pepper."

Marked changes are now occurring in pasty; it is rediversifying. One used to hear about individuals who put peas, for example, into pasty secretly, knowing neighbors would not approve. Now similar "violations" of U.P. tradition are openly admitted: pasty with kidneys, pasty with condensed onion or mushroom soup, pasty with gravy. These variants are still repugnant to many Yoopers and often are attributed to specific groups or to other areas, i.e., "it's those other guys." Dousing pasty with gravy, for example, is said to be Cornish (by Finns), French Canadian (by others), Mennonite (by a pasty shop owner who learned to make pasty from Finns), eaten only in the eastern U.P. (by those in the western end) or eaten only by non-Yoopers. These views, however, are exoteric beliefs about "them" and attempt to explain a drastic change in tradition.[18]

Further signs of rediversification are appearing as a consequence of commercialization. Both health food stores and a few standard pasty shops now offer a vegetarian version, often with whole wheat crust. Other less-than-traditional versions are found in establishments that cater largely to tourists. For example, some restaurants offer pasty with cheese, bacon, or chili topping. Some pizza parlors offer "pizza pasty"— pasty ingredients enfolded by pizza dough, much like calzone. Thus, the pasty, which became standardized within relatively narrow limits, is again appearing in greater variation.[19]

The first pasties available outside the home were sold at church pasty sales. In addition to raising funds, the church pasty preparation and sale is a popular social event. Despite long hours of work, participants speak of these activities both as enjoyable and as an effective way to initiate newcomers into church functions and U.P. tradition. In this context, knowledge about pasties is exchanged between individuals, thus reinforcing pasty tradition. Even women who bake their own pasties will buy at church sales. The product is regarded as homemade and "the real thing," because older women usually dominate at these affairs. Either they are deferred to because of their experience and age, or they take an active supervisory and authoritative role and monitor the work of younger women. As a consequence, in one town young women are intimidated and hesitate to volunteer because of possible criticism from the older women. One of these guardians of tradition, a ninety-year-old Cousin Jenny, stated emphatically that she could not eat any pasties but her own and those from her church because the others are only poor imitations.

The first commercial pasty shops began to appear just before World War II. Yoopers recall that in Hurley, Wisconsin, located at the Michigan state line and then known as "sin city," an Italian-American entrepreneur baked pasties in his kitchen and peddled them from bar to bar in the early-morning hours. About 1938, he opened a pasty shop. After the war other shops appeared across the border in Ironwood. Today pasties are made and sold in at least one outlet in nearly every U.P. community: pasty shops, bakeries, restaurants, bars, fast food counters, Dairy Queens, and grocery stores. Often they can be purchased hot, cold, partially baked, frozen, and day-old.

Yoopers regard homemade pasties as better, but on occasion even people who regularly make their own pasties buy commercial ones when they are too tired to cook; when they need a large number, as for a wedding supper; when they go fishing or hunting; or when they are feeling lazy—like sending out for a pizza elsewhere in the United States.

During its decades of industrial development, the U.P. experienced an economic boom. But because the economy was based on extractive industries—the primary production of iron, copper, and lumber—the area was directly and immediately affected when production fell off and large corporations were pulled out by their absentee owners. The U.P. had been exploited and then abandoned. The economy began a gradual but steady decline about 1920 and, despite occasional spurts of activity, never recovered.[20] The subsequent secondary status felt by U.P. residents has contributed negatively to their self-image and has resulted in an inferiority complex.[21] Since completion of the Mackinac Bridge in 1957, access to the U.P. has been easier, and tourism has become increasingly important in the local economy. One result is that pasty shops have proliferated. Along a seven-mile stretch of highway leading west from the bridge, some thirteen pasty shops, advertising in three-foot-high, glow-in-the-dark letters, exist to the virtual exclusion of other eateries. The personal names of the establishments, such as Granny's, Lehto's, and Suzy's, assure strangers of a homemade treat. Thus, the pasty has come to symbolize the Upper Peninsula. This consciousness of the regionalization of pasty is used, in effect, as a rhetorical strategy to enhance U.P. self-image.[22] According to Kenneth Burke, rhetoric serves to imbue individuals with heightened awareness and to persuade them by manipulating materials and ideas in an aesthetically pleasing manner.[23]

Traditional forms of culture are especially effective as persuasive devices because they bear the test of time and elicit a sympathetic response. Members of the media, restaurateurs, and other U.P. residents have used the power of traditional expression to their advantage in creating a strategy for regional identification. The strategy includes editorializing on the use, meaning, and significance of the pasty for regional inhabitants.

Narratives about pasty emphasize ties with occupation and environment, as well as with specific groups. Legends tell of hardworking miners who warmed pasties on shovels held over the candles of mining lamps. Others recall that miners carried hot pasties wrapped in cloth sacks or newspaper in their shirts and were kept warm on cold U.P. mornings and in damp, chilly mines. As they worked, miners, in turn, kept their pasties warm. Undoubtedly a warm pasty is comforting carried next to the body in severe temperatures; hunters and fishermen, possibly influenced by this workers' tradition, carry pasties in this way today. But one might assume that the physical exertion of mine work would transform any pasty so carried into a crumbled mess. One explanation is, of course, that pasty crust of fifty years ago was tougher and not as flaky as that of today. Also, it is possible that over time pasties have become larger. Both features would explain why pasty is not as durable today as folklore describes it.

Much of the folklore about pasty concerns the crust. The description above is of quite a different pasty than what meets present ideal standards of the perfect crust—not so flaky that it falls apart in the hand or so tough that it can survive a fall. Consider a narrative that explains the origin of pasty:[24]

> In Cornwall, the women searched for a good meal for the miners other than sandwiches; the men were tired of sandwiches. They experimented with potatoes, meat, and onions wrapped in dough and were pleased with the result. It was a whole meal in one. At meal time, the women brought their pasties to the mine and dropped them down the shaft to the men below. They didn't even break.

When Richard Dorson collected a variant in 1946, it was told in jest.[25] The above example was told to our informant by his Cornish neighbor as historical information.

Pasty as a missile is a recurring motif in popular expression. For example, a former resident of the U.P. expressed disbelief about the authenticity of this legend of the pasty's origin, but later recalled that his mother could toss her pasties into the air and catch them without breakage.[26]

Ritualizing events has been another strategy in the regionalization of pasty. The ultimate example of use of the missile motif occurred at the First Annual Pasty Throwing Contest in April 1983. Encouraged by the widespread saying that a "good pasty can be dropped to the bottom of a mine shaft without splitting open," the Finlandia Cafe and Bakery of Marquette sponsored the contest and also donated a batch of burned, unsalable, and inedible pasties.[27] The winner threw his pasty 155 feet, acquiring a trophy crowned with a gilded pasty and possible mention in the *Guiness Book of World Records*.

In addition to symbolic representation of the region, pasty lore is also manipulated to express group boundaries to distinguish Yoopers from outsiders. The folk terms "gut buster" and "ulcer bun," for example, communicate a shared knowledge about pasty that expresses social solidarity. These metaphors for pasty, although seemingly negative, are rather a good-natured, even affectionate, reference to pasty's substantial nature. It is a heavy food, one that goes a long way to satisfying hunger. But unless one is a Yooper, one might construe these terms as slurs. Shared knowledge also allows for in-group jokes. Based on awareness of the Catholic custom of meatless Fridays, the pasties of one Italian shop are known as "Catholic," because "they are skimpy on meat."

Lack of this knowledge by outsiders further reinforces pasty's link to the region. Enticed by the deluge of pasty advertisements, curious tourists identify themselves when they inquire about "pay-stee," thereby providing more grist for the folklore mill. U.P. residents never cease to be amazed by this pronunciation and its confusion with the accouterment for striptease dancers. Nor do they tire of recounting such incidents and ridiculing the outsider, who otherwise contributes to the Yooper's negative self-image. A prize-winning limerick by a U.P. resident focuses on this widely shared regional joke:

> A Casper widow named Patsy,
> Earned her living by selling of pasties,
> When a fudgy hasty demanded a pastey,
> Her response was rather nasty.[28]

The media and state government have played no small role in the rhetoric of regionalizing pasty. In 1968, Governor George Romney designated May 24 as Michigan Pasty Day. Local newspapers often feature articles about pasty. One such story sparked a long debate about what constitutes a real pasty.[29] In 1979, WLUC Television in Marquette aired a short Michigan promotional film, "Stay for It," featuring local folk historian Frank Matthews. Looking for all the world like a stereotypic miner, this senior Yooper informs viewers about pasty's Cornish origin and function. The film was an attempt to build regional pride by stressing pasty's aesthetic qualities and its historical and occupational tie to the U.P. As Mr. Matthews bites down on a tempting pasty, he urges viewers that "pasties are part of the Upper Peninsula heritage and that's why you should stay for it and try one!" Like Caucasian muses singing the praises of Dannon yogurt, this wizened regional authority promises a treat with a long and proud U.P. tradition.[30]

The use of pasties in cartoons attests to the food's ability to act as a commentary. At the time Cliff Wirth printed his cartoons in 1982, Michigan had suffered plant shutdowns that led to thirty percent unemployment in some regions, mass migration out of the area, and generalized psychological depression. Tradition may be antidotal to such problems.

Drawing on the Holland, Michigan, Tulip Festival, and the U.P. pasty, the cartoonist suggests we turn to these pleasurable, fulfilling regional cultural traits for comfort and to assist in revitalizing statewide pride.

The idea that pasty is unique to the U.P. is widely shared. Residents' esoteric beliefs about pasty's enigmatic qualities reinforce its symbolic regional meaning. For example, during and after World War II, many residents left the U.P. for industrial centers in the Midwest and West. With them went the pasty. Numerous stories are told about individuals who tried to start shops as close to the U.P. as Green Bay, Appleton, and Ashland, Wisconsin, but were unsuccessful, because, according to folk belief, people elsewhere were ignorant of pasty and would not eat it. A notable exception is a person who sold his pasties at factory gates at mealtime, thereby recalling pasty's working-class origin. In another case, a pasty shop owner in Ironwood enjoys telling about the problems he encounters when he orders matches printed with the name and address of the shop. Invariably, printers who are not local print "pastry" instead of "pasty."

The case of Yoopers moving tó Detroit, however, suggests a more successful transplantation of U.P. culture. During and after World War II, large numbers of Yoopers moved to Detroit to work in various industries. In the new urban context, they became more aware of their U.P. identity. Knowledge of regional esoteric folklife, such as that of the pasty, played no small part in the self-conscious awareness of membership in a regional folk group. Thus, Detroit became home to a U.P. social club, a U.P.-dominated Finnish social club, and an Episcopalian church, whose congregation consists almost entirely of Cornish Yoopers. Like their friends and relatives in the U.P., these groups continue the U.P. custom of sponsoring fund-raising pasty dinners and bake sales. Pasty shops owned by former Yoopers have been part of the Detroit scene for decades. According to one of these owners, about ninety percent of his customers are from the U.P. or have spent considerable time there:

> That's where the pasty came from. It didn't come to Detroit from Cornwall, but from the U.P. Pasty is the tie to the U.P. Invariably, a customer will tell me he is from the U.P., as if that's any surprise. I certainly didn't think he was from Alabama![31]

The ability of pasties to link the U.P. with other areas has contributed to the creation of a new self-consciousness in the Upper Peninsula. The same informants who remember business failures forty years ago are now predicting that pasty shops will soon exist all over the United States. Yoopers are witnessing the increasing fame of pasty among tourists; ski-

ers, hunters, anglers, and campers take as many as fifty pasties home
to freeze. Some residents now refer to pasty as "U.P.'s contribution to
American culture."

Pasty always seems to have been a link between generations and
among different groups. But, since the mid-1960s, it has emerged with
new meaning as a public, regional symbol that recalls the past, speaks of
the present, and implies the future. The Bicentennial was a significant
catalyst in this process. References to the history of the pasty, to its multiple ethnic associations, to its occupational and regional functions—as
well as descriptions of its aesthetic effects—have bestowed new status on
the pasty. Serving pasty to outside visitors is a conscious, predictable act
intended to impress and thereby persuade them about the good quality
of U.P. life. The tantalizing aroma, pleasing form and color, and delicious ingredients of pasty are often the focus of praise. The acceptance
of pasties by outsiders is symbolically a validation of U.P. culture in general. While participation in pasty foodways reinforces cultural tradition,
it also is a statement of regional identity.

Identity, however, is complex and always contextual. Pasty is symbolic
of the U.P., but it also is deeply rooted in ethnic and family traditions.
While it is available to anyone seeking to reinforce his or her ethnic
roots, pasty's ethnic associations are secondary to region. Thus, a certain
ambiguity exists regarding ethnic versus regional culture. But these two
categories of cultural expression need not be mutually exclusive; rather,
the separate identities, existing as they do at different levels of organization, are seldom in conflict. The adoption and transformation of the
Cornish pasty by other immigrant groups was an essential part of its
regionalization. As each group made the pasty its own, pasty became
both an ethnic specialty of each and, ultimately—first implicitly, then
explicitly—a specialty of the region.

Notes

1. William G. Lockwood and Yvonne R. Lockwood, "Ethnic Roots of American Regional Foods," in *Current Research in Culinary History: Sources, Topics, and
Methods,* proceedings of a conference sponsored by the Schlesinger Library of
Radcliffe College and the Culinary Historians of Boston, Radcliffe College, June
14–16, 1985, edited by Jillian Strang, Bonnie Brown, and Patricia Kelley (Cambridge: Culinary Historians of Boston, 1985), 130–37.

2. Doris B. Mclaughlin, *Michigan Labor. A Brief History from 1818 to the Present*
(Ann Arbor: Institute of Labor and Industrial Relations, 1970), 77; Willis F. Dun-
bar, *Michigan: A History of the Wolverine State* (Grand Rapids: William B. Eerdmans
Publishing Co., 1970), 498. Iron ore and copper mines became primary industrial employers in the U.P.

3. Jane Fisher, "Michigan's Cornish People," *Michigan History* 29 (1945): 379. See also John Rowe, *The Hard-Rock Men: Cornish Immigrants and the North American Mining Frontier* (Liverpool: Liverpool University Press, 1974), especially 62–95.

4. A. L. Rowse, *The Cousin Jacks: The Cornish in America* (New York: Charles Scribner's Sons, 1969), 168.

5. Fisher, "Michigan's Cornish People," 380.

6. Leonard Dinnerstein and David M. Reimers, *Ethnic Americans,* 2d ed. (New York: Harper & Row, 1982), 10–48.

7. Cultural geographers have argued that in the United States the first European population that established the economy and society of an area usually had decisive influence on later patterns that defined it as a cultural region, e.g., Wilbur Zelinsky, *The Cultural Geography of the United States* (Englewood Cliffs, N.J.: Prentice Hall, 1973), 5–35, and Raymond D. Gastil, *Cultural Regions of the United States* (Seattle: University of Washington Press, 1975), 26–27. Cf. George Foster's explanation in *Culture and Conquest* (Chicago: Quadrangle Books, 1960) of why the cultural patterns established in Mexico were nearly all Andalusian in origin even though immigrants from throughout Spain contributed to the colonial population of Mexico. Foster calls this phenomenon *cultural crystallization.* Since Andalusians were the first to arrive in Mexico, it was they who established the cultural patterns for later arrivals.

8. See, for example, Philip Harben, *Traditional Dishes of Britain* (London: The Bodley Head, 1953), 9–13; R. R. Roberts, *Cornish Recipes* (St. Ives, Cornwall, England: James Pike, Ltd., 1977), 3, 16; Marika Hanbury Tenison, *West Country Cooking* (London: Mayflower Granada Publishing, 1978), 77–105; Kathleen Thomas, *West Country Cookery* (London: B. T. Batsford Ltd., 1979), 57–58; Adrian Bailey, *The Cooking of the British Isles* (New York: Time-Life Books, 1971), 20–21.

9. Harben, *Traditional Dishes of Britain,* 9–10.

10. Roberts, *Cornish Recipes,* 3; Tenison, *West Country Cooking,* 78; Bailey, *Cooking,* 20. Also see Richard M. Dorson, *Bloodstoppers and Bearwalkers* (Cambridge: Harvard University Press, 1952), 117–18, for folk narrative associating the pasty with mining.

11. Arthur E. Puotinen, "Early Labor Organizations in the Copper Country," in *For the Common Good,* edited by Michael G. Karni and Douglas J. Ollila (Superior, Wis.: Tyomies Society, 1977), 123; Matti E. Kaups, "The Finns in the Copper and Iron Ore Mines of the Western Great Lakes Region, 1864–1905: Some Preliminary Observations," in *The Finnish Experience in the Western Great Lakes Region: New Perspectives,* edited by M. G. Karni, M. E. Kaups, and D. J. Ollila, Jr. (Turka, Finland: Institute of Migration, 1975), 59.

12. There is no way to document this claim except possibly through oral tradition, examples of which we did not find. No doubt the recipes were passed on orally. The Finnish cookbooks from that period were not published in the region and, therefore, do not contain pasty recipes. See, for example, Toinen Painos, *Keittorkirja* (Fitchburg, Mass.: Suomalainen Sosialistinen Kustannusyhtiö, n.d.); Mina Wallin, *Suomalais-Amerikalainen Keittokirja* (New York: By the author, 1914); Recent Finnish-American community cookbooks published in Michigan

inevitably include pasty recipes, e.g., *We Thank Thee, Lord* (Hancock, Mich.: Franklin Street Church, 1973) and *Ethnic Flavors* (Farmington Hills, Mich.: Finnish Center Association, n.d. [1990]).

13. Kirsti Tolvanen, *Finnish Food* (Helsinki: Kustannusosakeythiö Otava, 1959), 81–85.

14. "Tasty Pasty in Michigan, a Cornish Delicacy Is Given a Finnish Flavor," *Natural History*, 89, no. 1 (January 1980): 101–3.

15. Tenison, 78; Bailey, 20.

16. Cookbooks published in Great Britain refer to this process as "the Cornish crimp."

17. The origin of this saying might be attributed to a few popular pasty shops with Italian bakers at the time of this study. However, recalling Catholic church pasty sales, U.P. residents of different ethnic groups did not regard Italian-made pasties as different from others.

18. People who do put gravy over pasty—individuals belonging to different ethnic groups in the central U.P.—reason that pasty would otherwise be dry. No one seems to know exactly where the idea came from. Some suggested possibly an influence from meat pies or restaurants.

19. The former Madelyne's Original Foods of the U.P. had provided commercial pasties in the region for decades. According to the *Green Bay Press Gazette* (September 11, 1983), Madelyne's began to market pasty in California as a convenience food. Encouraged by orders ranging from 4,000 to 7,000 pasties a day from food distributors in Los Angeles and San Francisco, Madelyne's decided to vary its "original" recipe (meat, potatoes, rutabagas, and parsley) and offer chicken with cheese, Italian sausage with mozzarella cheese and potatoes, vegetable and cheese, and apple.

20. Jess Gilbert and Craig Harris, "Unemployment, Primary Production, and Population in the Upper Peninsula of Michigan in the Great Depression," in *A Half Century Ago: Michigan in the Great Depression,* edited by Frederick Honhart and Victor Howard (East Lansing: Michigan State University Archives and Historical Collections and the American Studies Program, 1980), 23–24.

21. For a folk perspective on this economic and social decline, see William Ivey, "The 1913 Disaster: Michigan Local Legend," *Folklore Forum,* 3 (1970): 100–114.

22. See Roger Abrahams, "Introductory Remarks to a Rhetorical Theory of Folklore," *Journal of American Folklore* 81 (1968): 143–58.

23. *A Rhetoric of Motives* (New York: 1950), 46.

24. Middle-aged Italian-American pasty shop owner in the western U.P. 1980.

25. See Dorson, *Bloodstoppers,* 107, 109, 117–18, for folklore collected about pasty. He also presents the folk explanation of the origin of pasty on 117.

26. Cornish, middle-aged male residing in the Detroit area, 1981.

27. *Ann Arbor News,* April 10, 1983.

28. This limerick appeared in an Upper Peninsula paper, *The Pick and Axe,* 1976. "Fudgy" is a pejorative term for tourists who, while on vacation, purchase large quantities of Mackinac Island fudge.

29. "U.P. 'Adopts' Miners' Meal," *Upbeat,* the Sunday magazine section of the *U.P. Times,* April 16, 1978.

30. Mr. and Mrs. Matthews also served as informants for *American Cooking: The Eastern Heartland* (New York: Time-Life, 1971), 25–29.

31. Wayne State University Folklore Archive, 1970 (No. 119). This shop, however, like those in Colorado, California, northern Minnesota, and Florida, where Cornish and Yoopers have moved, serves pasty as a specialty; i.e., pasties have not been recognized in these areas.

2

Rocky Mountain Oysters

James F. Hoy

Certain kinds of food are often associated with certain parts of the country—baked beans with Boston, or crawfish with Louisiana. Beef, of course, is the staple of the Great Plains, but more particularly our special culinary offering is the Rocky Mountain oyster, the polite term for the bovine testicle.

I had never really appreciated that term until the summer of 1983, when our family spent a leisurely week on a boat off the coast of British Columbia. Some mornings, when the tide was out, we would gather oysters. Whether raw, fried, or cooked in the shell over charcoal, these fresh oysters had an exquisite taste, far better than I have ever experienced in a restaurant. It is this richness and delicacy of taste that sea oysters share with the Rocky Mountain variety.

Although the squeamish won't touch them, the aficionado knows that Rocky Mountain oysters are one of the world's great delicacies. Like many things associated with a folk group, names will vary. I have heard them called mountain oysters, prairie oysters, bull fries, and lamb fries. This latter term, I assume, comes from the use of lamb testicles, although it is just as often applied to those from cattle. I have never eaten lamb oysters, but I have tried some from pigs and young goats. I have even heard of turkey fries. Nothing, however, beats genuine calf oysters.

Roundup was the traditional time for gathering mountain oysters in the Great Plains of a century ago. Today most calves are worked before they reach weaning age. While such oysters are smaller, they are also more tender. Another prime gathering time occurs when a rancher has

Reprinted by permission from *Plains Folk: A Commonplace of the Great Plains* by Jim Hoy and Tom Isern (Norman: University of Oklahoma Press, 1987), 77–79.

just received a shipment of short yearlings, some or most of which have not yet been castrated.

As the animals are worked, the oysters are tossed into buckets half full of water. Later, the testicles are washed and cleaned of extraneous skin and cords. They are then soaked in salt water overnight. Some people freeze the oysters at this point, reserving final cleaning (i.e., peeling away the outer skin) until the oysters are about one-fourth thawed. This is definitely the easiest way to clean them, but many people prefer fresh oysters to frozen ones. Either way, the next step is to cook them.

Small oysters are best fried whole; large ones must be sliced into pieces that are one-half inch or so thick. Recipes vary, but the best, in my opinion, is the simplest: roll the oyster in a mixture of salt, pepper, and flour and pop it into a skillet of hot grease. Other recipes include batters of Seven-up and pancake flour or of cracker crumbs and butter. Some people deep fry rather than using a frying pan.

Craig Claiborne, of the *New York Times*, credits Helen Dollagan, of the *Denver Post*, with this recipe: soak oysters in milk, dip in fresh bread crumbs, and brown in butter. Serve with ketchup or lemon wedges. To a real plainsman, though, pouring ketchup on good, tender mountain oysters is a sin comparable to smothering a prime, charcoal-broiled, medium-rare T-bone with ketchup.

When I was growing up, we often had mountain oysters for breakfast as a side dish with pancakes. At other times I remember mountain oysters as the main course for informal community gatherings. These were usually stag affairs (no pun intended) at which area ranchers and cowboys would celebrate the end of the calf-working season with a party that would include oysters, beer, and poker.

A few parting words of advice—novice mountain-oyster cooks should be prepared for a strong cooking odor. The cooked oyster will have no trace of this odor, but first-time eaters should be aware that this delicately textured, exquisitely flavored dish is also extremely rich; do not overeat.

3

Loco Moco: A Folk Dish in the Making

James L. Kelly

Because of their universal character and potential variability, foodways ought to be useful indicators of cultural contact and borrowing. It would seem also that the process of changing foodways, because of contact of cultures, is analogous to language change because of culture contact. As a result, the term and methods used in linguistic analysis may be applicable to the study of foodways.

After a discussion of relevant linguistic terminology and language change in Hawaii, this paper describes changing foodways in Hawaii and notes the similarity of these changes with language change. Finally, the paper reports on the creation of the loco moco, an entirely new dish derived from contact of different foodways, and therefore, comparable to a pidgin language.

Language Change

When culture groups and languages come into contact, immigrant families tend to continue to speak their native tongue, often the only language they know (Weinreich, 1974:87). Gradually, however, people with the most outside contacts, such as children and young adults, begin to speak other languages or parts of other languages. The acquired words or phrases may then spread among the large population of the native group. This is called the pre-bilingual period. Essentially what is happening is that a small group of people are borrowing words and structures from one or more languages and slowly disseminating them to others.

Reprinted by permission from *Social Process in Hawaii* 30 (1983), 59–64.

Following this, a stage of adult bilingualism is reached where the parts of one language are systematically substituted in the native language. In this case, these substitutions become a regular part of the everyday native language and their use is fairly widespread among the population of the native group; the same words or phrases being consistently employed by the members of the language group (Haugen, 1972:87). In many cases loan blends may occur in which the parts of another language that are substituted into the native language are changed. Pronunciation, for example, may be changed although the meaning remains the same.

If language contact continues, a pidgin language may result. A pidgin has structure and lexical items from two or more contact languages, but it is a new language (Fromkin and Rodman, 1978:269). Such a pidgin language developed in Hawaii largely as a result of the necessity of plantation workers of different language groups to communicate with each other and with their English-speaking overseers (Lind, 1960:44). As this was occurring, however, the use of native languages declined and became "Americanized." Local Chinese, for example, had increasing trouble with Chinese tones, while the Japanese "r" round changed to something more like the English "r" or "l" (Hormann, 1960:13).

Foodways in Hawaii

Hawaii makes an interesting laboratory for the examination of the thesis of changing foodways because of culture contact. It is an isolated group of islands to which have come successive waves of people each bringing their own native foods and ways of cooking. The variety includes: American, Hawaiian, Japanese, Chinese, Korean, Filipino, and Portuguese. In the beginning most immigrants continued to eat their own kinds of food, cooked in the same ways as in the old country, subject to availability of food, spices, and kitchen utensils. Major ethnic groups continued to maintain contact with the old country and, because they arrived in Hawaii in fairly large numbers, a market was created for the importation of foods into Hawaii. In addition, many of the early plantation workers lived in separate camps, arranged by ethnic group. Each camp or each family, then, could raise or exchange food and, therefore, maintain traditional food habits.

Gradually, however, a system of borrowing other foods began, somewhat comparable to borrowing in language change. Especially in restaurants, people began to try other kinds of foods. Restaurants that served only Chinese or Japanese food, for example, began to have customers from other ethnic groups. This system of borrowing foods continued until a stage, somewhat comparably to adult bilingualism in language, was reached in which standard foods were borrowed on a consistent basis.

Today in Hawaii, and for the past several decades, most residents eat a combination of borrowed foods from several ethnic groups. *Sashimi,* Japanese raw fish, is a common dish during holidays and as a party snack for almost all households, regardless of ethnic background. Teriyaki steak, another Japanese contribution, is almost as common. The teriyaki sauce is well known and many residents buy prepared teriyaki steak already marinated in the special sauce. Rice is served at many tables, and for many people arriving from the mainland, rice has replaced potatoes and bread. At the same time, however, rice in the diet of those people of Oriental ancestry has declined, replaced by breads, macaroni, and other Western starches (Miller, 1947:768).

Sandwiches are common for Orientals, while hot noodles are equally common for Westerners. Westerners generally have adopted the short cooking period for vegetables, while Orientals have begun to use more dairy products and meats. In addition, Orientals have increasingly used more candies, other sugar foods, and soft drinks.

Perhaps the most conspicuous change in diet is the change to Western style breakfast by all groups. Instead of an elaborate breakfast with vegetables and rice, both Orientals and Westerners now eat toast and coffee. On the whole, then, there seems to have been a trend toward fast foods: sandwiches, coffee, and toast. One of the reasons cited for the decline of Japanese food, for example, is that it takes too long to prepare and that it is too troublesome (Masuoka, 1945:765).

As in language change, such borrowing of different foods by different ethnic groups could not occur without some change in the borrowed foods themselves. Saimin, a hot noodle dish popular in Hawaii, is served in many small restaurants including McDonald's. But, this saimin is not a truly Oriental noodle dish. It is instead a modified, even Westernized, version. Similarly, Korean *kim-chi* is produced and consumed locally and, though it is "hot," Hawaiian *kim-chi* is far from being as hot as the true Korean *kim-chi.* The teriyaki steak sometimes appears in a different form also: "teri-burgers" are served at many fast food outlets. The Japanese plate lunch, a prepared takeout lunch, has also been modified from the Japanese original. In Hawaii the plate lunch may include such Western ingredients as macaroni salad as well as sushi.

The Loco Moco

Not surprising, continuous contact of different foodways has produced at least one new dish, something comparable to a pidgin language. The item is called a loco moco and its invention and diffusion is a good example of the changes in foodways resulting from contact of different culture groups.

The loco moco is prepared by putting a scoop of rice in a bowl, often a waxed, paper bowl, adding a hamburger patty and an egg, fried over-easy, and then pouring gravy over everything. It sells, usually, for $1 to $1.75.

The loco moco originated in a small cafe, called the Lincoln Grill, in downtown Hilo on the island of Hawaii. It was invented by the restaurant's owners and operators, Mr. and Mrs. Richard Inouye in 1949. It originated as an attempt to provide a snack for a group of teenage boys who were tired of eating American sandwiches, yet did not want to bother with time-consuming Oriental food. The contents of the loco moco were suggested by Mrs. Nancy Inouye. Rice was a staple of the cafe as was the gravy that was poured over it. Mr. Inouye had formerly worked at the Royal Hawaiian Hotel in Honolulu and there learned to make sauces and gravies. The hamburger patty, of course, was also a fairly common part of the cafe's menu because all types of food were served and American hamburgers were popular.

The final product is instructive in many ways. Not only do the ingredients suggest origins in different ethnic foods, but the way they are put together also reveals some blending of foodways. The rice is mixed with the other foods and the gravy, not kept separate as in Japanese food. And the gravy that was added at the end gives the entire dish a wetter taste compared to the dry hamburger. The egg, which was added a few years after the initial invention of the loco moco, seems to add flavor, perhaps in cases where less attention was paid to the gravy, and nutrition.

Overall the loco moco appears to have origins in Oriental and Western food habits. The rice and the use of a sauce are more Oriental and the ground meat and fried egg are mostly Western. Moreover, it is a mixture of eating habits: the slower eating style of Oriental food served in a bowl and the Western style of fast food and simplicity with less chances of messiness.

The name loco moco was chosen by the teenagers themselves. They tried to compose a name made up of their own initials. When this failed they used the nickname of the boy who first ate a loco moco. His nickname was "crazy," which is loco in Portuguese and in the local pidgin. Moco has no meaning and was chosen because it rhymed with loco and sounded better than loco soko, loco doko, or loco koko.

After its invention, the loco moco spread to other neighborhood restaurants in Hilo, to other parts of the Big Island, and more recently to Honolulu and other islands. It is a popular dish at school cafeterias and lunch counters. Inquiries about the origin of the loco moco reveal that most people think it was invented on the plantations. Thus, the image of most people is that the loco moco has the same origin as Hawaii pidgin. Moreover, the loco moco, like pidgin, lacks prestige. It is sold mostly in small local restaurants, in contrast to a dish like *sashimi* that is often served in the most expensive restaurants and at parties. Already it seems to have been adopted as local by some places. A restaurant on Maui, for example, has advertised the loco moco as "Maui's Own." Given this current status and image, the loco moco could become a symbol of localness in the same way as pidgin.

References

Fromkin, Victoria, and Robert Rodman. 1978. *An Introduction to Language.* New York: Holt, Rinehart, Winston.

Haugen, Einer. 1972. "The Analysis of Linguistic Borrowing," in his *The Ecology of Language.* Palo Alto, Calif.: Stanford University Press.

Hormann, Bernhard L. 1960. "Hawaii's Linguistic Situation: A Sociological Interpretation." *Social Process in Hawaii* 24.

Lind, Andrew W. 1960. "Communication: A Problem of Island Youth." *Social Process in Hawaii* 24.

Masuoka, Jitsuichi. 1945. "Changing Food Habits of the Japanese in Hawaii." *American Sociological Review* 10.

Miller, Carey. 1947. "Foods and Food Habits in the Hawaiian Islands." *Journal of the American Dietetic Association* 23.

Weinreich, Uriel. 1974. *Languages in Contact.* The Hague: Mouton.

4

The Cincinnati Chili Culinary Complex

Timothy C. Lloyd

It is common to read that developments in food processing, refrigeration, and transportation, which have made foodstuffs from any region of the United States available throughout the country and throughout the year, have contributed to the demise of regional foodways.[1] The availability of a great number of foodstuffs, however, does not in and of itself guarantee the elimination of traditional food habits. The most significant obstacle to this process of homogenization is the existence locally of associations and identifications surrounding food, food habits, and food events. These associations and identifications come from a variety of sources and, as nutritionists, applied anthropologists, and folklorists have found, are crucial to the choice and maintenance of what is customary in diet and in food-related activities.[2] On the other hand, these factors are not immune to development or change. It is possible for new foods to be introduced, or even to be invented, and then over time to have their own system of custom and identification build up around them. Cincinnati-style chili is such a food.

Cincinnati chili may be distinguished from other varieties of chili in two main respects: by its ingredients and by the way it is served. Generally speaking, Cincinnati chili is made by boiling ground lean beef, often under pressure, until it is browned through; adding a mixture of twelve to eighteen herbs and spices (depending on the specific recipe), including cinnamon, allspice, and bay leaves; and then cooking this mixture for three or four hours until it is reduced to the proper consistency. This food, served alone, is called a "bowl of plain." Few people in Cincinnati,

Reprinted by permission from *Western Folklore* 40, 1 (January 1981), 28–40. © California Folklore Society.

however, eat this version of the dish—they eat a "three-way" or a "four-way" or some other "way."

There are at least five Cincinnati chili "ways": a "two-way," or "chili spaghetti," is chili on top of a bed of spaghetti; a "three-way," the most popular "way," is spaghetti topped with chili and grated yellow cheese; a "four-way" is spaghetti, chili, cheese, and diced white onions; and a "five-way" is spaghetti, chili, cheese, onions, and kidney beans. Some stories tell of one of the chain of Dixie Chili parlors across the river in Kentucky that experimented with six-ways by adding sliced hot dogs to a five-way, but apparently this idea never became popular. A common option is a cheese coney, which is constructed of bun, hot dog, chili, onions, and cheese, plus a side bowl of oyster crackers (never regular saltines).

In Cincinnati, this system of chili service, organized around the proper order and terminology of "ways," tends to be taken for granted as part of the local, traditional culinary complex. Thus, although it is possible to be served "spaghetti with chili, cheese, and onions," the correct term for this order is a "four-way." The correspondence between the order of additional ingredients and higher-numbered ways follows a strict rule of cheese = three, onions = four, and beans = five, and although changes may be made to the menu, the formula by which they are made is itself organized around this rule. For instance, let us say you want spaghetti, chili, and onions, but no cheese. You would not, in this case, order a "three-way with onions instead of cheese," or a "two-way plus onions"; you would order a "four-way no cheese." According to the rule, onions = four, so if you want chili that has onions on it you must start with a four-way (the highest-numbered way corresponding to the ingredients you want) and then subtract those ingredients that you do not want. In like manner, spaghetti, chili, cheese, and beans comprise a "five-way no onions," not a "three-way plus beans." The only general exceptions to this rule are the "chili spaghetti" mentioned above and the combination of spaghetti, chili, and beans which, in the interest of economy, is called a "chili bean," not a "five-way no cheese no onions."[3]

Cincinnati chili is made and served in 65 chain chili parlors (the chains are Empress, Gold Star, Skyline and, in the Kentucky suburbs, Dixie); in individually owned chili parlors; in restaurants which serve chili, but do not specialize in it; and in private homes. The process by which chili is made and served is, as one might expect, most precise and mechanized in the chain parlors.

Each of these chain operations began as a single restaurant, and its chili was prepared by, or under the strict supervision of, the restaurant's founder. Expansion and franchising began in the late 1940s and early

1950s, and now all of the chili for each chain is prepared in one centrally located kitchen and is sent by truck to the individual restaurants. This method of production and distribution is common among chain restaurant businesses, since it is more cost-effective and ensures a standardized product. In this case, however, it also ensures that the formula for the mixing of chili spices, which is the key to any Cincinnati chili recipe, will continue to be available only to a select few—and the secrecy of the recipes is as important a matter as cost-effectiveness in the Cincinnati chili business. Joe Kiradjieff, the son of the inventor of Cincinnati chili and the head of the Empress chain, maintains that the only two people who know his father's original formula for the kinds and amounts of spices for Empress chili are himself and his mother, that he will pass it on only to his daughter, and then only when he is ready to retire.[4] Alone in his basement, he mixes all of the spices for every order of chili served in the eleven Empress parlors. The five Lambrinides sons, who run Skyline Chili, and the Sarakatsannises, of Dixie Chili, mix the spices for their recipes at their offices, and the Davids, of Gold Star, at their commissary.

None of the restaurant managers or owners I interviewed would divulge his recipe, or for that matter, would reveal any information about his spice formula except that it called for more than a dozen spices and that the secret of good chili was a proper balance among the spices, with no one ingredient overshadowing the others. They did, however, provide a good deal of information about the other aspects of chili preparation, which further indicates that the spice mixture is the crucial part of this process. Although the amount of cinnamon used in a particular chili recipe is about the same as the amount of any other spice ingredient, cinnamon is the essential ingredient in the recipe's spice mixture. It is the link to the Old World foods which are among the ancestors of this chili; it marks the divergence of this version of chili from other American regional recipes; and it sets the general tone for the interplay of sweet and hot spices that make up the mixture. The basic Cincinnati chili recipe contains the following ingredients: ground lean beef, water, onions, garlic, white vinegar, worcestershire, peppers or tabasco, bay leaves, chili powder, cumin, tomato sauce, cinnamon, and allspice (which, although it tastes like a combination of cinnamon, cloves, and nutmeg, is itself a separate spice). Since many Cincinnatians know enough about the basic recipe to make their own versions of the dish at home, we must assume that this matter of "secret" recipes has less to do with culinary knowledge than with family and regional pride.

The primary difference among the chilis served at the outlets of these three chains seems to be one of hotness—that is, the total amount, rather than the relative proportions, of spices in each recipe. Skyline is the mildest, Empress hotter, and Gold Star hotter still, though nothing

like many of the hot Texas or southwestern chilis. Although considerable controversy exists among local chili connoisseurs as to the particular chain, individual chain location, and specific time of day at which
the best chili can be found, for many Cincinnatians the best chili is
determined not by criteria of authenticity, secrecy, or spiciness but by
considerations of habit or by childhood remembrance. A significant
number of my informants felt that the best chili was that which happened to have been served either at the parlor around the corner from
where they were raised, or at a downtown parlor where chili meals were
part of the family ritual of a regular Saturday's shopping trip.

In any event, at the central kitchens, the mysterious spice mixture is
added to the partially cooked beef and the chili is cooked until done
and then chilled for shipment. At the restaurants, the chili is mixed with
a small amount of water, reheated, and then placed toward one end of
a long steam table in a large ceramic crock. Along each side of the steam
table is a line of smaller crocks containing, in order, spaghetti, cheese,
onions, and beans; a chili order is dished up as one of the servers moves
along in assembly-line fashion, adding the proper ingredients for the
"way" ordered. The buns and wieners for the coneys are at the other
end of the steam table and are assembled in the same manner.

In the individually owned parlors, such as Blue Ash Chili or Uncle
Steve's Camp Washington Chili, the cooking and serving processes are
less rationalized and mechanized, but the spice formulae are no less
secret. The menu is essentially the same: chili in the various "ways,"
coneys, and oyster crackers. Although some of these parlors also serve
breakfast and short orders (including another Cincinnati specialty, the
"double-decker" ham, roast beef, and cheese sandwich), their recognized specialty is chili. Many of the owners of these parlors claim that
their chili is bound to be better than that of the chains, since it is prepared in smaller quantities and is given the kind of attention often impossible in a more institutional setting. Because of this attention, and
the fact that most of these parlors have been in the same neighborhoods, if not the same locations, for many years, they attract a large
regular neighborhood clientele. For their customers, these parlors also
serve as meeting-places in much the same way as would a neighborhood
grocery, beauty parlor, barbershop, or tavern.

The quality of chili served at Cincinnati restaurants which do not specialize in chili is generally not as high as it is in the parlors. It is especially
interesting that many of these restaurants go to the trouble either of
making their chili, whatever the quality, in the Cincinnati style, rather
than buying canned regular "meat and bean soup" chili from a food
service distributor or of serving this regular chili in the local manner (a
variation known nationally as the "chili mac"). This is even true of some

restaurants that are part of other chains with their own standardized distribution system. Serving regular chili in the regular manner (meat and bean soup in a bowl with saltines) in Cincinnati, although practiced, is evidently not a smart business decision.

With some 200 restaurants serving chili in town and with frozen Empress and Skyline and canned Dixie products available in the groceries, it is possible to eat chili anytime anywhere in Cincinnati; it thus seems unlikely that anyone would go to the trouble of making chili at home— but many people do. In fact, the invention, testing, and transmission of chili recipes is an important activity in Cincinnati. Despite the fact that most of the specific restaurant recipes are ostensibly secret, the general idea of what goes into Cincinnati chili is well known in the area and serves as the basis for individual experimentation.

The ingredients for three of the recipes I collected in Cincinnati are given in Figure 1. The first is the recipe used earlier as a good basic standard. The second adds cayenne and unsweetened chocolate ("For body," I was told by my informant). The third adds everything else on the spice shelf. The woman from whom I collected this recipe told me that she and a couple of her friends arrived at it by sitting down with five or six different recipes and adding together into one list every ingredient that was in any one of them.[5] While this third list of ingredients probably represents the ultimate complexity that Cincinnati chili can attain, it also gives an idea of the range of ingredients likely to be present in one version or another of the dish. A comparison of these three lists also shows the core ingredients which form the basis for chili experimentation—everything in the lists down to cinnamon—and some of the individual variants developed from this core.

Most regionally characteristic foods derive from the plants and animals common to a region, are then shaped by individual choice in daily meal habits, and only later may enter regional restaurant offerings. Cincinnati chili, however, began as the outgrowth of a commercial enterprise. In the early 1920s, Tom Kiradjieff, born in Macedonia, came to Cincinnati by way of New York City, where he had spent several years working in restaurants and selling coney islands from storefront stands. When he arrived in Cincinnati, he opened a coney island stand on Vine Street in downtown and named it after the Empress Theatre next door. Seeking to make his business unique, Kiradjieff experimented with different recipes for the sauce for his coneys, or, as they were often called, chili dogs. In 1922 he developed the original recipe for what is now Cincinnati chili.

Nick Sarakatsannis, the head of Dixie Chili, has called Kiradjieff "an Edison, a Firestone." In a *Cincinnati Magazine* interview in 1978, he said:

Recipe 1	Recipe 2	Recipe 3
beef	beef	beef
onions	onions	onions
garlic	garlic	garlic
tomato sauce	tomato sauce	tomato sauce
white vinegar	white vinegar	white vinegar
worcestershire	worcestershire	worcestershire
peppers or tabasco	tabasco	
bay leaves	bay leaves	bay leaves
chili powder	chili powder	chili powder
cinnamon	cinnamon	cinnamon
allspice	allspice	
cumin	cumin	
	cayenne	
	unsweetened chocolate	
		curry powder
		ginger
		paprika
		powdered mustard
		cloves
		oregano
		basil
		nutmeg

Figure 1. Lists of ingredients for three chili recipes.

Everybody, in the old days in the regular restaurants, they had roast beef, roast pork, roast lamb; they didn't sell it today. So the next day they scrape up all that meat, they grind it and they make it chili. They put beans in it, and they call it chili con carne. But in 1923, the Empress, they buy freshly ground beef and they cook it. No roast pork or roast beef or leftovers. They use pure beef, no beans. The idea was to have plain meat chili to prove it wasn't leftovers. And they add the spaghetti. From then on, we all copied. I had my own chili, but I copied the spaghetti.[6]

In developing his recipe, Kiradjieff began with the sauce he was using on his coneys with the coney nickname of chili dogs, and with the dishes of the same name, but of the different substance described by Sarakatsannis. The origin of the essential elements of his new chili recipe—the choice, number, and combination of spices, the inclusion of cinnamon in the recipe, and the serving of chili with spaghetti—cannot be explained by reference to these sources alone. For this explanation, we must also look to the foodways of the Levant and of the Balkans—the area where Kiradjieff was born and where, we may assume, some of his culinary inclinations were developed.

Although there is no one dish in the eastern Mediterranean area which corresponds to Kiradjieff's chili, there are three characteristics of Balkan and Levantine foodways which appear to have influenced his innovation. The first is the extensive use in main dishes throughout the area of the most important spice in this chili—cinnamon—and, to a lesser extent, allspice: in Greek *moussaka* and *pastitio,* in Bulgarian *ghivetch,* in stews and other lamb dishes in the Arabic countries, and in curries. The second is the combination of many spices with contrasting effects of sweetness (cinnamon, allspice, cloves, and nutmeg) and hotness (garlic, cumin, peppers, and chilies), in the stews, soups, and other dishes of the area. Most of these spices are used for the same effect in Cincinnati chili. The third is the characteristic combination of such spice mixtures, tomatoes or a tomato-based sauce, cheese, a pasta, and very often beef or lamb in one dish, as is the case with some versions of *pastitio* and *moussaka.*[7] It is also possible that Kiradjieff's idea of serving chili with spaghetti was derived from Italian pasta and sauce dishes. These foreign foodways and foods must be included in a full account of the sources of Kiradjieff's invention, since he would have been likely to draw heavily upon his prior culinary experiences for a solution to the problem of developing a new chili recipe.

At first, the various "ways" in which Cincinnati chili is now served did not exist. The only dish that Kiradjieff served was a mixture of chili and spaghetti; that is, the chili was not served on top of the spaghetti, but was prepared separately and then stirred together with it when served. Around 1930, according to Joe Kiradjieff, his father's customers suggested that for a more attractive product, he might do better to serve the chili on top of the spaghetti. He tried it, found it successful, and then proceeded, over the following few years, to make cheese, onions, and beans available for the more elaborate chili constructions.

The original Empress parlor was the only Empress parlor until shortly after World War II, when Joe Kiradjieff entered the business and when he and his father began to open other stores and, eventually, to franchise. The Empress chain now has eleven parlors, fewer than any of the other chains except Dixie. Empress, though the oldest, is not the largest because Joe Kiradjieff is the only family member involved in the business and is reluctant to assign franchises or to divulge the chili recipe or other business secrets to anyone outside the family. As he told me, the Lambrinides family of Skyline Chili has an advantage over the Kiradjieffs because they have five sons, each with a family, and thus are able to manage a large restaurant business by themselves.

In 1949, Nicholas Lambrinides, who had worked for the Kiradjieffs for a few years, left to open the first of the Skyline Chili parlors. His five sons now operate eighteen of them. For the last thirty years, there have been rumors in Cincinnati that Lambrinides learned the secret Kiradjieff recipe and took it with him when he left; although both principals deny these stories, many people in Cincinnati still believe them to be true. Kiradjieff maintains that the Skyline recipe is not the original one and therefore is not as good; the Lambrinides family, on the other hand, maintains that their recipe, though not the original, is the better. All of this supports the contention made earlier that the "secret recipe" controversy has more to do with family pride than with cooking itself.

Family pride is important because, with the exception of the Gold Star chain owned by a Jordanian-American group, the chili parlors in Cincinnati are essentially Greek family business. (It should be noted that the Kiradjieffs, who are from Macedonia, consider themselves to be Bulgarian.) The restaurant business has always provided employment opportunities for newly arrived Greeks and for members of many other ethnic groups in the northern and midwestern urban centers of the United States. Such potential employment has very likely been a force for greater emigration to this country, since it has assured work and pay in an environment populated by one's countrymen, who could help the new immigrant with the problems of acculturation. For the past fifty years, the major (though not the only) restaurant employment opportunities for Greeks in Cincinnati have been in chili parlors, and the chili business has sent a considerable number of young Greek-Americans to college and to graduate and professional schools. The importance of chili to the Greek community in Cincinnati is attested to by Calvin Trillin in the chapter of his *American Fried* which looks at Cincinnati. He says:

> When the Kiradjieff family, which introduced authentic Cincinnati chili at the Empress in 1922, was sued several years ago by a manager who alleged that he had been fired unfairly, one of his claims amounted to the contention that anyone fired under suspicious circumstances from a chili parlor with Empress' prestige was all through in the Greek community.[8]

In a 1979 newspaper interview, Father Constantine Mitsos of the Holy Trinity Orthodox Church recited some of the names of his parishioners:

> Of course there are the Lambrinides brothers of Skyline Chili. And there are others who own Skyline franchises. The Georgeton brothers. Chili Time in St. Bernard is run by Harry C. Vidas—you've got to say the middle initial because there are so many of them—and his brother Pete, and a nephew Ted. Chili Town across from Shillito's is the Demas brothers, George and Tim. There is Camp Washington Chili, and Price Hill Chili—oh yes, and Delhi Chili. White Oak Chili and Blue Ash Chili. Across the river there is Covington Chili and Dixie Chili.[9]

While the business of making and selling chili is largely a Greek domain, the dish itself is not defined in Cincinnati as an ethnic food. None of the chili-makers I have interviewed, including the Greeks, has felt that Cincinnati chili is a Greek food or has been able to trace it to any Greek or Balkan source. In much the same way, chili parlors are not considered to be Greek restaurants. Only a handful of the parlors have the customary markers of Greek restaurants, whether visual (conspicuous blue-and-white decoration, Greek travel posters, Greek design motifs), verbal (restaurant names such as Acropolis or Aegean), or culinary (recognized Greek menu items); and the chili served at these locations is generally not very highly regarded. Since these restaurants are all of recent origin, we must suspect that the original intention of their owners was to open Greek restaurants to serve *gyros* and *souvlaki* and that the addition of chili to their otherwise ethnic menu was done in consideration of local custom. This is itself an indication of the strength of local chili tradition. The sort of place where Cincinnatians go to eat chili is a parlor run by Greeks—and that is not the same thing as a Greek restaurant. This situation is paralleled in Los Angeles, where Greeks own a large number of local non-chain hamburger businesses,[10] and in the East and Midwest, where there are many urban Greek short-order restaurants, caricatured by the "cheeseburger and Pepsi" joint portrayed on the television program *Saturday Night Live*.

The definition and identification of chili in Cincinnati are not primarily ethnic—they are regional. Many Cincinnatians are aware that the amount of time they spend eating, cooking, and talking about chili is unique and that chili is not only different there, it is also more important than it is in most other places. Some take considerable personal pride in their testing and exchange of chili recipes, but they take a greater, almost civic, pride in the fact that Cincinnati is a place where such activity is highly regarded. All of this has not been lost, of course, on the local Chamber of Commerce, which recently printed a "scratch and sniff" cover section on chili, including a rating of local parlors, in their monthly magazine,[11] or on local newspapers, which regularly print chili stories and recipes. The "scratch and sniff" section of *Cincinnati Magazine* also contained an admittedly tongue-in-cheek listing of the prices and distributors for the tables, chairs, salt-and-pepper shakers, china, ashtrays, and other items used by local parlors so that readers could create their own Skyline or Empress setting at home. Evidently, the most common design features of the parlors, as well as the chili they serve, are locally significant.

Chili and chili parlors contribute in another way to regional identity: they help to identify the various neighborhoods of the metropolitan area and serve as markers for orientation within the city. Many of the

individual parlors, which, as mentioned earlier, are neighborhood land-
marks, carry the name of the neighborhood or suburb in which they
are located and from which the bulk of their business comes—Camp
Washington Chili, Blue Ash Chili, Price Hill Chili. The chain parlors
are locally identified by neighborhood—the Kenwood Skyline, the Mt.
Washington Gold Star, the Downtown Empress. South of the Ohio River
(the Ohio equivalent, in some ways, of the Mason-Dixon line), in the
Kentucky suburbs, the major chain parlor is Dixie Chili. This combination of culinary and geographic significance makes chili parlors an important part of individual map-making and of neighborhood and
regional identity.

In fact, this identity has often worked against the development of the
Cincinnati chili business outside of the area. The failure of some chain
parlor franchises in other areas of the state and Midwest has been due,
according to the owners, to the fact that the product is advertised as
"Cincinnati chili," an association that may not be so attractive in To-
ledo, Columbus, or Detroit. From now on, they plan to call their product
"gourmet chili."[12] One of the few areas outside Greater Cincinnati
where parlors have been successful is central Florida, where a significant
amount of the business has come from retired or vacationing Ohioans,
who seem to welcome the opportunity to make contact with a bit of
Ohio in the South.

Cincinnati chili has become such an important regional food not simply because it is made and eaten within a particular area, but also (and
perhaps primarily) because it has been adapted to suit general local
taste, just as the chili recipes of the southwestern United States have
come to be culinary expressions of local tastes in that hybrid border
area. This is so because of the manner in which the chili is served. The
least popular Cincinnati chili dish is the bowl of plain chili, which, interestingly enough, is the way almost all chili is served outside of Cincinnati. This dish is the least popular because it is considered to be too hot,
too strong, too spicy—a dish for true aficionados which must be
"worked up to." In the most popular chili "way," the three-way, the
spicy and exotic chili is served between two layers of bland, plain food—
spaghetti and cheese—which tames the chili's strength and spiciness
and brings the dish as a whole into a balance more acceptable to local,
mid-American palates.[13]

What is more, the spaghetti, chili, and cheese of the three-way are
prepared and placed on the plate separately, thus creating a separation
of discrete meal elements. As Joe Kiradjieff said, his father's chili became
much more popular when he stopped stirring the chili together with
the spaghetti. The adaptation to local tastes is thus made possible by the
use of the spaghetti and cheese, which balance the chili, and by the

layering of separate foods on the plate, which preserves, even in chili, the typically American idea of a "steak, potatoes, and carrots" assemblage of separate and distinct food items that make up a proper meal.

The ingredients, method of preparation, and organization of the chili meal in Cincinnati are unique to the area and comprise one of the most distinctive foodways systems in the United States. Although the most significant part of its spice recipe comes from a Balkan-Levantine source, this chili has been adapted, in serving and substance, to American tastes. Unlike other urban foods which have been the object of scholarly attention, it is regionally, not ethnically, defined. It is served in restaurants and in homes, rather than strictly in private settings, and a particular combination of traditional and institutional factors influences its preparation and serving in each context. It is available all day, every day, and thus it does not have the special significance of foods which are part of holiday or other important meals. At the same time, this style of chili and the activities surrounding the making and eating of it are central to the regional identifications of many Cincinnatians. These activities are significant, in fact, precisely because they have come to be ordinary, everyday occurrences within the area. They have become customary elements of this culinary complex.

Notes

A preliminary version of this paper was read at the 1979 Annual Meeting of the American Folklore Society in Los Angeles, California.

1. See, for instance, Richard Osborn Cummings, *The American and His Food: A History of Food Habits in the United States* (Chicago, 1940); and Waverly Root and Richard de Rochemont, *Eating in America: A History* (New York, 1976), ch. 16–18, 30–31.

2. See, for instance, John W. Bennett, Harvey L. Smith, and Herbert Passin, "Food and Culture in Southern Illinois—A Preliminary Report," *American Sociological Review* 7 (1942): 645–60; *The Problem of Changing Food Habits*, ed. Committee on Food Habits (Washington D.C., National Research Council Bulletin 108, 1943); *Manual for the Study of Food Habits*, ed. Committee on Food Habits (Washington D.C., National Research Council Bulletin 111, 1945); Margaret Cussler and Mary Louise de Give, *Twixt the Cup and the Lip: Psychological and Socio-Cultural Factors Affecting Food Habits* (New York, 1952); Margaret Mead, "Cultural Patterning of Nutritionally Relevant Behavior," *Journal of the American Dietetic Association* 25 (1949): 677–80; and Marjorie Sackett, "Folk Recipes as a Measure of Intercultural Penetration," *Journal of American Folklore* 85 (1972): 77–81. I am indebted to Charles Camp for information leading me to these references; see his "Food in American Culture: A Bibliographic Essay," in *Journal of American Culture* 2 (1979): 559–70.

3. Barbara Jo Foreman, "No speak-a da Chili," *The Enquirer Magazine* (Cincinnati, Ohio), 1 October 1978, 28–31.

4. Interview with Joe Kiradjieff, Cincinnati, Ohio, 16 August 1979.

5. Interview with Edna Davis and Mamie Jackson, Cincinnati, Ohio, 3 October 1979.

6. "The New York Chili Connection," *Cincinnati Magazine,* October 1978, 62.

7. See, for instance, Hassalevris, *Constantine Cooks the Greek Way* (Los Angeles, 1962), 37, 39–41, 44, 48; Sylvia Windle Humphrey, *A Matter of Taste: The Definitive Seasoning Cookbook* (New York, 1965), 48–50; Inge Krananz, *The Balkan Cookbook* (New York, 1972); Olympia Marketos, *Athens a la Carte: The Best of Greek Cooking* (Chicago, 1963), 32–34; Sophia Skoura, *The Greek Cook Book* (New York, 1967), 45, 50–51; and Theresa Kanas Yianilos, *The Complete Greek Cookbook* (New York, 1970), 62–63, 65, 213–14.

8. *American Fried* (Garden City, New York, 1974), 130.

9. Lonnie Wheeler, "The Greek Connection," *Cincinnati Enquirer,* 11 February 1979.

10. John McKinney, "A Fortune From Grease," *New West,* Southern California Edition, 5 November 1979, SC 37–41.

11. "The Red Hot Guide to Cincinnati Chili," *Cincinnati Magazine,* October 1978, 61–66.

12. Interview with Frank David, Cincinnati, Ohio, 16 August 1979.

13. Octavio Paz, "Eroticism and Gastrosophy," *Daedalus,* 101, No. 4 (1972): 74.

5

A Pound of Kenya, Please or a Single Short Skinny Mocha

Stephen Frenkel

During the past decade, the growth of specialty coffee businesses in the Pacific Northwest has been phenomenal. The sale and promotion of these coffees—whole beans as contrasted to vacuum packed tins of Folgers—has created a new landscape of consumption. On the one hand, specialty coffee is an economic success story, the fad that succeeded frozen yogurt and gourmet cookie stores. There are more than 6,000 commercial espresso machines in the state of Washington alone, roughly 1 for every 750 people. Neon signs, vinyl advertising banners, and corporate logos announce espresso at every corner. The specialty coffee industry, on the other hand, is more than a business opportunity, it is a phenomenon with cultural, social, political and environmental ramifications.

The Coffee Landscape

Perhaps the best place to begin this story is with the development of the cultural landscape of specialty coffee. It's not that mass-marketed coffee has disappeared from the landscape. There are still plenty of coffee shops serving bottomless cups. Likewise, espresso is nothing new; fancy coffee products have long been sold in upscale restaurants and in urban and ethnic enclaves. Cities such as San Francisco and New Orleans have been regional coffee roasting entrepots since the nineteenth century.

Reprinted by permission from *Pacifica: The Association of Pacific Coast Geographers* (Fall 1995), 1, 12–15.

What is new is the availability of specialty coffee from Petaluma to Peoria. Still, the Pacific Northwest remains the cultural hearth of this new coffee landscape.

Today's espresso bar is part of a coffee revolution that began about twenty-five years ago. Its earliest offspring were (and still are) located near major universities and in a few urban areas. These are the counter-culture inspired coffee houses of woody interiors, and clientele ranging from pierced people to philosophy-spouting Euro-wannabees, drinking shots of strong espresso and smoking hand-rolled cigarettes. Such meeting grounds owe symbolic allegiance to coffee houses as haunts of idle chatter and free expression, an identity that reaches back to medieval Turkey although more immediately traceable to European cafés of the last century. Geographically, these coffee house outposts are entrenched near their places of origin, the streetscapes surrounding bohemian and university quarters.

Nevertheless, a significant change occurred in the early 1980s as the bohemian aspect of specialty coffee began to be replaced by a corporate identity. Standardized form replaced individuality. Where bohemian coffee-houses were typically in low-rent districts or in run-down houses with a pony-tailed proprietor, espresso is increasingly sold in strip-malls. Corporate coffee houses—perhaps best exemplified by Seattle's Starbucks—are sanitized, and their employees made to conform to codes of behavior and dress. The result is the transformation of the counterculture coffee house to an up-market retailing outlet, the espresso bar.

The built landscape reflects this economically rationalized mass-production of coffee. Starbucks, for example, divides their coffee stores into functional categories: there are Urban Beverage Stores (places that specialize in early morning lattes for harried office-workers); Urban Bean Stores (shops that specialize in a "european" experience with small tables and outside seating); and Suburban Bean Stores (these are located on commercial strips, and are rapidly replacing the coffee shop of old). Coffee sales also occupy non-fixed locations. Department stores and malls intent on upgrading their image, place chic mobile espresso carts in prominent locations. There are machines scattered across college campuses, and even inside some of the Seattle area's more upscale high-schools.

Reflecting the American predilection for automotive culture, gas stations pump espresso and cappuccino, and coffee is sold at drive-thru windows throughout the Seattle area. Near my house I can choose between the Java Junction, Cruis'in Coffee, or Cafe GoGo. Even rural areas embrace the landscape of cappuccino. There, one finds the seeming incongruity of signs advertising "Tackle and Ammo," along with "Espresso."

Selling Class

Specialty coffee is not just a landscape feature, and the new corporate coffee shops are not just feeding an addiction. They represent an idea, coffee as high culture. Viewed as a symbolic activity, drinking specialty coffee raises the social status of both seller and consumer. The location of coffee shops in upscale bookstores and art-galleries further enhances the perception of coffee as a high status drink. Thus, for the consumer, drinking a double short cappuccino is valued both for its material quality and for the message that it communicates. This can be explained using Pierre Bourdieu's concept of "cultural capital," which is gained from knowing how a given item, object, or action is constituted in terms of "taste." People in the know signify their high status by denigrating the wrong sort of coffee as "institutional" "weak" or simply "bad." This raises their level of cultural capital. The language of specialty coffee separates those who know from those who don't. What exactly is a single short skinny mocha? Insiders needn't ask.

Yet, the very popularity of specialty coffee works against it as a valued item of cultural capital. Given the intensification of gourmet coffee sales, some feel the need to differentiate themselves further from the millions of other drinkers. They may register for classes on espresso making, read books on the history of coffee, and participate in coffee-making demonstrations at stores. Virtually every Starbucks store offers pamphlets ranging from "The Story of Good Coffee from the Pacific Northwest" to a taxonomical field primer called "A Quick Guide to Starbucks Specialty Beverages." Selling coffee is thus all about selling an image.

Selling Place

While individual identity is important, regional identity has become another selling point. Despite a nationwide diffusion, specialty coffee is linked to the Pacific Northwest, particularly Seattle. Walk the streets of Chicago, San Francisco, or airports nationwide, and espresso machines produce "Seattle-style coffee." Turn on the television and Frasier can be seen working through life's problems in Seattle's coffee shops. Pick up a travel magazine and read about espresso on the Puget Sound.

CRUISIN					
		WITH 2 SHOTS	WITH 3 SHOTS	WITH 4 SHOTS	
ESPRESSO	8oz	12oz	16oz	20oz	32oz
LATTE		1.50	1.75	2.00	2.25	4.00
MOCHA		1.75	2.00	2.25	2.50
ICED MOCHA			2.25		4.50
BREVE		1.75	2.00	2.25	2.50
CAPPUCCINO		1.75	2.00	2.25	2.50
ICED LATTE			2.00		4.00
STRAIGHT ESPRESSO					.75
fresh brewed COFFEE .49 .69 .89 .99					
Bibi Caffé ESPRESSO SODA 1.50					
COOL COFFEE CREAM 2.50					
AMERICANO/HOT TEA any size 1.00					
DECAF available/BRING OWN CUP save .10					
SODA · fib. COFFEE w/THERMOS 4¢oz					
FRAPPÉ Cool Coffee Cream 2.50					
EXTRA FIXINS					

What exactly is a single short skinny mocha?

How did Seattle become the coffee capital of America? Is it the prover-
bial rainy climate that makes people desire the stimulation of coffee? Is
it the promotional skills of Starbucks? Is it an alternative to alcohol? Is
it addiction? Or is it the relatively remote nature of the region that
allows for independent invention?

While all these ideas have some merit, I want to suggest an added
explanation: the growth in the popularity of coffee in the Pacific Northwest constitutes a response to patterns of modernist consumption. As we
live and work under a fairly uniform economic system, the desire for
local difference is systematically stymied. Commercial products are increasingly global and homogeneous. Traditional coffee fits this trend. It

is a uniform product with only slight regional variation. We respond to this uniformity by developing a nostalgia for the local and particularistic.

The psychological urge for localism in the face of an increasing glob-alism creates a condition conducive to the celebration of specialty cof-fee. Because coffee proliferated early on in the Pacific Northwest, the perceptual recognition of Seattle as a center of innovation fulfills the nostalgia for regional identity. To mention coffee in the context of Seat-tle gives residents something to boast about.

In this search for difference and diversity, regional identity falls well short of the ideal. Specialty coffee is now mass-marketed all across the country. The cappuccino landscape is highly standardized and rational-ized. Starbucks, for example, with more than 500 outlets nationwide, is now attempting to develop links with Pepsico, and there is talk of selling their products through McDonalds.

Selling Development

But what of coffee production? Coffee is, after all, a tropical crop, yet my double tall latte is a long way from Kenya's coffee plantations. As Robert Sack has recently argued in *Place, Modernity and the Consumer's World,* "the very act of consuming mass-produced products . . . makes us agents of production by perpetuating places and processes of produc-tion."

In fact, growing coffee has many negative consequences: the wide-spread use of nitrogen/phosphorous/potassium fertilizers; the regular application of herbicides; and the contamination of water from the processing. Further, despite high profits in the United States, in produc-ing regions the realities are malnutrition, poor sanitary conditions, and inadequate medical facilities. Coffee consumers certainly benefit from the land and labor of coffee growers. Put in the context of one's morn-ing coffee, however, too much knowledge detracts from enjoyment. Per-haps for this reason, as Sack suggests, factors of production are relegated "to a hidden back stage."

Even so, while the separation of consumption and production is com-mon, the production of coffee can be an attractive story, an advertiser's dream. Pictures of coffee plants, and the image of hard-working small-holders personally growing and selecting your beans, present a pleasant vision. Likewise, there is an element of exotic adventure in choosing beans. Buying a pound of Kenya, Sumatra, or Costa Rica can seem more like a form of vicarious travel than a consumer transaction. Starbucks has even issued coffee passports with a visa stamp given for country "vis-ited." In this manner, coffee companies make a very clear separation between images of production and the politics and economics of production.

Two approaches command our attention in this back-staging process. In the first, the focus is on physical geography. Places are de-peopled and "othered." New Guinea, for example, is reduced to certain attributes: its altitude and soil type lead to a specific bean. There, according to Starbucks brochures, "the equatorial climate and volcanic soil create a highly favorable setting for raising coffee." In such descriptions, the realities of a developing nation are not an issue. Instead, the beans are magically grown, picked and processed without benefit of humans.

In the second back stage approach, there is some mention of the producer, but only in a favorable light. Starbucks advertising descriptions read like the romanticized colonial experiences portrayed in early Banana Republic catalogs. For example, in Guatemala where conflict over productive land is common, the reader learns: "Nestled high in the premier growing area of Antigua, these estates are operated by dedicated horticulturalists." Or in Ethiopia, where a civil war has reduced production over the past two decades: "Here, much of the coffee is still harvested in the traditional manner from wild trees." The fact that harvesting in the traditional manner might imply poverty is never suggested. Thus, the individual is represented as a sanitized and caricatured image.

Recently, there is a countervailing trend where consumption of coffee is intentionally linked to political questions of power and inequality. Some in the coffee community are deliberately attempting to destabilize the separation of production and consumption and specifically link coffee consumption to development issues. These development links have both an idealistic and a pragmatic side.

From a practical standpoint, social consciousness is a selling point. Take the case of Starbucks: For the past five years, the company has been in a partnership with CARE, the international aid and development organization. Starbucks presently donates $100,000 a year, earmarking the money for projects in developing countries from which they buy coffee. While this is philanthropy, it is also advertising. The CARE connection is advertised in newsletters, on cups, by pamphlet, and in annual reports. Readers of "Coffee Matters," Starbucks publicity journal, learn that the company provides clean running water in a village in rural Guatemala, comic books in Kenya with basic information on health and environmental matters, and reforestation efforts in Ethiopia.

For others, the issue of development is more idealistic. An example is the experience of Coffee Kids, a development organization dedicated to improving the quality of life for children and families of coffee-growing communities. Founded in 1988, Coffee Kids begins with the proposition that what to us is simply a cup of coffee, is to others a product with a profound effect on their lives. The organization uses advertising associated with the sale of coffee drinks in the United States to actively educate consumers about the politics of coffee, and to fund development efforts. With an annual budget of $350,000, Coffee Kids implements small-scale, participatory community development projects around the world.

This essay contextualizes the cultural landscape of coffee. It demonstrates how a seemingly mundane activity, selling and drinking coffee, is fundamentally tied to issues that range from local identity to a global economy. The themes of individual identity, regional identity, and cultural politics offer a broader understanding of the meaning of coffee in a consumer's world.

6

The Maine Lobster as Regional Icon: Competing Images Over Time and Social Class

George H. Lewis

Most people in America, when presented with the image of a fresh-cooked lobster, think almost automatically of the coast of Maine. In image *Homarus americanus* is wedded to the state, even though technically it can be found along a 1,300-mile stretch of the Atlantic coast from Cape Hatteras to Labrador and is caught, commercially sold, and shipped from many sea-bordered American states, as well as from Canada. In fact, Canadian lobstermen outnumber Americans (Maine and other states combined) by more than two to one. They provide at least half the lobster sold in the United States, whether or not it is sold under the name of "Maine lobster."[1] Yet no matter how many lobsters are caught, shipped, or eaten out-of-state, the lobster is a symbol of Maine in much the same way maple sugar is of Vermont (though Maine has more maple trees than does Vermont). The spiny crustacean has become a symbol—a regional icon, if you will—of the state, one called upon with light-hearted reverence in passages such as the following, taken from a regional cookbook devoted to *Homarus americanus:*

> It is . . . for the traveler who returns again and again to the rocky coast of Maine, charting his course by the aroma of freshly boiled lobster. His landmarks include the fancy seafood restaurants, the converted bait shacks where lobster rolls are served, and the picnic areas where a Yankee "clambake"[2] can be found on a Sunday afternoon. His heart is unashamedly in

Reprinted by permission from *Food and Foodways* 3, 4 (1989), 303–316. © 1989 Harwood Academic Publishers.

his stomach, but let no one who has not dined upon the lobster make light of this passion.[3]

Regional Character and Meaning of the Lobster

As Howard Marshall has said in his study of special foods of Missouri, "like dialect and architecture, food traditions are a main component in the intricate and impulsive system that joins culture and geography into regional character."[4] In this way, the lobster joins with the "down east" accent, Maine humor, and the distinctive architecture of the area to contribute to a regional character.

And a strongly defined region it is, being bounded on two sides by Canada and on one by the Atlantic Ocean. During the nineteenth century the makeup of Maine's population remained relatively stable, with little immigration either from Canada or from the rest of New England (with the exception of some migrants from Quebec and the Maritimes in the latter years of that century to a select few manufacturing towns, such as Biddeford, Saco, and Lewiston). Most Mainers traced their lineage from English Protestant stock who had settled the area from 1750 to 1800, arriving from Britain or from settlements in southern New England. Except in centers such as Portland, Maine was not thickly settled. Communities across the state were scattered and separate. Because of this combination of isolation and stability,[5] as folklorist Edward Ives has pointed out, Maine's culture can be said to have developed along its own lines.

Interestingly, this peculiar Maine mix of culture and geography did not at first include the lobster, which early New Englanders viewed as cheap, low-status—even poorhouse—fare. Lobsters were many times donated to widows, orphans, and others in the spirit of public charity. Showing up in local fishing nets as early as 1605, lobsters were a common catch along the Maine coast. However, so devalued were they as a food source that there are reports of saltwater farmers gathering them in carts after storms, when they would be piled a foot or so deep along the coast, and either feeding them to the pigs or plowing them by the ton into their rocky fields as fertilizer. Although some historians feel this usage of the lobster has been exaggerated for effect—that any food so easy to obtain and so cheap would have been consumed by thrifty Yankees—all agree that lobster *was* a low-status food.[6]

This abundance of lobster, and its definition as low-status food, continued into the early 1800s. Not until a well-defined urban market for cheap lobster began to develop in centers such as Boston was there any real thought of creating a lobster industry. And even then, rapid spoilage and slow transportation limited it to coastal waters adjacent to Boston. In Maine, at the time too far away to be realistically fished for lobster for export, the lobster remained a low-status food item, often used as pig feed, fertilizer, and fish bait. The fishing and shipbuilding industries were the important things; one ate lobster only because one could get more money at market for fish. In a depressed economy such as that of the Maine coast, this was more than good sense, it was economic necessity.

Soon after the Civil War, two very important things occurred with respect to the lobster and Maine. First, demand for lobster meat rose dramatically in urban areas of the east coast, in cities such as Boston, Baltimore, and New York. It was now feasible to ship lobster to these expanding markets because of technological advances in the still new canning industry and the advent of steam-powered transportation— railroads, steam-powered tugs and barges, and the swift lobster smack.[7] These advances also allowed the more efficient canning of fish and helped Maine, by the 1800s, replace fished-out Cape Cod as the center of these maritime food industries.

Second, a wealthy new national elite, rising from the ashes of the Civil War on wings of monopoly capitalism, began buying up land in Maine in order to establish summer homes, especially along the coast in places such as Bar Harbor, Boothbay, Kennebunkport, and Camden.[8] These wealthy "summer people" formed a distinct social group, visiting among themselves and associating with local residents mostly when in need of goods or tradespeople and servants for their lavish summer homes.

Jean Curtis Frost, a resident of Bar Harbor, remembers as a child in the 1920s passing out towels to the rich kids at the exclusive Bar Harbor Club. And the story of that era she tells still circulates in the town, of a local who jumped in the club pool. "They drained it. Cleaned it right out. It was that kind of place."[9]

These first summer residents, who already had fallen in love with the Maine land- and seascape, began to look for ways to set themselves apart from others in their winter worlds of Boston, New York, and Philadelphia. They brought home stories of the Maine "rustics," imitated their accents, and spoke lovingly of Maine lobster, purchased from a local fisherman and eaten fresh-boiled and straight out of the shell, not from a can—an experience available only to those who could summer in Maine.[10]

Thus were the roots established for two distinct cultural views of the lobster—that of the economically poor Maine local and that of the rusticator or wealthy summer resident. The food and foodways of a group, as anthropologist Mary Douglas has pointed out, comprise a code with multiple meanings that lie in a "pattern of social relationships."[11] Foodways are interaction, encoding a highly ritualized, although taken-for-granted, set of behaviors. Linda Keller Brown and Kay Mussell have explained in their study of ethnic and regional food in the United States that these "foodway codes" change as social interactions between groups evolve and change. "When members of different groups come into contact in a multi-cultural society, the sharing of traditional food items may take on a variety of new meanings, depending upon the motivation of the giver and the response of the recipient."[12]

This change in meaning seems to be especially important to understand with respect to the lobster in Maine. Originally an extremely low-status but abundant food along the coast, lobster was made popular in canned form in urban areas outside Maine, where it took on status as a "new" food item packaged in a relatively new way. Finally, when the wealthy urban elite "discovered" Maine, they appropriated the lobster along with Maine real estate. To them, the lobster represented the natural bounty of the land—something that at their social class level was available only to those who summered in Maine.

Gradually the significance of the lobster as a part of the regional culture of Maine began to be defined. But this definition was crafted more by literate summer visitors who had adopted the state and saw in the lobster a symbol of uniqueness than it was by local residents, who saw lobsters traditionally as a low-status food item but one that was now, due to outside demand and heavy fishing, becoming both scarcer and higher-priced. To the locals, a common symbol of their hand-to-mouth everyday existence had been taken over by outsiders and, like their land, priced beyond their means. In addition, their culture was being redefined for them by these outsiders, who insisted on the lobster as a symbol of the state and its residents. By the 1940s even the educated and cosmopolitan Maine poet-in-residence at Bowdoin College, Robert P. T. Coffin, had come to help redefine the lobster as part of Maine culture:

TABLE 1
Socioeconomic Class and Orientation to Region

	Residents	Visitors	Out-of-staters
High	Older-established families	Summer residents	Upper-class
Mid	Newly arrived professionals	Tourists	Middle-class
Low	Working Class Coastal Resident	Day trippers	Lower-class

He travels fastest ahead who keeps his eyes on the past. For this thorny Yankee of the crab family goes away from you and other danger tail-end-first. . . . As my best New England uncles used to do, he protects his brain by advancing with his rear into the unknown. He gazes still on tradition and authority, and goes forward backward, as best Yankees do. . . . He is the archest of arch-conservatives, the Republican of the deep. He is a Yankee, all right.[13]

Socioeconomic Class and Relationship to Region

Among the factors involved in the definition of the lobster as a symbol of Maine culture, two major discriminating variables stand out: (1) the socioeconomic class level of the defining group, and (2) the relationship of this group to the cultural-geographic region—in other words, are members residents, visitors, or physically unacquainted with the region? If one posits three very general class levels and plots them against these three possible relationships, nine general conditions emerge, each with a different combination of socioeconomic and regional orientations, and each containing social groupings with differing views of the lobster as representative of themselves and/or the state. Obviously, in such a scheme there are exceptions to the rule, as well as social groupings that "spill over" from one socioeconomic/regional category to another. For example, many older-established families and some summer residents today are economically middle-class, and some lower-class visitors to the state do not fit the "daytripper" pattern as they camp out or stay in older cabins or motels in less sought-after areas in the state. Even with these exceptions and spillovers (noted in Table 1), however, the general pattern of the effects of class and relationship to region, taken together, on a social group's orientation to *Homarus americanus* and the State of Maine seems strong and distinct.

Maine Residents and the Lobster

Maine has a history of being, economically, the "weak sister" of New England. Even today, for many year-round residents, living takes on an almost hand-to-mouth character. On the coast, where the tourist pressure of the summer months of July, August, and early September creates a large number of temporary jobs in the service industry, locals scramble to try to hold two or even three jobs for this short, intense period—some working up to twenty hours a day for the generally low wages that characterize these sorts of jobs. They do so to try to "build a kitty" that will hold them through the long, lean winter months when many of them may hold no job at all.[14]

For those who do not live on the coast, things are generally even leaner. With the exception of some tourist industry along a few accessible lakes in western Maine and the fall hunting trade, the sorts of jobs common along the coast are not available. In all, the latest Department of Commerce figures show 13 percent of the state's population lives below the poverty line. This is the highest figure in New England, and it is higher than the national average of 12.4 percent.[15]

When one examines per capita income, one finds that a similar picture emerges. In 1986 per capita income in Maine was ranked thirty-second in the nation and, at $11,106, was the lowest in New England— nearly $3,500 below the average for the area. The latest U.S. census figures on median housing values follow the same pattern—at less than $38,000 Maine values are nearly $12,000 lower than the national average.

And even these figures are misleading. The urban area of Portland and the southern county of York, where a large number of newly arrived urban professionals have located, tends to inflate state averages. For most of Maine, with a population classed by the U.S. Census as still 52.5 percent rural (compared with a national average of 23.4 percent) and with the highest number of citizens below the poverty line of any New England state, these figures are lower still.[16]

Growing up poor along the Maine coast, as contemporary regional writer Sanford Phippen put it,

> meant eating a lot of clams we dug ourselves, and in winter a lot of deer meat. Being poor was getting a box of a summer boy's used clothes to wear to school. . . . Our house was filled with cast off furniture. My mother, who did domestic work for the summer rich, took in laundries, sewed, and did any other odd job she could find. . . . This Maine is frustrating; it is hard on people. It is a life of poverty, solitude, struggle, lowered aspirations, living on the edge.[17]

Although Phippen's account may contain an element of romantic literary exaggeration, it has a lot of truth to it as well. He describes a life in which lobsters, with their inflated prices, are way out of the economic reach even of the people who catch and handle them. In the high season a lobsterman has to think twice, and seriously, about dipping into his catch to put this high-priced food on his own table.

When one moves inland, away from the less economically depressed coast, one leaves behind the lobster as even a relatively unattainable symbol. A century and a half ago, when lobster was an affordable food source, technology had not been developed that would allow its efficient storage and transportation inland. In addition, many residents did not look on the lobster as even edible—something that is true of many inland people's reactions to shelled sea creatures. By the time the lobster had been redefined as a special food, and one that could be transported commercially, its price had risen so astronomically that inland Maine people, in general, could not begin to think of buying it as a serious foodstuff. Today, it is seen as a symbol of the economically more affluent coast. And although most inland Mainers recognize that the year-round residents of the coast can scarcely afford to eat lobster regularly, they also are aware that, in a relative sense, the coastal economy is stronger than their own, and there is some feeling of resentment about it—a resentment that can be, and at times is, focused on the lobster if it is being proposed or used as a symbol of the state. As one inland Mainer from Aroostook County remarked in an interview:

> If them tourists want to come up from Boston and pay them prices, then, by Christ, let 'em. Damn fools. Lobsters, hell, they're big cockroaches, that's what they are. You ain't gonna catch me eatin' one, even if I could afford the damn thing.[18]

For this large proportion of the year-round residential population, the lobster may well serve as a constant and telling symbolic reminder of how economically disadvantaged they are, in relation to the summer people and the increasingly middle-class tourist trade of the coastal areas.[19] Thus resentment can surface whenever the lobster is used, officially, to serve as an icon *of* the people of Maine, as occurred in the mid-1980s, when the state legislature adopted a new design for the Maine license plate—one featuring a red lobster against a white background.

This design—and the explicit incorporation of the lobster as a state symbol—was inspired by a project undertaken by fourth-grade students in the "gifted program" of Kennebunk, a relatively affluent town on the southern Maine coast which, along with next door Kennebunkport, is also a traditional stronghold of the summer wealthy.

Many of the well-to-do citizens of Kennebunk, whose children make up the largest proportion of enrollees in gifted programs such as this one, are recent arrivals to Maine. They are likely to be white-collar professionals, trained in an urban setting such as Boston, who are looking for a quieter, simpler life. From Kennebunk they can easily commute to Portland, the largest urban area in Maine (thirty minutes away), or, in the other direction, the Boston area (a bit over an hour away). These people, the new Maine professionals, have been brought up to see the lobster as a symbol of Maine and the coast. In addition, persons of this socioeconomic class *can* afford to eat lobster, and do. In their eyes, there could be no more appropriate symbol of the state.

For long-time and less affluent residents, however, the lobster as license plate image only took on more negative symbolic meaning than the lobster had before its image was legislated onto the plates. The idea was seen as having originated with a class of persons who are looked on suspiciously by "native" Mainers. They have not been in the state long enough to be thought of as residents, nor do they live within the same socioeconomic means and conditions as long-term residents. In addition, they are urban professionals in a traditionally rural state.

As if that weren't enough, this legislative decision, made by the central authority of a state whose residents have traditionally distrusted and resisted the power of central authority, has had immediate impact on everyone in the state who owns a vehicle. New license plates, with red lobsters imprinted on them, have had to be personally affixed to all vehicles for which they were issued. Given that many people view their automobile as a valued extension of self and self-image, the state was, in effect, forcing residents to display a symbol for which their feelings ranged from neutral to highly negative—and they had to display this symbol for all to see, as an extension of themselves. As Maine author Carolyn Chute has said, "Personally, the decision to use the lobster on the plates is insulting. I mean, the lobster has no reality for most real Mainers. If you wanted to show typical Maine food, you'd be more accurate with the potato. Or better still, how about macaroni and cheese?"[20]

Vocal opposition against the new plates has appeared all across Maine, especially in the interior of the state. Some people have begun to white out the lobsters on their new plates. The state, citing a probable constitutional question involved in prosecuting such actions, has advised district attorneys it would not stand behind any decision to bring charges in instances where only the *lobster* is painted out and not the identifying numerals and letters of the license itself.[21] Thus painting out the lobster in Maine has become a politically and legally acceptable response to the new plates—it is not being prosecuted as an illegal action.

Although the media have made light of the "lobster license plate war," the charge has stirred up resentment and bitterness. Proponents and opponents seem to divide along socioeconomic class lines, where one resides (coast or inland), how long one has been a resident, and whether one is urban or rural in orientation and lifestyle. In general, a person of lower socioeconomic class, rural, long-time resident, and *especially* not living on the coast is most likely to oppose the new plates. On the other hand, a person of middle-to-upper socioeconomic class, more recently arrived in Maine, urban-oriented, and a coastal resident is most apt to see the lobster license plates as appropriate and to be actually pleased and proud to display them.

This breakdown of attitudes is similar to feelings about the lobster in general. Longtime residents, who are more likely to be of lower socio-economic class, view the lobster with some degree of resentment. Histor-ically, the lobster represented cheap food for the poor and was nearly as likely to be used as fish bait and fertilizer along the coast. Inland, the lobster had little relevance to the lifestyles of Mainers. The lobster has now been elevated by outsiders from a symbol of neutral or negative status into a symbol of good living and taste—but one that is economi-cally beyond the reach of many local citizens. Add to this the widespread distrust of ingesting strange, shelled sea creatures and the ambivalence locals feel about outsiders and the tourist trade, and we have a poten-tially volatile and negative image of the lobster for many long-term resi-dents of Maine. The wry joke that passes through the culture of these people is that "the politicians down to Augusta voted for the lobster as the state bird," underscoring both the inappropriateness of the choice and the foolishness of the choosers.

Newer residents of the state, for the most part urban-oriented profes-sionals, are affluent enough to eat lobster and, usually before moving to Maine, have "bought" the image of the lobster as representative of the state. To them lobster indicates both a unique and local taste *and* one that, by price and reputation, has been validated by the cosmopolitan upper class of the country. Thus it fits their needs perfectly—validating their status level and, at the same time, pointing out the individuality of their residential choice.

Older Maine residents of these higher socioeconomic class levels, though few in number, share to some extent the cosmopolitan orienta-tion of the newcomers, as they also share the economic concerns of the larger body of local residents. Being able to afford to eat lobsters themselves on special occasions, and aware of the special status lobsters have acquired in the eyes of affluent outsiders, these people can enjoy the sense of identity the lobster gives yet, at the same time, not take it as seriously as either the less economically well-off long-term residents or the newer professionals. As one local lawyer remarked:

We'll go out for lobster for special family occasions, like birthdays. And certainly order them for out-of-state visitors and business contacts. It's like I'd expect a good steak when I visit Kansas City, or cajun food down in New Orleans. It's that kind of symbol of recognition of the area. But, other than the tourist trade, lobsters don't mean much to an awful lot of people in Maine. Sure, they know what they are, but they can't afford them. That's about it.[22]

Visitors to Maine

The literature on the social impacts of tourism contains an effort to identify different *types* of visitors to vacation areas. Many studies focus on the changes in tourists and tourism as an area is first discovered, later visited, and still later institutionalized with the advent and spread of a tourist industry.[23] Another area to attract examination has been the socioeconomic class of the tourist. How do tourists from different class levels affect the type, quality, and impact of tourism on the visited region?[24] With respect to tourism in Maine, sociologist Peter Rose has analyzed the social structure of the summer trade, identifying groups ranging from "colonists" (the gentry who put the place on the social map and who expect the natives to do their bidding) to "coneheads" and bus tourists near the bottom of the prestige ladder.[25]

From this perspective, three major—and quite different—types of summer visitor can be identified in Maine. Like local residents, each of these groups has its own relationship with the lobster as symbol of the state.

Those who have been visiting Maine longest, the upper socioeconomic *summer residents,* were the ones to originally develop the idea of the lobster as symbolic of Maine. The *middle-class tourist,* who comes to Maine to stay for a week or two in the summer, or who perhaps visits on a prepackaged tour, represents a second form of visitor to the state. Finally, the *daytripper* is the lower-class visitor who comes in by car, usually for the day only—or possibly overnight on a weekend—a third and distinctly different form of tourist in Maine.

The summer residents first infused the lobster with a special, romantic significance. Eating lobster became a symbolic way of communing with the state—of identifying with the natural bounty of its coast while summering in Maine. At the same time residents of the state were romanticized, by some of the more literary-prone summer residents, as characters both hardy and noble, simple and rustic. These summer residents fleshed out the image in short stories, poems, and novels that often focused on the Maine lobsterman who braved the storms of the great Atlantic to bring the lobster to market.[26]

The image is seen in the following excerpt from Arthur Train's 1927 story "The Viking's Daughter," with the caveat that here, uniquely, we have a lobsterfisher who is female:

> At that instant the sun broke though the grey bank of cloud upon the eastern horizon and the leaden world became one of purple and bronze. It shone through Desire's wind-tossed hair, turning it and her oilskins to bright gold. Suddenly Mr. Dingle felt an immense and reposeful confi-

dence in the stalwart, erect, fearless young figure beside him. She was strong, brave and resourceful. She would not let him down.[27]

This earlier mythos of both the lobster and the noble lobsterman has been passed down to the present from its inception in the late 1800s and its romantic translation in regional literature, especially that of the 1920s and 1930s.

But in reality, what has happened in Maine since that time has been its development as a middle-class tourist destination. No longer is the state an exclusive haven in the summer for the rich, as it was at the turn of the century. In 1985, for example, nearly 6.5 million tourists visited the state of Maine,[28] a fact that is highly upsetting to older summer residents. Additionally, the romance of the lobster, initially developed by these summer residents, has been successfully marketed as a pop cultural image to the middle-class tourist. It, too, is no longer something special and unique to the summer resident.

So although lobster is still eaten in the privacy of those large summer homes which still exist, and in the dining rooms of the few surviving exclusive summer hotels, it has lost most of its potency as a symbol of identification for these people. For many, it is now no more than an expensive regional food that, at most, evokes memories of a past when the coast was rugged, isolated, and unspoiled by the crass weight of middle-class commercial tourism.[29]

For the middle-class tourist, the lobster is not only the appropriate symbol of Maine in terms of foodstuff, it is also desired in many other forms in the large souvenir market that has developed. With over six million tourists visiting the state annually and spending nearly $1.5 billion on their visits,[30] tourism is, for Maine, a huge industry.

Tourists eat lobsters at summer establishments that advertise competitively on large outdoor signs, trying to lure tourists with the lowest price for a lobster. Sometimes, in two- or even three-lobster "specials," the price per lobster is lower still (although one is warned that these specials "must be ordered and eaten by only one person"—that is, not shared among several at a table to save money). Usually the lobsters served in these establishments are the smallest that can legally be caught and kept (0.75 to 1 pound) and are not nearly the bargain the advertised price per lobster suggests. Still, if one wishes to "do Maine right," these are the least expensive places to eat the obligatory lobster dinner.

Another part of "lobster lore" seems to have arisen with the middle-class tourist: the complex code of instructions involved in how to shell the creature and eat it properly. Waiters will explain and, if necessary, help. Placemats are printed with step-by-step instructions. Plastic bibs are provided to protect the tourist's clothes and to identify him or her to other diners as both financially able to afford lobster and enough of a novice to allow the "native" Maine waiter (in reality, most often a college student from out-of-state) to tuck the bib—a clear symbol of infancy—under his or her chin. Thus the eating of the first lobster can serve as an initiation ritual, or rite of passage, for the tourist who is likely to believe this initiation is into some sort of "culture of Maine," even though in reality it is more of a commercial ritual developed by the tourist industry than it is any sort of inclusion ritual involving native Mainers.

The lobster image has also been appropriated by the tourist industry, as a centerpiece to the souvenir business. Lobster traps are sold as coffee tables, lobsters are found on tee shirts, as gold, silver, and pewter jewelry, as stuffed toys, as weathervanes, as Maine "handcrafts." John Palmer, head of Down East Crafts (which has about two thousand products in its line), explains why the lobster is central to what they produce:

> Lobster is one of the main things people think of when they come to Maine, and so, in our market and in our product line, we try to give them enough lobsters to keep them happy. We have a network of home workers that assemble products for us. We give them the materials, and specifications, and show them how to assemble products. Therein lies the hand-crafted aspect of a lot of our stuff. Where we can't get products made in this country, we do import from overseas—Japan, Korea and Taiwan to a certain extent.[31]

These souvenirs can range in price from art forms, sculpture, and jewelry focused on the upper-middle-class tourist to the cheaper tee shirts and mass-produced "handcrafts" of Down East Crafts, a good deal of which is geared for impulse buying in the two-to-four-dollar range— lobster plaques for the wall, miniature lobster traps, Christmas ornaments ("Lobster Claus"), salt and pepper shakers. Thus because of (1) the expense of the authentic lobster for this socioeconomic class; (2) its perishable nature as a food item; (3) the difficulty of transporting it home for show; and (4) its symbolic link to Maine as almost a part of the state itself, the image of the lobster has successfully been transferred to cheaper, nonperishable, easy-to-transport items.[32] For the authentic and ceremonial ingesting of *Homarus americanus* as a part of the Maine gestalt, then, can be substituted (if the meal is too expensive) the purchase of a souvenir.

With souvenirs available on a sliding price scale, everyone, no matter what his or her economic constraints, can purchase a copied image of the authentic. Moreover, anyone can also take the souvenir home, an advertisement or material "memory" rather than the authentic sight or experience left behind in Maine.[33] As a salesperson interviewed in the tee shirt shop at the Maine Mall in South Portland said:

> I personally wouldn't buy a shirt with a lobster on it, but you wouldn't believe how many of these we sell. Everybody says you have to go to Maine to get real lobster, and they want to take something home with them, to remember Maine by.[34]

In this souvenir industry, even the inauthentic *image* of the lobster can take on value as a symbol of Maine. The only *authentic* souvenirs become those purchased in the state (and supposedly crafted there, even though many are actually made by cheaper, overseas labor). Scarce souvenirs, then, take on importance as collectibles. When a young tourist couple from Raleigh, North Carolina, was interviewed, the woman proudly displayed her tee shirt, with the word MAINE and a large red lobster displayed on the front. Asked where she had obtained the shirt, she replied: "Rockland. Last year. You know I haven't been able to find any like it in the stores here this year." Her companion agreed. "Nice, isn't it?" he asked, with more than a hint of pride in his voice.[35]

Not only has the image of the lobster been separated from the authentic object, the image has begun taking on significances of its own, as a symbol of "Maine-ness." Last year's tee shirt, no longer available, becomes a mark of identity, of inclusion in the category of "frequenter of Maine" as opposed to "novice traveler." For many who cannot afford to purchase *Homarus americanus* itself (or are culturally too timid to attempt to eat this strange creature), the image of the lobster offers a representation of reality that can be, in some ways, more compelling than the reality itself. As Stuart Ewen, in his more general discussion of style and popular culture, has remarked: "Freed from the encumbrances of matter, the *look* of the visible world can now be easily, and inexpensively, reproduced . . . matter as a visible object is of no great use any longer, except as the mould on which form is shaped."[36]

The cheaper lobster souvenirs are the central component of the daytripper's experience with the lobster in Maine. On the lowest level of the socioeconomic scale, people drive to Maine for the day or possibly the weekend, if they can afford a motel overnight. Because of their budgets and culturally shaped food preferences, they are more apt to purchase a crab or fried clam roll than the more expensive and exotic lobster (or lobster roll)—if they venture beyond the franchised fastfood stands at all. For them the souvenir market has created "Claws" (an inexpensive video tape of inauthentic Maine humor and lobster images), the ubiquitous tee shirt, lobster lollipops, claw-shaped harmonicas, hats with stuffed furry lobster claws hanging from them, "Lobster

Lover on Board" bumper stickers, paintings of lobsters on velvet, and racks and racks of lobster postcards.

Many of the inexpensive lobster images purchased by daytrippers poke fun at the more traditional commercial image of the lobster. If a real lobster is too expensive and exotic for these people to experience, and if it is a symbol both of Maine and of gracious, upper-class living and dining, then why not, in the good old American prole tradition, have some fun with the image? Thus there are canned "lobster farts" for sale, as well as soft plastic lobster "noses" to be worn as gag masks.

Several lobster postcards are in this vein. One series, called "Lobstercards," features trick photographs of real lobsters in bizarre situations. In one, a lobster is attacking a Barbie Doll, who reclines on the beach in true upper-middle-class tourist fashion. Another lampoons the gourmet image of the lobster by portraying a live lobster in a frying pan with four eggs. The instructions or recipe on the card direct one to heat the pan until the thrashing around of the dying lobster scrambles the eggs, creating the world's finest omelet. Finally, lobsters, sitting in a gourmet restaurant, point to people (clearly dressed in upper-middle-class attire) who are swimming in a display tank. "I'll take that one," says a lobster to the black-tie-and-tux-clothed lobster waiter.

Clearly such lobster images, inexpensively purchased, serve the daytripper as advertisements, or material memories, of Maine that can be posted home and shown to friends to authenticate the fact that he or she indeed did travel to Maine—a status-enhancing trip, both because of the expense of recreational travel and because of the tradition of Maine as summer home for the wealthy and, more recently, as a desired middle-class tourist destination. At the same time many of these images serve to deflate the status of the lobster user, to poke fun at the use of the lobster as symbol by socioeconomic classes higher in status than that of the daytripper.[37]

Out-of-State Images of the Lobster

The lobster, as regional image and as symbol of expensive, gourmet dining, has been successfully marketed out-of-state by some of Maine's largest lobster dealers—companies such as Homard, Inc., and the Great Maine Lobster Company. As Bob Wakefield, owner of the Great Maine Lobster Company, puts it:

> We have a reputation for being craftsmen. Maine has an image, and that image is quality. We're not a bunch of hayseeds up here. We do have some

sophistication. We certainly have a product that is renowned throughout the world—recognized as the king of shellfish.[38]

Homard, Inc., ships lobsters to Japan and to the European market. The company has joined six of the largest lobster dealers in Maine, so they can charter planes to fly their product. A promotional tape that Bruce Saunders, head of the company, put together documents one shipment in 1987 of 170,000 pounds of lobsters, chartered to a single overseas customer—to his knowledge, the largest such shipment ever made.

The Great Maine Lobster Company, focused more on the American market, targets individual, upper-class customers for its products. Bob Wakefield explains:

> We ship live lobsters in a kettle with a cooking pot. We give you everything, from the pot to the metal crackers, picks, bibs, wet naps, potholders—all of the accoutrements. All you do is add water. . . . I wanted to go to the upscale, premium buyer. So we started with the outer box . . . white with bright red [lobster] graphics. Very vibrant. Vibrant colors just jump out at you.[39]

The pot that fits inside this box has an abstract, hi-tech lobster logo on its side. The box also contains a twelve-page booklet about the early days of lobstering, something "to entertain with while the lobsters are cooking." Wakefield explains that his product is available on order from six to seven hundred gourmet foodstores across the country, "from Bloomingdale's to Neiman-Marcus to many lesser-known but high-quality places."

In export form, then, the lobster is marketed as a rare and expensive product. In the balance between symbolizing Maine and reflecting discriminating and expensive taste, the balance on out-of-state marketing clearly shifts to emphasize taste and the ability of the customer both to recognize the quality of a relatively rare foodstuff and to afford to serve it far away from the coastal waters of Maine. This out-of-state market is particularly important because the best lobster catch in Maine is in the late fall and early winter months, when the tourists are gone.

As one moves downward in the American socioeconomic class structure, one sees lobster retain its image as a status foodstuff. To be affordable to the middle class, however, the actual lobster eaten usually takes the form of frozen Australian lobster tail, many times served along with steak as a part of a standard middle-class status meal known as "surf and turf." Thus the image of rarity and status is retained, but a cheaper product that has no relationship to Maine—or to *Homarus americanus* (Australian lobster being, biologically, a different creature entirely)—is substituted for the authentic foodstuff. Like so many other imitations of status products, the Maine lobster has been replaced with something cheaper and more easily adaptable to the mechanics of mass distribution—something onto which the aura of the authentic object can be, and has been, successfully projected.

In sum, the meaning of the Maine lobster as icon depends heavily upon what socioeconomic group one is focusing on, as well as that group's physical location with respect to the State of Maine. As Marshall Fishwick has remarked, "objects in general, and icons in particular, are the building blocks of reality. They are sensitive indicators of who we are, where we come from, where we intend to go."[40] Nowhere is this truth more evident than with the Maine lobster, whose image has been used to reinforce social class, define cultural insider and outsider, and sell status and self-esteem in the mass marketplace. The lobster has been variously praised and damned, copied and rejected, romanticized and ridiculed. It has served as fish bait, fertilizer, and gourmet food. It has appeared in literary short stories, on license plates, and on tee shirts. It has been envied and loved, steamed and boiled. But like all true cultural icons, *Homarus americanus* has never been ignored.

Notes

I thank the anonymous reviewers whose insights and critical comments have improved this article a good deal.

1. Joy Dueland, *The Book of the Lobster* (Somersworth: New Hampshire Publishing Co., 1973), p. 22. See also Marcia Spencer, *Lobsters Inside and Out* (Orono: University of Maine Press, 1987).

2. Already tradition is being tampered with. The original clambake did *not* contain lobster, but Raymond Sokolov of the American Museum of National History points out that the more commercial ones today do, as "even some of the clambake's most devoted adherents . . . succumb to the proddings of their sensual natures and embellish the bake with lobsters." Only a few traditionalists now "hold the line against lobster fancification." Sokolov, *Fading Feast: A Compendium of Disappearing American Foods* (New York: Farrar, Straus, Giroux, 1981), p. 139.

3. Dueland, *Book of the Lobster*, p. 7.

4. Howard Marshall, "Meat Presentation on the Farm in Missouri's 'Little Dixie,' " *Journal of American Folklore* 92 (1979), p. 400.

5. See Edward Ives, "Maine Folklore and the Folklore of Maine," *Maine Historical Society Quarterly* 23 (Winter 1984), p. 115.

6. See Dueland, *Book of the Lobster*, p. 45, and Mike Brown, *The Maine Lobster Book* (Camden, Me.: International Marine Publishing, 1986).

7. See Carol Bryant et al., *The Cultural Feast* (New York: West Publishing, 1985), pp. 58–59.

8. See George H. Lewis, "Mass Society and the Resort Town: A Case Study of Bar Harbor, Maine" (master's thesis, University of Oregon, 1968), pp. 13–28, and Richard Hale, Jr., *Story of Bar Harbor* (New York: Ives Washburn, 1949), pp. 52–60.

9. Quoted in Pamela Wood, "Mt. Desert Island," *Salt: Journal of New England Culture* 5 (January 1982), p. 3.

10. See Ives, "Maine Folklore," for an account of this phenomenon, especially with respect to the development of the down east "accent," the image of the Maine rustic, and "Maine" humor, by the wealthy summer people of that time. See also Hale, *Story of Bar Harbor,* for how Bar Harbor's summer colony interacted with the natives. How Maine summer folk set themselves off from others of their socioeconomic class is reflected in Louis Auchincloss's story "Greg's Peg," in which the summer colony in Bar Harbor is visited by "outside" yachtspeople: "I noticed several young men who were not in evening dress and others whose evening clothes had obviously been borrowed, strong, ruddy, husky young men. It was the cruise season, and the comfortable, easy atmosphere of over-dressed but companionable 'Anchor Harbor' was stiffened by an infiltration of moneyed athleticism and arrogance from the distant smartness of Long Island." Reprinted in Sanford Phippen, ed., *The Best Maine Stories* (Augusta, Me.: Lance Tapley, 1986), pp. 125–126.

11. Mary Douglas, "Deciphering a Meal," in Clifford Geertz, ed., *Myth, Symbol and Culture* (New York: Norton, 1971), p. 61.

12. Linda Keller Brown and Kay Mussell, *Ethnic and Regional Foodways in the United States* (Knoxville: University of Tennessee Press, 1984), p. 7.

13. Robert P. Tristram Coffin, *Mainstays of Maine* (New York: Macmillan, 1944), pp. 1–2.

14. Personal observation and interviews along the Maine coast, 1955 to 1988. In addition, see the more formal data contained in *Maine Tourism Study, 1984–85*, vol. 2 (Augusta, Me: State Development Office).

15. Poverty, income, and housing value data are drawn from the Bureau of the Census on-file data disk, Atlanta, Georgia, August 26, 1988, by the author, as well as from information contained in the *1988 Statistical Abstract of the United States* (Washington: U.S. Dept. of Commerce).

16. That the growing affluence of the Portland/York County area has been a large factor in raising the per capita income level of the state can be seen by the upward movement of Maine from 39th to 32nd in the nation in this category, from 1980 to 1986. This period coincides with that of the move of young professionals to the southern urban areas of the state.

17. Sanford Phippen, "The People of Winter," in *The Best Maine Stories*, pp. 311–312.

18. SALT interview with George Hoag, July 1988. Several interviews quoted in this article were conducted by the author or Lou Brown, a student in a SALT-sponsored research project directed by the author, of the interface between regional and mass culture in Maine. Interviews were conducted in the summer and fall of 1988. The SALT Center for Cultural Studies is located in Cape Porpoise, Maine 04046.

19. Although the people of Maine are economically disadvantaged in comparison to summer residents and tourists, this does not imply any concomitant feelings of inferiority or lack of self-esteem or importance on their part. Indeed, most "Mainiacs" would not swap places with urban tourists for all the lobsters in the Atlantic. Although life in Maine is, in comparison, sparse and spare, most natives like it that way and see it as morally and emotionally a better life than that to be found in the city. As Draper Liscomb, a long-time resident of Town Hill, Maine, said about moving back to the state after a time spent in Connecticut, where economics forced him to go look for work: "I didn't want to raise my kids down in that god damn mess, you know. Yeah, that was one of the big reasons I came back home. . . . I really like to go outdoors and piss holes in the snow. . . . You know, all those doctors and lawyers work their hearts out, so they can come up here and live like I do." SALT Archives, Kennebunkport, Maine. Interview conducted by Bethany Aronow, Summer 1981.

20. Interview with Carolyn Chute, SALT, Summer 1988.

21. *Bangor Daily News*, November 7, 1988, p. 31.

22. Author interview with Merle Carroll, October 1988.

23. See Edward Cohen, "Toward a Sociology of International Tourism," *Social Research* 39 (1973), pp. 164–182, and David Nash, "Tourism as a Form of Imperialism," paper delivered at the American Anthropological Association Annual Meeting, 1974, as examples of this concern.

24. See David Greenwood, "Tourism as an Agent of Change," *Ethnology* 9 (1978), pp. 80–90, and Dean MacCannell, *The Tourist: A New Theory of the Leisure Class* (New York: Schocken, 1976).

25. Peter Rose, "Colonists and Coneheads," *Salt: Journal of New England Studies* 30, 2 (1987), p. 6.

26. See the works of Sara Orne Jewett and Elizabeth Ogilvie as examples. See also Rachel Field, *Time Out of Mind* (New York: Macmillan, 1935), and Mary Ellen Chase, *A Goodly Heritage* (New York: Henry Holt, 1932).

27. Arthur Train, "The Viking's Daughter," in *The Best Maine Stories*, p. 39.

28. *Maine Tourism Study, 1984–85*, vol. 1 (Augusta, Me.: State Development Office).

29. Discussion with Pam Wood, Director of SALT studies. Also informal discussions with guests at the Colony Hotel, Kennebunkport, Maine, July 1988.

30. *Maine Tourism Study*, vol. 1.

31. John Palmer, SALT interview by Lou Brown, July 1988.

32. For the upper-middle-class tourist, lobsters are available—live and boxed to travel—in the major Maine (and Boston) airports. Thus, for a fairly steep price, the air traveler who takes less than 24 hours to reach his or her destination can take lobsters home—though they must be cooked and consumed immediately, and thus are not durable as souvenirs or as proof of a Maine experience.

33. See MacCannell, *The Tourist*, pp. 145–160 for a good discussion of authenticity and the souvenir industry.

34. SALT interview by Lou Brown, July 1988.

35. SALT interview by Lou Brown, August 1988.

36. Stuart Ewen, *All Consuming Images* (New York: Basic Books, 1988), p. 25.

37. These images are also purchased by those higher on the socioeconomic ladder who, while visiting Maine, do not wish to think of themselves as tourists or to be labeled as such. Thus they find public identification with the messages of these cards to be effective in distancing them from the middle-class tourist who "buys" the symbolic, status image of the lobster. In a sense, they can effectively be tourists and, at the same time, deny this image by poking fun at it symbolically.

38. SALT interview by Lou Brown, July 1988.

39. Ibid.

40. Marshall Fishwick, "Icons of America," in R. Browne and Fishwick, eds., *Icons of America*, (Bowling Green, Ohio: Popular Press, 1978), p. 8.

7

Patterns of American Rice Consumption 1955 and 1980

James R. Shortridge and Barbara G. Shortridge

The opening sentence in "The American Heritage Cookbook" serves as a beacon and a challenge for scholars interested in the variety of American society. "Ours is not a 'cuisine' such as homogeneous nations boast, but a rich potpourri of dishes and drinks that have evolved from the native bounty of this country and the cultures of dozens of others."[1] A host of terms suggest the regional expression in this potpourri. Boston baked beans, Southern fried chicken, Cajun crawfish, San Francisco sourdough, Maine lobster, Texas chili, and Virginia ham immediately come to mind. Foodways clearly can tell much about the people of the United States and their cultural geography.

The focus of this article is the consumption of rice, one of the few footstuffs for which detailed data are available. We survey state patterns for 1955 and 1980 with an emphasis on the process of change between the two years. Our basic argument is that these patterns are important not only in their own right but also as general cultural indicators. The eating of rice like food habits in general is both tenacious and dynamic.[2] Changing intensities of regional usage may provide important clues about hearths of innovation, diffusion routes, and the relative strengths of processes creating diversity and homogeneity in society.

The lack of data is the bane of research on foodways in the United States. Detailed information exists for the production of most crops and animals at the state and county levels, but for some reason data on consumption by human beings are usually summarized for the country as a

Reprinted by permission from the American Geographical Society for *Geographical Review* 73, 4 (October 1983), 417–29.

whole. Some detailed information on consumption may be found in the work of nutritionists, folklorists, and anthropologists, but their samples tend to be limited either in terms of population (for example, pregnant women) or area (for example, an urban neighborhood). Nutritionists frequently translate "food eaten" into some dietary equivalent like proportion of protein. The National Food Consumption Survey, conducted three times since 1955, avoided these problems, but the sample is adequate only for a gross, four-part regional division of the country.[3] Another measure of food consumption is needed, something between the individual dietary surveys and the countrywide statistics.

Unique and almost ideal data for geographical analysis exist for rice. Thirteen times since 1955–56 officials of the U.S. Department of Agriculture have surveyed rice mills and repackagers to ascertain shipments of rice made to each state.[4] The studies, intended to help the traditionally regional rice industry to expand domestic consumption, are made possible by the relatively small network for milling and repackaging rice. For the 1980–81 survey, forty-eight of fifty-three mills and six of twelve repackagers responded; they accounted for 90 and 93 percent respectively of the rice shipped for domestic, direct consumption.[5] The figures were higher in previous surveys, for example, 98 percent for 1955–56.[6]

Because almost no rice is grown for subsistence in the United States, domestic shipments provide a good measure of consumption. The data sets include rice for direct food use, or approximately 61 percent of the total rice shipped in 1980–81, but exclude statistics about rice destined for breweries (25 percent of shipments) and for cereal makers and other food processors (14 percent of shipments). Some distortion in the available data occurs where rice is not consumed in the state to which it was shipped. Imported rice, stockpiling, and free distribution of surplus government-owned rice constitute other, but minor, problems. Imported rice accounted for less than 1 percent of the total rice consumption in the United States in 1980, and stockpiles normally were held by producers and millers, not retailers.[7] Because recent figures are not available, distribution of government-owned rice was excluded from this analysis. The exclusion is not serious because the amount was small (.5 percent of total domestic consumption in 1974–75) and because consumption of that rice might not be strictly voluntary.

Rice-Consumption Pattern in 1955–56

The consumption of rice at the time of the first distribution study was very low and highly regionalized (Fig. 1). Americans consumed only 4.67 pounds of rice per capita, far below the range of 200 to 300 pounds

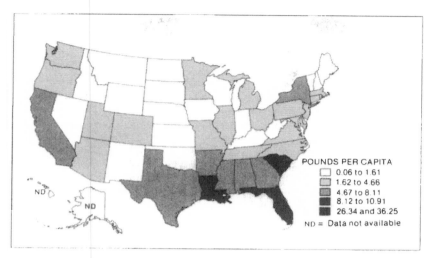

Figure 1 American rice consumption by state 1955–56.

in parts of southern and eastern Asia.[8] In thirty-eight states per capita consumption was below the nationwide average. Rice essentially was not a recurring item on menus in New England, the Middle West, the Great Plains, and the West outside of California. Rice was even avoided in the upland South. With so striking a regional pattern one might suspect the existence of strong prejudices against rice. According to a 1939 study in California, Ohio, and Oregon, no such situation existed. In a survey of 693 college students, no one listed rice as an "unfamiliar" food, and only 2 percent of them checked it as "disliked."[9] Apparently rice was avoided in most of the country because other sources of starch, particularly potatoes and wheat products, were entrenched food habits.

Relatively heavy consumption of rice in 1955–56 occurred in areas with a history of rice production and in areas with large numbers of immigrants or their descendants from traditional rice-eating cultures. Louisiana with 36.25 pounds per capita and South Carolina with 26.34 pounds were far ahead of the other states in rice consumption at mid-twentieth century. Rice production in the United States began in South Carolina about 1686 and continued to thrive there commercially until the Civil War. Louisiana rose to prominence as a rice producer later in the nineteenth century and led the country in rice production from 1890 to 1949. Most of the other states in the South with high levels of rice consumption also were longtime producers. The output in Georgia was usually just below that of South Carolina in the past, whereas Arkansas and Texas vied with Louisiana for dominance in this century. Modest acreages were found in Alabama, Florida, and Mississippi.[10]

It would seem reasonable that an affinity for rice eating would develop in rice-producing areas, especially in the past when long-distance ship-ment of foodstuffs was less common than now. Moreover, rival sources of starch like Irish potatoes and wheat have never been important crops in the South because of plant disease and storage problems.[11] The persis-tent use of rice was similar to the Southerners' substitution of corn for wheat flour and the retention of cornbread as a regional specialty. Rice remains a cornerstone of Charleston cuisine a century after South Caro-lina ceased growing rice on a large scale. It does yeoman work as a pilaf, or bed, for native varieties of shellfish, in soups, and in desserts. Cowpeas and rice are the main ingredients in Hoppin' John, the traditional New Year's Day dish. All things considered, the level of rice consumption in South Carolina and the rest of the South might be expected to be higher than the reported figures.

Florida, New York, and perhaps California are anomalies on the map for the 1955–56 pattern. Compared with other southern states, rice con-sumption in Florida was much higher than expected in the context of the state's history as a rice producer. New York had a moderate level of consumption—7.21 pounds per capita—but no production. The pres-ence of immigrant groups from traditional rice-consuming areas likely accounted for the New York pattern. New York City began to attract large numbers of Puerto Ricans in the 1950s. Although few studies exist about the diet of Puerto Ricans who live on the mainland, nutritionists have suggested that rice remains a staple, which is eaten twice a day.[12] By 1960 the Puerto Ricans in New York City numbered approximately 600,000. The combination of this number with the totals for rice-eating populations associated with previous immigrations seems adequate to account for the annual per capita consumption of rice in the state.[13] Similarly the presence of Cuban and other Caribbean immigrants in Florida was the likely factor that pushed the average consumption figure to 10.91 pounds.

The relatively high consumption of 7.71 pounds per capita in Califor-nia has no simple explanation. Because approximately one-fifth of the American rice crop was produced in California during the 1950s, one is tempted to attribute consumption to the thesis of local use through iso-lation that was suggested for the South.[14] This interpretation may be true in part, but the diversity of agriculture in California argues against dependence on any one foodstuff. Eastern Asians and their descendants who constituted 5 percent of the population of the state, were another factor.[15]

Rice-Consumption Pattern in 1980–81

The patterns of rice consumption in the United States changed dramatically between 1955–56 and 1980–81 (Figs. 2 and 3). The traditional, strongly regional pattern observable for 1955–56 became much more complex and more nearly nationwide by 1980–81. Interpreting the changing patterns involves questions at several levels of analysis. What do the patterns tell about the consumption of rice? What do they indicate about other foodways and American culture generally?

Per capita annual consumption of rice for the United States rose from 4.67 pounds in 1955–56 to 8.12 pounds in 1980–81.[16] Because Hawaii was added to the data set between the surveys, this increase should be discounted from 74 to 66 percent, but the change is still remarkable. Persons in twenty-six states now ate rice in at least modest quantities: four or more pounds per capita annually. Fifteen states had gains at or above the nationwide rate of increase. A large increase occurred in seven of those fifteen states. The gains were almost entirely outside the South, the traditional region of rice consumption in the United States. Consumption in Louisiana and South Carolina, which were in a class by themselves in 1955–56, dropped nearly in half by 1980–81. Alabama and Georgia had modest declines as anomalously did Rhode Island. The rise nationwide is thus even more striking.

Only one change in the distributional patterns between 1955–56 and

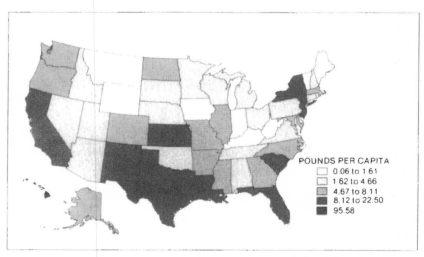

Figure 2 American rice consuumption by state 1980–81.

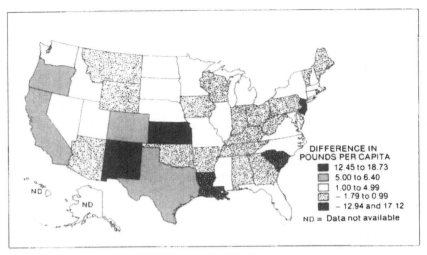

Figure 3 Change in rice consumption by state 1955–56 to 1980–81.

1980–81 seems attributable to traditional factors. Greatly increased consumption in New Jersey, one of the seven states with the large boom in rice eating, was probably caused by the immigration of large numbers of Asians, Puerto Ricans, and American blacks between the years in which the data on rice consumption were collected. These groups constituted 1.4 percent, 6.7 percent, and 12.6 percent respectively of the population for the state in 1980. The pattern in the six other "boom" states is less easily explained than that for New Jersey. All were in the West, but the distribution there at first appears to be almost random. States like Kansas-Nebraska and Arizona-New Mexico, which are often paired on standard socioeconomic measures, were strikingly dissimilar in rice consumption. A series of gross statistical analyses confirmed this assessment. Rice consumption for the seventeen states of the Great Plains and Mountain West regions was unrelated to median age ($r = .06$), median income ($r = .02$), and the proportion of persons with four or more years of college education ($r = .09$). The pattern of rice consumption was slightly related to the proportion of persons who lived in urban areas ($r = .35$).

Cultural characteristics provide a better explanation of the pattern of rice acceptance in the West. The map evidence that we display here, the information from the national food-consumption surveys, and indications of consumer-preference trends from advertisers and popular literature suggest that rice has become a part, perhaps even a symbol, of a new American lifestyle. This lifestyle does not have a generally accepted name, but it is widely recognized in the popular press and is often associated with California. Features of the lifestyle include informality, ecologically minded thinking, strong concern for physical well-being, and a rejection of dietary and other habits associated with traditional American culture. Quality of life is the byword of this lifestyle.[17]

There were several ways by which rice could have become associated with this lifestyle. If potatoes symbolized the Middle Western and eastern United States, rice could provide an equally nutritious substitute. The grain was readily available in the West, because the Central Valley of California had been a major area of production since the 1920s. Methods to prepare and to consume rice were easily available from the large Asian population in California. Certain aspects of Asian religion and philosophy had been highly regarded by Californians and other Americans who were disenchanted with their own society. It seems reasonable to expect similar borrowing of food habits. We even suggest a sequence: rice was a crop that was familiar yet exotic to America and hence was a relatively early adoption. Less familiar offerings like bean curd and sushi followed.

It seems clear that elements of the idealized "California" lifestyle have diffused to the rest of the country. Assertions have been made for various art forms, religious and social philosophies, and arcadian attitudes together with many other cultural traits, but data are too scarce to document the path of expansion. The patterns of rice eating may provide clues to the general process of diffusion.

After the linkage of rice eating to an alternative American lifestyle, growth in consumption would be interpreted as follows. Californians ate more rice than most Americans in 1955–56; the level of consumption rose at an above-average rate during the 1960s and 1970s so that the state was one of the leading consumers of rice by 1980–81. Persons in Colorado, New Mexico, and Oregon—other states commonly identified as foci of the new lifestyle—also increased their consumption of rice. The increased consumption in these states is probably stronger evidence than the rise in California for the hypothesized linkage between rice and the new lifestyle. Rice was not produced in these three states, and none had large ethnic groups with rice-eating traditions. Consumption of rice in the three states was virtually nil in 1955–56. A changing lifestyle seems to be the most plausible explanation for the increased use of rice as a food.

New Mexico led the country in the rate of increased rice eating during the period 1955–1980. Consumption in that state rose from .81 pound per capita to 17.48 pounds per capita annually. It is probably not coincidental that this state with its Native American-Hispanic heritage has achieved an image of a slow-paced, ecologically minded way of life that has come to rival California's as the epitome of the alternative lifestyle. A correlation exists, for example, between the growth areas for rice consumption and the western states favored for 1960s-style communes. California and New Mexico led in both; Colorado and Oregon were next.[18]

The eating of rice was not prevalent among residents of Arizona, Nevada, and Utah. For the most part, this pattern was consistent with the theory of rice eating as an indicator of an alternative lifestyle. Utah and Nevada may be neighbors of California, Colorado, and New Mexico, but much evidence indicates that they differ culturally.[19] Mormon Utah has always marched to its own particular drummer. The wanton atmosphere of Nevada shares a rejection of American traditionalism with the California-New Mexico model, but the resultant styles differ. The avoidance of rice in Arizona seems unexpected at first, because the state is frequently identified as neo-Californian in several ways. Arizona may be exceptional, and its resistance to rice eating may indicate a refinement in the theory. Arizonan development is more imitative of southern California than of the state as a whole. The adoption of rice as a food was likely more characteristic of the northern portion of California than the southern part.

The thesis of rice as an indicator of a general cultural diffusion from a southwestern hearth is generally concordant with the map evidence, although the southern states with a tradition of rice growing and eating are exceptions. New York and New Jersey may also be anomalies, although one could hypothesize that these states are a secondary cultural hearth where the eating of rice moved from ethnic associations to general public acceptance. Data are not available to evaluate this theory adequately, but spaghetti provides a precedent. Once a rarity in American diets, this food diffused throughout the country from initial ethnic bases in New York City and San Francisco.[20]

As one surveys the rest of the map of rice consumption in 1980–81, the patterns of avoidance and change generally match commonsense expectations based on the lifestyle theory and traditional associations with rice. The conservative, still somewhat isolated upland South has resisted the adoption of rice eating, as have the similarly conservative northern plains and Rocky Mountain states. Missouri, Illinois, and other industrial states of the eastern Middle West showed slight gains in rice consumption since 1955. The migration of southern blacks who brought with them the practice of eating rice to the northern states undoubtedly has been a major factor. The proportion of blacks in the 1980 population of these eight states is highly correlated with rice consumption ($r = .62$). An advertising survey in Chicago indicated that blacks there ate four times as much rice as did whites.[21]

The high level of rice consumption in Texas can be related either to the state's southern heritage and its recently increased production of rice or to the southwestern lifestyle theory. Both forces probably operate. Kansas is the most glaring anomaly. Kansans are neither rice producers nor traditional rice eaters; few people would associate them with alternative lifestyles. If anything Kansas stands for conservatism and tradition, supposedly a land of meat and potatoes.

Changing Image of Rice

Americans have traditionally viewed rice as a nutritious, inexpensive, but unglamorous source of starch. Rice was basic fare for lowland southerners, but not much appreciated outside that region, except in certain ethnic enclaves in northern and western cities. This evaluation is partially borne out by the pattern on the 1955–56 map and is supported by several socioeconomic surveys. The first National Food Consumption Survey in 1955 revealed a strong relationship between the use of rice and income level. Whether measured by percentage of households using rice or by quantity used by household, the numbers were highest for low-income families (Fig. 4).[22] Households with annual incomes under $2,000, for example, consumed rice at a rate of .54 pound a week, while ones in the $8,000-$9,999 range used only .16 pound a week. Data from the second survey of consumption in 1965 revealed a similar trend but with added overall consumption of rice. The highest rate was .70 pound a week for households with incomes between $3,000 and $4,000; the low was .22 pound a week for the $9,000-$9,999 income category.[23]

A 1965 survey of homemakers' opinions by the U.S. Department of Agriculture probed the image of regular, uncooked rice. Respondents agreed that it had a low cost per serving and was high in food value. There was a slight tendency to consider rice fattening to the eater, but opinion divided on the issue of the necessity or the excitement of rice as food.[24] Additional insight about the image of rice came from nonusers who were asked why they avoided rice. Seventy-one percent responded vaguely that they disliked rice; 12 percent stated that it was too much trouble to prepare; 9 percent considered it too starchy and fattening; 8 percent found it tasteless; 6 percent preferred potatoes; 4 percent thought it unhealthy, and 2 percent considered it a Chinese food.[25]

The prevailing image of rice in the 1950s and 1960s was traditional and unglamorous, but the surveys hinted at a change. The rates of rice consumption in 1955 generally fell as household income rose with the notable exception of the highest income category (Fig. 4). A similar shift occurred with the percentage of households using rice at the

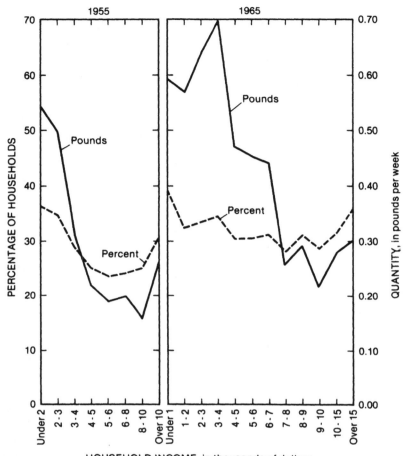

Figure 4 Household consumption of rice.

$6,000-$7,999 category. This trend was substantiated by the data from 1965.[26] The appeal of rice to the affluent could not be its traditional image as a low-cost source of starch.

Nationwide consumption of rice had been stabilized for decades when the Rice Council, a nonprofit promotional organization, was founded in 1959.[27] Initially the council's approach to increasing rice consumption was traditional: advertisements in homemaking magazines stressed the versatility of rice, and packets of recipes were distributed to food editors at newspapers. Innovation, particularly the ease of preparing so-called instant, or precooked, rice, was emphasized. Increased sales led to an expanded advertising budget and a shift in sales tactics.[28]

The Rice Council in 1967 decided to launch an advertising campaign against potato eating. By then rice was assumed to be chic, easy to prepare, and nonfattening in contrast with potatoes. Slogans stressed these features. Although it is impossible to assess whether the campaign set or followed trends in society, the success of the drive indicated a sharp shift in American attitudes.[29] Complaints led to the abandonment of the antipotato advertisements in 1968, and a new campaign that stressed sophistication and youthfulness began. In advertisements a young woman in suggestive poses replaced the happy family and its wholesome meals, while slogans with double entendres supplied the message. This campaign was judged to have been successful.[30]

The sophistication theme in combination with the idea of nontraditional American culture has continued in recent advertising. In the late 1970s one important firm, Riceland Rice, filmed a series of commercials in several quality southern restaurants. The locales emphasized the association of rice eating with Charleston, the French Quarter of New Orleans, Cajun cookery, and the Ozarks.[31] The choice of the last location, we argue, is significant. The Ozarks are not a traditional area of rice consumption, but the region carries an image of homespun self-reliance—another variation of the arcadian alternative lifestyle.

The associations generated by advertisers for rice—sophistication, youthfulness, and a sense of arcadian antiestablishment—all correspond to traits that generally characterize the idealized lifestyle of the new West (and now perhaps parts of the South). A recent, heightened perception of rice as a health food is making the correspondence with this lifestyle even stronger. Advertisements and articles stress rice as a source of protein to encourage eaters to reduce the intake of meat.[32] They assert that rice is low in fat and sodium—excellent for person on low-cholesterol and low-sodium diets. "Eminently digestible" and nonallergenic, rice is ideal for babies, the elderly, and everyone in between these age groups. The old image of rice as a fattening food seems to have changed. Several current sources emphasize that rice is excellent for weight-control diets because it has only eighty-three calories per half-cup.[33]

A direct linkage between the eating of rice and the western arcadian lifestyle occurs in the Americanization of a French-cooking movement known as *nouvelle cuisine*. Nouvelle cuisine arose in the early 1970s as a reaction to the sumptuous, even gluttonous, tradition known as *la grande cuisine*. The theme of the nouvelle cuisine was simplicity: light, fresh foods in their natural forms. It was a search for the innermost flavors of fresh foods from local sources—the elevation of folk dishes to an art form.[34]

Beginning in the 1970s, the nouvelle cuisine was widely accepted in the United States. After a period marked by widespread consumption of bland, convenience foods, many Americans were ready to return to diet of quality eating. Concerns about calories and cholesterol led them to the sophisticated, yet simple French model. The new cuisine was adopted earliest and most vigorously in the San Francisco area. According to Alice Waters, the owner of Chez Panisse, the acknowledged hearth of the movement in Berkeley, the cuisine can be traced to the counterculture of the 1960s and a general arcadian ambiance as much as to nouvelle cuisine proper.[35] Rice fitted easily into the cuisine. A strong oriental influence was acknowledged in both the French and the Californian versions.

"California cuisine" as this tradition is becoming known has captured the consciousness of the Bay area "like nothing since fitness." Food in the area is as much an indicator of status as are theater and fashion.[36] Waters and her protégés have been termed pioneers, and their foodways are predicted to become the "state's greatest export since jogging."[37] Our data for rice suggest that the diffusion is already under way.

Conclusion

Rice, one of the few foods for which detailed data on consumption in the United States are available, seems to be diffusing across the country as a part of a widely recognized, but little analyzed, cultural movement. Data availability began in 1955–56, just before the important diffusion started. The recent statistics from 1980–81 indicate that the movement is still expanding. Rice consumption in 1955–56 was limited primarily to southern rice-growing states, especially South Carolina and Louisiana. Outliers with moderate levels of rice consumption were New York and California where rice eating was associated with traditions of certain ethnic groups. Data for 1980–81 revealed that rice consumption declined in the South but increased generally throughout the country.

The pattern of that increase together with data from socioeconomic surveys, the thrust of advertising campaigns, and the evidence in popular literature on rice and nouvelle cuisine suggest that the diffusion of rice eating is linked to a new American lifestyle. California and New Mexico form the hearth of this lifestyle, which is characterized by casualness, youthfulness, ecologically minded thinking, concern for physical health and proper diet, and empathy for elements of nonstandard American cultures.

Rice eating as an indicator of a broad cultural movement is a theory that cannot be proved conclusively. The concept is consistent with available data and our knowledge of American cultural regions. Even if the theory is rejected, the changing pattern of rice consumption indicates much about the contemporary United States. Rice seems to be in the process of being accepted as a regular, nonexotic part of the American diet. The decline of a regional pattern for rice eating is demonstrated not only by the acceptance of rice as a foodstuff outside the South but also by the relative reduced use in the South.

Notes

1. *The American Heritage Cookbook* (New York: American Heritage Publishing Company, 1964), p. i.

2. Kathleen Ann Smallzried, *The Everlasting Pleasure: Influences on America's Kitchens, Cooks, and Cookery, from 1565 to the Year 2000* (New York: Appleton-Century-Crofts, 1956), pp. 4–5.

3. Food Consumption of Households in the United States, *Report No. 1, Household Food Consumption Survey 1955,* U.S. Department of Agriculture, Washington, D.C., 1956; Food Consumption of Households in the United States, Spring, 1965, *Report No. 1, Household Food Consumption Survey,* Agricultural Research Service, U.S. Department of Agriculture, Washington, D.C., 1968; Food Consumption: Households in the Northeast, Spring, 1977, Human Nutrition Information Service, Consumer Nutrition Center, U.S. Department of Agriculture, Washington, D.C., 1982; Food Consumption: Households in the North Central Region, Spring, 1977, Human Nutrition Information Service, Consumer Nutrition Center, U.S. Department of Agriculture, Washington, D.C., 1982; Food Consumption: Households in the South, Spring, 1977, Human Nutrition Information Service, Consumer Nutrition Center, U.S. Department of Agriculture, Washington, D.C., 1982; and Food Consumption: Households in the West, Spring, 1977, Human Nutrition Information Service, Consumer Nutrition Center, U.S. Department of Agriculture, Washington, D.C., 1982.

4. The thirteen surveys in 1955–56, 1956–57, 1960–61, 1961–62, 1966–67, 1969–70, 1971–72, 1972–73, 1973–74, 1974–75, 1975–76, 1978–79, and 1980–81 are contained in ten reports. Harry O. Doty Jr., Patterns of Rice Distribution in the United States and Territories, Agricultural Marketing Service, U.S. Department of Agriculture, Washington, D.C., 1959; Edward J. McGrath, Distribution Patterns of Rice in the United States, Economic Research Service, U.S. Department of Agriculture, Washington, D.C., 1964; J. C. Eiland, Distribution of Rice in the United States: 1966–67, Economic Research Service, U.S. Department of Agriculture, Washington, D.C., 1969; J. C. Eiland and Theodore F. Moriak, Distribution Patterns for United States Rice: 1969–70, Economic Research Service, U.S. Department of Agriculture, Washington, D.C. 1972; J. C. Eiland and Theodore F. Morak, Market Patterns for Rice: 1971/72, Economic Research Service, U.S. Department of Agriculture, Washington, D.C., 1973; J. C. Eiland, U.S.

Rice: Distribution Patterns: 1972/73, Economic Research Service, U.S. Department of Agriculture, Washington, D.C., 1974; Shelby Holder, Alberta Smith, and J. C. Eiland, Distribution Patterns for U.S. Rice, 1973/74, Economic Research Service, U.S. Department of Agriculture, Washington, D.C., 1976; Shelby H. Holder Jr. and Alberta Smith, Analysis of U.S. Rice Distribution Patterns, *Agricultural Economics Report No. 413,* Economics, Statistics and Cooperatives Service, U.S. Department of Agriculture, Washington, D.C., 1978; Shelby H. Holder Jr. and David Martella, U.S. Rice Distribution Update, *Statistical Bulletin No. 640,* Economics, Statistics, and Cooperatives Service, U.S. Department of Agriculture, Washington, D.C., 1980; and Shelby H. Holder Jr. and Douglas Dorland, U.S. Rice Distribution Patterns, 1980–81, *Statistical Bulletin No. 693,* Economic Research Service, U.S. Department of Agriculture, Washington, D.C., 1982.

5. Holder and Dorland, footnote 4 above, p. 1.

6. Doty, footnote 4 above, p. 5.

7. Food Consumption, Prices, and Expenditures, 1960–1980, *Statistical Bulletin No. 672,* Economic Research Service, U.S. Department of Agriculture, Washington, D.C., 1981, p. 74.

8. Doty, footnote 4 above, pp. 14–15. The figure presented here is slightly lower than the statistic in Doty, because we excluded the government-donation program.

9. Irene S. Hall and Calvin S. Hall, A Study of Disliked and Unfamiliar Foods, *Journal of the American Dietetic Association,* Vol. 15, 1939, pp. 540–548.

10. Lewis C. Gray, History of Agriculture in the Southern United States to 1860 (2 vols.; Washington, D.C.: Carnegie Institution, 1932), Vol. 1, pp. 277–290 and Vol. 2, pp. 721–731; Duncan C. Heyward, Seed from Madagascar (Chapel Hill: University of North Carolina Press, 1937); Sam B. Hilliard, Antebellum Tidewater Rice Culture in South Carolina and Georgia, in *European Settlement and Development in North America: Essays on Geographical Change in Honour and Memory of Andrew Hill Clark* (edited by James R. Gibson; Toronto: University of Toronto Press, 1978), pp. 91–115; and James M. Clifton, The Rice Industry in Colonial America, *Agricultural History,* Vol. 55, 1981, pp. 266–283.

11. Sam B. Hilliard, *Hogmeat and Hoecake: Food Supply in the Old South, 1840–1860* (Carbondale: Southern Illinois University Press, 1972), pp. 161–168 and 176.

12. Diva Sanjur, Social and Cultural Perspectives in Nutrition (Englewood Cliffs, N.J.: Prentice-Hall, 1982), pp. 241–250; and Roberta L. Duyff, Diva Sanjur, and Helen Y. Nelson, Food Behavior and Related Factors of Puerto Rican-American Teenagers, *Journal of Nutrition Education,* Vol. 7, No. 3, July-September, 1975, pp. 99–103.

13. Sanjur, footnote 12 above, p. 242; and Terry J. Rosenberg, Residence, Employment, and Mobility of Puerto Ricans in New York City, *University of Chicago, Department of Geography, Research Paper No. 151,* Chicago, 1974, p. 40.

14. Shelby H. Holder Jr. and Warren R. Grant, U.S. Rice Industry, *Agricultural Economics Report No. 433,* Economics, Statistics, and Cooperatives Service, U.S. Department of Agriculture, Washington, D.C., 1979, p. 2.

15. Jane S. Lewis and Maria Fe Glaspy, Food Habits and Nutrient Intakes of

Filipino Women in Los Angeles, *Journal of the American Dietetic Association,* Vol. 67, No. 2, August 1975, pp. 122–125; Louis Evan Grivetti and Marie B. Paquette, Nontraditional Ethnic Food Choices among First-Generation Chinese in California, *Journal of Nutrition Education,* Vol. 10, No. 3, July-September, 1978, pp. 109–112; and Sanjur, footnote 12 above, pp. 276–283.

16. Consumption figures for 1980–81 calculated from state totals in Holder and Dorland, footnote 4 above, pp. 26–28; per capita figures based on 1980 federal census. Suspected errors in rice data for Delaware and Wyoming were confirmed in conversation with Shelby Holder Jr., an agricultural economist at the U.S. Department of Agriculture. Reported total for Delaware was 50,000 cwt. too high, for Wyoming 210,000 cwt. too high. Our calculations were reduced accordingly.

17. Carey McWilliams, California: The Great Exception (New York: Current Books, 1949); James E. Vance Jr., California and the Search for the Ideal, *Annals of the Association of American Geographers,* Vol. 62, 1972, pp. 185–210; D. W. Meinig, Symbolic Landscapes: Some Idealizations of American Communities, in *The Interpretation of Ordinary Landscapes: Geographical Essays* (edited by D. W. Meinig; New York: Oxford University Press, 1979), pp. 164–192; and Joel Garreau, *The Nine Nations of North America* (Boston: Houghton Mifflin, 1981), pp. 245–286.

18. Vance, footnote 17 above, p. 201.

19. D. W. Meinig, American Wests: Preface to a Geographical Interpretation, *Annals of the Association of American Geographers,* Vol. 62, 1972, pp. 159–184.

20. Evan Jones, *American Food: The Gastronomic Story* (New York: E. P. Dutton, 1975), pp. 118–119.

21. Don Wirth, Riceland Rice: Seeking out the Scattered Market, *Broadcasting,* Vol. 93, July, 1977, p. 8; N. W. Jerome, Northern Urbanization and Food Consumption Patterns of Southern-Born Negroes, *American Journal of Clinical Nutrition,* Vol. 22, 1969, pp. 1667–1669; and Sanjur, footnote 12 above, pp. 250–255.

22. Household Food Consumption Survey 1955, footnote 3 above, p. 52.

23. Household Food Consumption Survey 1965, footnote 3 above, p. 18.

24. Evelyn F. Kaitz, Homemakers' Preferences and Buying Practices for Selected Potato, Rice, and Wheat Products, *Marketing Research Report No. 939,* Statistical Reporting Service, U.S. Department of Agriculture, Washington, D.C., 1971, p. 12.

25. Kaitz, footnote 24 above, p. R51.

26. Household Food Consumption Survey 1965, footnote 3 above.

27. *The Southern Rice Industry* (edited by Marshall R. Godwin and Lonnie Jones; College Station, Texas: Texas A&M University Press, 1970), p. 211.

28. Rice Council Sets $600,000 Budget for 1964–65 Promotion, *Advertising Age,* Vol. 35, June 29, 1964, p. 8; and Rice Ads Aimed at Consumers, Restauranteurs, *Advertising Age,* Vol. 37, September 12, 1966, p. 6.

29. Rice Council Mashes Potatoes in New Campaign, *Advertising Age,* Vol. 38, July 17, 1967, p. 82; and Rice Council Agrees to Soften Anti-potato Ads, *Advertising Age,* Vol. 29, June 17, 1968, p. 10.

30. Sexy Approach Aims to Sell More Rice, Baby, *Advertising Age,* Vol. 40, September 29, 1969, p. 52.

31. Wirth, footnote 21 above, p. 8.

32. Allen Simon, Versatile Rice—The Almost Perfect Health Food, *The Saturday Evening Post,* Vol. 254, May-June, 1982, pp. 102–104.

33. Rice, *Family Health,* Vol. 11, February 1979, pp. 40–44; E. Kessler, Notes from a Rice Paddy, *Mother Earth News,* Vol. 57, May, 1979, pp. 92–93; and Rice, the Do-it-all Food, *Changing Times,* Vol. 34, March, 1980, p. 85.

34. Roy A. deGroot, French Cooking Is Dead; the New French Cooking Is Born, *Esquire,* Vol. 83, June, 1975, pp. 131–140; Joseph Wechsberg, Profiles: Michel Guérard, *The New Yorker,* Vol. 51, July 28, 1975, pp. 34–38; Linda B. Francke and others, Food: the New Wave, *Newsweek,* Vol. 86, August 11, 1975, pp. 50–57; and Raymond Sokolov, A Tasteful Revolution, *Natural History,* Vol. 92, July 1983, pp. 82–84.

35. Charles Michener with Linda R. Prout, Glorious Food: The New American Cooking, *Newsweek,* Vol. 100, November 29, 1982, pp. 90–96; and Lacey Fosburgh, The New Cuisine's Palace, *The New York Times,* June 19, 1983.

36. Fosburgh, footnote 35 above.

37. Michener, footnote 35 above, p. 90; and Fosburgh, footnote 35 above.

8

Food-Place Associations on American Product Labels

Cary W. de Wit

Associations between food and place are common in the United States. Examples include Idaho potatoes, Washington apples, Hawaiian pineapples, Maine lobsters, Florida orange juice, Wisconsin cheese, Georgia peaches, Boston baked beans, and Kansas wheat. Such juxtapositions are taken for granted by most people, but a close examination of specific food-place associations could further understanding not only of food patterns but also of popular perceptions of their allied places. One could argue that place imagery generated by and reflected in food associations is a significant and growing aspect of overall regional perceptions.

Data on collective perceptions of places usually must be gleaned indirectly, such as through surveys, personal interviews, or prolonged literature searches. For the study of food-place associations, place-names as they appear on food labels in the grocery store provide a convenient and readily available source of data. The validity of food labels as documentation of popular food-place alliances is based on two assumptions: food producers and marketers use specific place references because their popular images lend an air of distinctiveness, authenticity, or quality to the products (Gray 1992); and marketers' choice of labeling accurately reflects popular perceptions and associations. Assuming that marketers are sensitive to popular culture, the associations found on food labels may serve as an indicator of some common American food-place affiliations.

Reprinted by permission from the American Geographical Society for *Geographical Review* 83, 3 (July 1992), 323–30.

Place-Names on Labels

Data for this study were collected from the goods displayed on the shelves of five grocery stores in Lawrence, Kansas. These five included two large units of a statewide chain, two independently owned stores (one large and one medium-sized), and one small, nonprofit, cooperatively owned natural/health-food market. These were a representative selection from the total of nine grocery stores in Lawrence. The extent to which they are representative of the United States as a whole is not certain, and readers should keep a few possible biases in mind. First, this survey was conducted in a midwestern university town, so the actual variety of products, and their consequent labeling with place-names, may well be skewed toward midwestern tastes. Certainly, the location of a city in the country affects what kinds of brands of food appear in stores, dependent on the proximity of processors and distributors. The eclectic tastes and sizable foreign population of a university community are likely to put an exotic twist on the type of products appearing on shelves, so that gourmet and foreign items are more available than in a typical American community. On the other hand, the relatively small population of 66,000 may limit the variety as well as the number of brands available, compared with what might be found in a large city.

Another possible limitation is timing. All the data were collected during March and April of 1990. There is a seasonal cycle to the availability of, and customer demand for, fresh produce and certain other foods. The sources of foods change with the seasons, too, and both cycles bring changes of unknown magnitude in the occurrence of place-names.

I inventoried all food products that used a place-name either in the product name or in the brand name, for a total of two hundred seventeen items. These place references fell into twenty-eight categories: twenty-one states; the regions of New England, the South, and Cape Cod; and the cities of Milwaukee, New York, Kansas City, and Boston. Nicknames were categorized according to the places to which they referred. For instance, Land O' Lakes was considered a Minnesota reference. To map and compare the food-label data, I developed four measures of association: the total number of items, the number of varieties, the number of false associations, and the number of double-name items. Each of these is explained in more detail below.

A simple measure of association is the total number of food items that use a given place-name (Table 1). For the simple total count, I considered each brand a separate item, except when products of the same brand and general type varied in their essential ingredients. For example, I counted as separate items the three differently flavored mustards

TABLE 1
Association Scores

PLACE	ITEMS (N)	VARIETIES (N)	ASSOCIATION TYPE		DEGREE OF ASSOCIATION
			True	False	
Texas	40	27	19	21	65
California	52	33	47	5	59
Vermont	15	6	14	1	19
Oregon	16	13	14	2	18
Idaho	13	1	13	0	13
Louisiana	11	7	9	2	13
Milwaukee	7	2	1	6	13
New England	6	1	2	4	10
Kansas	8	5	8	0	9
Pennsylvania	8	3	8	0	8
New York State	4	2	1	3	7
New York City	3	3	0	3	6
South	3	2	0	3	6
Washington	6	6	6	0	6
Florida	3	2	2	1	5
Kansas City	2	2	0	2	4
Wisconsin	3	2	2	1	4
Hawaii	3	2	3	0	3
Iowa	2	2	1	1	3
Minnesota	3	3	3	0	3
Boston	1	1	0	1	2
Cape Cod	1	1	0	1	2
Georgia	1	1	0	1	2
New Mexico	2	2	2	0	2
Illinois	1	1	1	0	1
Nebraska	1	1	1	0	1
North Carolina	1	1	1	0	1
Tennessee	1	1	1	0	1

Source: Compiled by author.

of the Napa Valley Mustard Company: California Hot-Sweet, Green Chili and Garlic, and Herbs of the Valley. On the other hand, minor variations of a product, such as size and level of seasoning, were not counted separately. California and Texas are the undisputed leaders in total number of items, followed distantly by Oregon, Vermont, Idaho, and Louisiana (Fig. 1).

A second measure of place association, the number of varieties using a place-name, is more restrictive than the item count. Each variety is a basic food type into which one or more individual items may be categorized. Texas, for instance, appears on three different brands of salsa, but these were only counted as one variety, as were Vermont's seven different kinds of salad dressing and New England's six brands of clam chowder.

The variety scores change the ranks from the item count somewhat and close the gap between the two leaders, California and Texas, and the rest of the sample. Texas and California had only about two-thirds as many varieties as total items. Twenty of the forty Texas items were reduced to the eight variety categories of barbecue sauce, hot sauce,

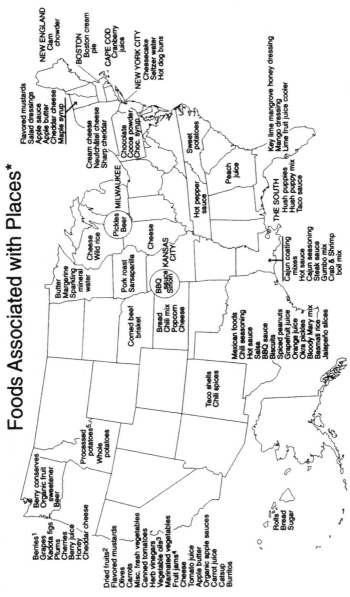

Foods Associated with Places*

NEW ENGLAND
Clam chowder

BOSTON
Boston cream pie

CAPE COD
Cranberry juice

NEW YORK CITY
Cheesecake
Seltzer water
Hot dog buns

Flavored mustards
Salad dressings
Apple sauce
Apple butter
Cheddar cheese
Maple syrup

Cream cheese
Neufchâtel cheese
Sharp cheddar

Chocolate
Cocoa powder
Choc. syrup

Key lime mangrove honey dressing
Mango dressing
Lime fruit juice cooler

Sweet potatoes

Peach juice

THE SOUTH
Hush puppies
Hush puppy mix
Taco sauce

Hot pepper sauce

Cajun coating mixes
Hot sauce
Cajun seasoning
Steak sauce
Gumbo mix
Crab & Shrimp boil mix

MILWAUKEE
Pickles
Beer

Cheese
Wild rice

Cheese

Butter
Margerine
Sparkling mineral water

Pork roast
Sarsaparilla

KANSAS CITY
BBQ sauce
Sirloin

Corned beef brisket

Bread
Chili mix
Popcorn
Cheese

Mexican foods
Chili seasoning
Hot sauce
Salsa
BBQ sauce
Biscuits
Spiced peanuts
Grapefruit juice
Orange juice
Okra pickles
Bloody Mary mix
Basmati rice
Jalepeño slices

Taco shells
Chili spices

Processed potatoes[5]
Whole potatoes

Berry conserves
Organic fruit sweetener
Beer

Berries[1]
Grapes
Kadota figs
Plums
Cherries
Berry juice
Honey
Cheddar cheese

Dried fruits[2]
Flavored mustards
Olives
Carrots
Misc. fresh vegetables
Canned tomatoes
Herb vinegars
Vegetable oils[3]
Marinated vegetables
Fruit jams[4]
Cheese
Tomato juice
Apple butter
Organic apple sauces
Carrot juice
Catsup
Burritos

Rolls
Bread
Sugar

Compiled 1990 by Cary de Wit, University of Kansas.

Figure 1 Food-place associations

[1]Gooseberries, boysenberries, blackberries, strawberries, red raspberries. [2]Apples, peaches, figs, prunes, raisins. [3]Walnut, olive, pecan. [4]Black raspberry, strawberry, apricot, kiwi. [5]Hash browns, tater tots, golden fries, potatoes O'Brien, crinkle cuts, homestyle potatoes, cottage fries, shoestrings, potatoes au gratin, scalloped potatoes, instamash potatoes.

*Listed in order from most to least frequent occurrence.

salsa, chili seasoning, taco shells, biscuits, spiced peanuts, and nonalcoholic malt beverages. Vermont's variety score was only six, because seven of its fifteen items were salad dressings and three others were mustards. Idaho had a variety score of one because each of its thirteen items was a variation on potatoes. Milwaukee had far fewer varieties than items: five of its seven items were pickles; the other two were beers.

Two revealing distinctions among the labels were items that did not actually originate in the places named on their labels, which I term false associations, and items that used a place-name in both product and brand nomenclature. Both of these distinctions suggest a very strong place alliance, a point that I discuss elsewhere. Some examples of false associations were New York Seltzer Water, which comes from California; Vermont Cheddar, from Wisconsin; and Oregon Berry Juice, from Vermont. The degree of falsity assumed here should be taken with caution. In some cases, an item is produced at the location named on its label, but the owner of the facilities for production and distribution is located elsewhere. This legal and economic tie is not always the case: the Vermont attorney general's office has recently taken legal action against the use of Vermont names and imagery on products actually coming from Maine, New Jersey, and Canada (Calta 1991).

Some false associations use a place-name to indicate a preparation style. Examples are southern-style hush puppies, Boston cream pie, and New York-style cheesecake. False associations stand in contrast to true associations, those that use a place-name consistent with the item's place of origin. Examples of these are California Raisins, Kansas Wheat Bread, and Vermont Maple Syrup.

To make overall comparisons, I compressed the data into a single index value that combines the scores for total items, false associations, and double names to create a degree-of-association score for each of the twenty-eight place categories. This index is intended to reflect the extent to which an affiliation with a place can enhance a product's image. My reasoning is that a food producer or marketer would be more likely to add a place-name to a label if it is likely to enhance the perceived distinctiveness, authenticity, or quality of a product (Schlosberg 1989; Walker 1989). Therefore, a place reference that appears frequently on labels generally indicates that the place has a strong image-enhancing ability. The degree-of-association score was calculated as follows. Each place started with a base score the same as its total item count. To this was added one extra point for each false association and one for each double name. The rationale is that a place reference is most likely to be used falsely or used twice on the label when it has an unusually strong image-enhancing effect (Calta 1991).

The association measure is obviously arbitrary, especially because a place that actually generates a large number and variety of items will tend to have a high score as a result of its unusual productivity, but, when this factor is kept in mind, the measure still reveals some interesting contrasts between places. California and Texas were the leaders again on this scale, but because its score was boosted by four double place-names and twenty-one false associations, Texas surpassed California. Thus, a link with Texas seems to offer more image enhancement than does one with California, in spite of the plethora of California products. The runners-up on this index were Vermont, Oregon, Idaho, Louisiana, Milwaukee, New England, and Kansas. Kansas results were exaggerated because several Kansas products that were included, such as popcorn, chili mix, and locally made cheese, probably are not available countrywide.

Specialty and gourmet foods were most commonly labeled with place-names. Ninety-three of the survey sample, or 43 percent, were gourmet or specialty items. California and Vermont, specifically, were popular on specialty labels.

Interpretation

The evidence from food labels confirmed the popular perceptions of Idaho potatoes, New England clam chowder, California raisins, Milwaukee beer, Wisconsin cheese, and Texas chili, but I found no verification for other popular affiliations such as Washington apples, Maine lobsters, Boston baked beans, or Florida orange juice. The absence of some of these expected connections is likely caused by the bias in food labels toward highly processed foods. Fresh produce, grains, meats, and seafood are usually not sold in factory-prepared packages and labeled with brand names. Thus California's link with canned olives, a processed and packaged item, becomes much more prominent in a study of labels than such equally real connections as those between Kansas and wheat, between Iowa and corn, and between Maine and lobsters. Likewise, the affiliation of Oregon with canned berries becomes more prominent than that of Washington with fresh apples or of Florida with fresh oranges.

The high degree-of-association score of Texas is consistent with its reputation for strong self-identity (Meinig 1969, 85–86, 124). One aspect of this identity is food, and food labels suggest that Texans are very proud of their culinary heritage. On the Texas roster appeared many foods it would be hard to imagine coming from anywhere else, including Texas Caviar, a blend of salsa and other spicy vegetables; Killer Hot Texas Bar-B-Q Sauce; Wild Bull Chili Seasoning; Crisp Okra Pickles; and

Red Eye Texas Style Bloody Mary Mix. Texas brand names also showed a distinctive flair, with entries like Hot Cha Cha!, Shotgun Willie's, Talk 'O Texas, and Tres Chic of Texas. Texan products were the most likely to incorporate the state name into the product name, to create hybrids like Texacali (hot spiced peanuts), Texapeppa (hot sauce), Texacante (salsa), Texsun (fruit juices), and Texmati (basmati rice). Texan product labels were often embellished with extra comments like "Taste of Texas," "Hot 'n Spicy, Texas style," and "Homemade in Texas. By Texans!" The liberal use of Texas place-names on product labels, whether they be true or false associations, put Texas far in the lead for both double names and false associations. This suggests that marketers are especially eager to adopt a Texas affiliation.

Vermont products also distinctively displayed the Vermont name, especially in the brand names. Twelve of Vermont's fifteen items fell under the brand names Anne's Vermont, Maple Grove Farms of Vermont, Blanchard & Blanchard Pure and Fancy Foods From Vermont, and Cherry Hill Vermont Made. Three of those items also used Vermont in the product name, which put them into the double-name category and boosted Vermont's degree-of-association score. The frequency of the appearance of Vermont in brand names suggests an especially strong desire on the part of the producers to make the origin of their products apparent.

Vermont products were frequently packaged and labeled in such a way that they had a "homemade" appearance. They came in odd-shaped bottles or jars and bore illustrations of country farms, home kitchens, and folks collecting maple sap in buckets. These products gave the impression that they were homemade from home-grown products and produced on a small scale with personal care. The association of Vermont with this product type seems to be stronger than with any individual product, with the possible exception of maple syrup.

The New England area carries an image much like that conveyed by Vermont-labeled products (Meinig 1979, 165–166), but only Vermont-affiliated products distinguished themselves by communicating a strong image of homemade wholesomeness. New Hampshire and New York State are agriculturally very similar to Vermont, but no products labeled with New Hampshire place-names and only four labeled with New York place-names appeared in the survey. Products from New York also showed much less variety and distinctiveness than did those from Vermont; all four were some kind of cheese, lending no distinction to New York except as a dairy state. Apparently, having Vermont on the label communicates an image of authenticity and quality above and beyond that of New England as a whole. The evidence from food labels appears to verify Vermont's prominence in popular culture as a wholesome place of small rural communities, peopled with honest, down-to-earth, hard-working folks (Calta 1991).

High variety and degree-of-association scores and a low percentage of false association would indicate that a large number and variety of foods honestly come from California. This relationship is not surprising, given the importance of the state as an agricultural producer. Its prominence stands in contrast with the low index values of other important agricultural states, such as Iowa, Nebraska, Illinois, Florida, and Wisconsin. California, although its scores may be inflated, still gives a more positive image to foods than do the other states. California place-names on food labels are another indication of the position California holds as a national symbol of the good life, youth, freshness, and dreams fulfilled (Vance 1972, 193–204; Meinig 1979, 169–172).

California was also commonly linked with sophisticated and highly prepared foods such as marinated asparagus, dilled green beans, marinated dried tomatoes, kiwi jam, organic apple-raspberry sauce, herb vinegars, salsa cheese, and champagne mustard. The state had the second-highest proportion of gourmet and specialty foods as well, with twenty-five of its fifty-two items in this category. This may be due in part to the wide variety of unusual fruits and vegetables that can be grown in southern California, but it also suggests a link between certain kinds of foods and a certain kind of lifestyle. California is commonly perceived as a hearth for creative new lifestyles, and is often on the forefront of food innovations, such as health foods, organic produce and nouvelle cuisine (Shortridge and Shortridge 1989, 95). The food-label affiliations appear to confirm this popular lifestyle image.

Conclusions

Texas, California, Vermont, Oregon, and Louisiana are the places most associated with foods. California appears on the labels of the greatest number and variety of foods, while the appearance of Texas on the labels seems to offer the greatest enhancement of product image. Texas is primarily affiliated with miscellaneous Mexican-style foods, chili, hot sauce, salsa, barbecue sauce, and other hot and spicy things, and California with fresh, canned, and dried vegetables, dried fruits, mustard, and gourmet foods. Oregon is associated with fruits and berries, Vermont with maple syrup and homemade-style specialty items, and Louisiana with Cajun food and hot sauce. The assumption that certain place-names are perceived to enhance the distinctiveness, authenticity, or quality of a product is confirmed by the high proportion of place-named items in the gourmet-specialty category. It also appears that place images communicated by food alliances can accurately reflect the popular conception of these places, as they did in this study for California, Vermont, and Texas.

That marketers would use a place association to sell an item tells something about the place, as do the type of product and the style of packaging they choose to associate with it. In some cases, marketers may use place associations to persuade people that the place somehow comes with the product. The findings of this study uphold this idea, especially for Vermont, California, and Texas, each of which offers products that suggest a certain lifestyle. Vermont products communicate an image of wholesome, simple living, while California products suggest an easygoing, highly sophisticated, innovative culture, and Texas products connote a lifestyle of flamboyant individualism. Perhaps by putting place-names on product labels, marketers offer consumers an opportunity to buy a portion of the lifestyle that the place's image offers and a chance for the geographically bound to have a "taste" of what that place is like.

References

Calta, M. 1991. Made in Vermont: Some bottled myths good enough to eat. *New York Times* 4 December.

Gray, J. 1992. New Jersey label proves of little value. *New York Times*, 4 May.

Meinig, D. W. 1969. Imperial Texas. Austin: University of Texas Press.

———. 1979. Symbolic landscapes: Some idealizations of American communities. Interpretation of ordinary landscapes: Geographical essays, ed. D. W. Meinig, 164–192. New York: Oxford University Press.

Schlosberg, J. 1989. Green Mountain mystique. *American Demographics* 11 (September): 56–57.

Shortridge, B. G., and J. R. Shortridge. 1989. Consumption of fresh produce in the metropolitan United States. *Geographical Review* 79: 79–98.

Vance, J. E., Jr. 1972. California and the search for the ideal. *Annals, Association of American Geographers* 62: 185–210.

Walker, D. 1989. Vermont Distillers goes against the grain and promotes responsibility. *Adweek's Marketing Week* 30 (11 December): 30.

9

The Compiled Cookbook as Foodways Autobiography

Lynne Ireland

The compiled cookbook, also known as the fund-raising cookbook, first emerged on the American culinary scene during the Civil War.[1] Ladies Aid Societies, not content with mere bandage-rolling, gathered together favorite recipes of their members and sold the collections at Sanitary Fairs (fund-raising bazaars for war relief) throughout the Union. Proceeds went to the dependents of the numerous, "glorious war dead."

The success of these compiled "receipt books" did not escape the notice of other fund-raisers, and in the years following the Civil War every charitable organization from the Women's Poultry Club to the Auxiliary Society of the Hebrew Sheltering Guardian Society of the New York Orphan Asylum was selling cookbooks.[2] Well over two thousand titles were published by the end of the century, firmly establishing the place of the compiled cookbook in the hearts and kitchens of organized women everywhere.

Many of us have at one time or another contributed to, solicited for, bought, sold, received, given, or thrown away just such a collection. With their popularity undiminished from turn-of-the-century days, compiled cookbooks continue to be widely produced and sold. Renewed interest in the culinary arts, which has caused an explosion in the number of cookbook titles published professionally in recent years, has created a continual market for amateur-compiled work as well. And while the consumer continues to buy, the dedicated club woman (and now, man) continues to compile, produce, and sell. Many have taken a hint from

Reprinted by permission from *Western Folklore* 40, 1 (January 1981), 107–14. © California Folklore Society.

soft-sell advertisers and proclaim their compilation not strictly for fund-raising purposes, but for the commemoration of silver jubilees, bi-, ses-qui-, and demi-centennials, as well as any other historic occasion worth passing note.

These cookbooks are sometimes regarded as amateurish, which they may be, or as prime repositories for middle-class culinary kitsch, which many undoubtedly are. I would like to suggest, however, that besides giving five recipes for hamburger stroganoff and five times that many for the ubiquitous Jell-O[3] salad, the compiled cookbook has something to offer those of us interested in foodways research.

Whether twenty mimeographed and stapled sheets from the St. Ann's Altar Society or the magazine-slick, color-plate-studded, two-hundred-page Art Association effort, compiled cookbooks make a statement about the food habits of the groups which produce them. Much more than the magazines and cookbooks of the popular press which set stan-dards and attempt to influence consumption, the compiled cookbook reflects what is eaten in the home. It is, in a sense, an autobiography.

Perhaps unintentionally, compilers create a composite picture of what they allegedly eat. Admittedly, there are some pretentious compilations which proclaim themselves "part of the noble tradition in popular cul-ture which for decades has enriched the national cuisine with an ever-increasing variety and sophistication."[4] Much more common, however, is the preface:

The recipes in this book may not have been tested in laboratories, but their success has been established by friends and relatives, by church and civic groups and by the most critical group of all—husbands and families.[5]

If the compiled cookbook can be viewed as foodways autobiography, two questions arise: how complete an autobiography and how accurate?

While no replacement for direct contact and observation of cooking and eating patterns, the compiled cookbook can supply a good number of clues to the foodways puzzle. An examination of recipes can provide, for example, insights into food preference. In thirty-five middle-Ameri-can Great Plains cookbooks,[6] beef appears to be far and away the pre-ferred protein source. Chicken and pork tie for second place. Fish, save for carp and bass, is nearly impossible to obtain fresh in this land-locked region and is included in a very small percentage of recipes. Where it is found, it is primarily in the form of canned tuna or salmon.

Casserole dishes equal or outnumber meat and poultry suggestions, and make heavy use of "cream of _____" soup. Common examples of this type include "Hamburger Noodle Casserole," consisting of ground beef, cooked noodles, and cream of celery and cream of mushroom soup; "Baked Chicken Supreme," comprised of uncooked chicken, Minute Rice, and the "cream of" soups previously mentioned; and "Tuna Noodle Casserole," which follows the same inexpensive meat, starch, and condensed soup formula.

"Salad" rarely designates fresh or cooked fruits or vegetables in some sort of dressing, but rather a cornucopia of ingredients encased in jiggling gelatin. Sweets in the forms of pies, cakes, cookies, bars, and "desserts"—fluffs, delights, surprises, chiffons, and ambrosias where gelatin again reigns supreme—account for a full half of the recipes in these cookbooks, testifying to the astonishing annual sugar consumption of many Americans.

If preferred food can be seen by frequency of inclusion, disliked or even taboo foods are conspicuous by their absence. Again, in Great Plains examples, organs, or what the butcher euphemistically refers to as "variety meats," are, with very few exceptions, not to be found. Religious or philosophical proscriptions are also subtly made evident. In Methodist Church compilations, as well as in those produced by other groups advocating temperance, not only are there no recipes for frozen daiquiris, but nary a drop of cooking sherry is to be found. Lips that touch wine don't brag about it in such collections.

Commonly consumed and currently popular dishes are signaled by their repeated appearance, usually with only slight variation in ingredients or name. Meatloaf, spaghetti and meat sauce, baked beans, and green bean casserole are examples of these repeated dishes. Some compilers, rather than printing essentially the same recipe time and again, list the names of all those who submitted the dish under one composite recipe. Repeated recipes also denote "trendy" dishes: one year it's lasagne or cherry cola salad; another sourdough starter and spinach salad. Economical and easily accessible ingredients (ground beef, chicken, rice or pasta, canned vegetables, condensed soups) and uncomplicated preparation techniques ("Brown hamburger and onion, mix in other ingredients and bake in greased casserole one hour")[7] are further clues to everyday foods.

Festival, holiday, and special-occasion foods are included by cookbook compilers, often denoted by name: "Bohemian Christmas Balls" or "Lenten Cocoa Cake." Many such recipes are printed with explanations of their significance, use, and in some cases, ethnic origin. "This was my mother's Christmas candy which we loved."[8] "Jan Hagel is a historical cookie. He was a mercenary soldier and this cookie looks like it is covered with buckshots."[9] Dishes with special significance consistently contain more expensive, richer, or more difficult to obtain ingredients, and the required preparations separate them from everyday fare. Chesnica (a Serbian Christmas cake made from strudel dough, ground walnuts, raisins, and honey), toffee requiring more than a pound of butter, and crab souffle are examples of these extraordinary dishes.

Ethnic settlement and assimilation may be in part ascertained from compilations. A number of Dutch, Swedish, or German-Russian recipes in a book obviously point to continued ethnic identification. In communities where such identity is no longer strong, recipes from the old country may be found in the chapter titled "Foreign." Inroads made by mainstream American foodways may also be revealed, as in the Serbian cookbook in which recipes for traditional cabbage rolls are followed by "Southern Fried Chicken."[10]

If, as I suggest, compiled cookbooks can provide insight into preference and taboo, common and festival foods, ethnicity and assimilation, we are still left with the question of how clear an insight. The problem in examining compiled cookbooks as autobiographies is the same encountered with any autobiographical work. Do the facts presented in any way correspond to reality? Are cookbook compilers saying, "Here is what we eat? or "Here is what we would have you believe that we eat?"

There are a number of clues to the accuracy of the cookbooks, many of them obvious. First and foremost is the compilation's title. I doubt even the most skeptical among us would question the sincerity of the Ladies Aid Society of Albion, Nebraska, which straightforwardly proclaimed their collection *What Albion Congregationalists Eat*. The most frequent title, found in nearly fifty percent of the cookbooks examined, is *Our Favorite Recipes*, perhaps an indication that the dishes, if not the most spectacular from each individual's cooking repertoire, are among the best-loved. Clever titles have become more evident in the last five years, as in a church compilation entitled *Burnt Offerings, Tort Pleasers* (assembled by attorneys' wives), and a collection of noon-time offerings called *Thyme for Lunch*.

The nature of the recipe collection is another obvious clue. Hors d'oeuvres, main-dish, foreign-food, and club-luncheon cookbooks cannot by their very nature present an accurate picture of food habits. When considered with and contrasted to other more general compilations, however, they can help to identify everyday and special-occasion or company foods (barbecued chicken as opposed to lobster-broccoli quiche).

Group demographics can also aid in ascertaining accuracy. A rural Nebraska volunteer fire department auxiliary which included a number of lobster dishes in its work might seem less reliable than urban attorneys' wives who did the same (at least in terms of autobiography). Similarly, Czech recipes are more likely in a cookbook from Nebraska's "Bohemian Alps" than in one by a group from melting-pot Grand Island.

The best source of verification of actual usage of contributed recipes is, of course, the contributors themselves. In quizzing cookbook contributors and producers, I discovered with few exceptions that contributions fell into two categories: favorites frequently consumed and special-occasion foods. Few contributed "company only" recipes; those for special occasions were primarily family oriented (such as tunnel-of-fudge cake for a child's birthday), or were associated with holidays (Christmas baked goods like stollen and fruitcake, or the stereotypical Thanksgiving turkey and dressing). While this sampling was by no means scientific, I am confident in the conclusion that compiled cookbooks of a general nature, at least on the Plains, serve as a fairly accurate guide to the food habits of the group which produced them.

Some may view this approach as tangential to the study of traditional foodways. Admittedly, the compiled cookbook is a "popular culture" medium, originally produced locally, but now often published in standardized formats by regional printing and binding companies. Much of what is included in the cookbooks, however, seems at least partially determined by tradition. At the bottom line, of course, are the foodways themselves, undoubtedly influenced by popular culture, but basically folkloric.

Whether the compilation is locally or regionally produced, a standard format seems to prevail. Recipes are divided into general categories— appetizers, salads, vegetables, entrees, casseroles, desserts—often with chapter title pages illustrated by the group's resident artist. Fillers for page bottoms or blank space most often take the form of aphorisms, wise sayings which hearken back to traditional proverbs. Examples include "The surest thing to make us open our eyes is the alarm clock," and "Anger is only one letter short of danger."[11]

Recipes for successful marriages, happy families, and ideal homemaker, and even the American way are other traditional inclusions. Perhaps the ultimate such expression is as follows:

American Blue Ribbon Recipe

In your HOME mix:
2 parts love   1 part courage
1 part confidence   1 part security
Add a dash of humor, flavor with joy, season with consideration, respect and pride.

In your CHURCH, place:
        1 large square of sincerity
        2 heaping cups of vision
        3 full measures of faith
Sift these ingredients until a smooth, even texture results.

In your SCHOOLS, place:
    3 cups practical knowledge
    2 parts ambition
    1 full measure of self-reliance
Fold in 2 parts wisdom. Stir constantly until the ingredients blend.
Now combine all three mixtures. Add equal portions of Active-
citizenship and Free Enterprise. Be SURE these ingredients are
fresh and of the highest quality, since the success of this recipe depends upon them. Place finished mixture in container of Freedom,
warm in an oven of Understanding. This Blue Ribbon dish which
Americans can enjoy daily is considered a rare treat in many other
countries of the world.[12]

Inclusion of some recipes seems to be traditionally determined.
"Scripture cake" (variously called "Bible cake" or "Old Testament
cake"), which tests the cook's biblical knowledge (or tenacity) by listing
the ingredients as 2 cup Judges 5:25, 2 cups Jeremiah 6:20 and instructions as "follow Solomon's advice for child-rearing in Proverbs 23:14,"[13]
appear in over half the church compilations.

Some compiled cookbooks reveal a conservative adherence to traditional food habits despite change and innovation. Years after Vatican
II, fish recipes in Catholic cookbooks far outnumber those included by
Protestant brethren. Despite change in Methodist doctrine, which now
makes alcohol use a matter of individual conscience, even for clergy,
not a drop of spirits is found in many Methodist cookbooks.

In conclusion, while compiled cookbooks are no replacement for
first-hand foodways investigation, they can, I believe, serve as a useful
research guide in determining food habits of some groups. Although a
popular culture medium, the compiled cookbook can give insight into
traditional attitudes, usage and consumption. Like any autobiographical
work, the compiled cookbook has limitations, but when carefully examined it can supply helpful answers to many of our foodways questions.

Notes

An earlier and much shorter version of this paper entitled " 'What Albion
Congregationalists Eat': Cookbooks as Autobiographies," appeared in the *Center
for Southern Folklore Magazine* 3 (1980): 14.

1. Margaret Cook, *America's Charitable Cooks: A Bibliography of Fund-Raising
Cookbooks Published in the United States (1861–1915)* (Kent, Ohio, 1971), ii.

2. Ibid.

3. Also referred to as "gelatin" or by other brand names such as "Jell-well."

4. Nebraska Art Association, *The Sheldon Gallery Cookbook* (Lincoln, Nebraska,
1978), preface.

5. Women's Council United Church of Christ, *What's Cookin'* (Gering, Nebraska, 1977), frontispiece.

6. Cookbooks examined include the following compilations: Christ United Methodist Church Women, *Our Favorite Recipes* (Lincoln, Nebraska, 1972); First Christian Church Women, *75th Anniversary Cookbook* (North Platte, Nebraska, 1976); Cozad Women's Club, *Favorite Recipes* (Cozad, Nebraska, 1975); Ladies Auxiliary, Volunteer Fire Department, *Gering Cookbook* (Gering, Nebraska, 1974); St. Nicholas Serbian Orthodox Church Mother's Club, *Golden Anniversary Cookbook* (Omaha, Nebraska, 1975); Daughters of the Nile, *Recipes Old and New* (Hastings, Nebraska, 1975); and others noted throughout the paper.

7. Reformed Church Women, *Holland Reformed Church Cookbook* (Holland, Nebraska, 1977), 58.

8. Women's Council, *What's Cookin'* (Gering, Nebraska, 1977), 7.

9. Reformed Church Women, *Cookbook,* 78.

10. St. Nicholas Serbian Orthodox Church Mother's Club, *Golden Anniversary Cookbook* (Omaha, Nebraska, 1975), 43–44.

11. Cozad Women's Club, *Favorite Recipes* (Cozad, Nebraska, 1975), 24, 27.

12. Women's Society of Christian Service, *Good as Gold Recipes* (Blair, Nebraska, 1962), 67.

13. Ibid., 64.

Section Two

Ethnic Foods

Ethnicity is a concept almost impossible to define in the United States of the 1990s. Rules for group memberships are increasingly flexible and markers of distinction exist in constant states of construction and modification. Food, as the chapters in this section make clear, can be both a good measure for the distinctiveness of particular peoples and an important means by which their ongoing negotiation of meaning occurs. The issues involved are laid out nicely in the first reading of this section, the introduction to *The Minnesota Ethnic Cook Book* by Anne Kaplan, Marjorie Hoover, and Willard Moore. The other four readings are case studies, beginning with a brief descriptive account of the distinctive cabbage rolls known as bierocks or runsas that are made by German-Russian settlers on the Great Plains.

The remaining chapters in this section explore newer, more complex transformations of identity. First, C. Paige Gutierrez's study in the Cajun country of southern Louisiana demonstrates the influence of mass American culture on ethnic symbolism. The move of crawfish from unpretentious, everyday fare to cultural icon was not premeditated, she finds, and occurred in the 1960s as an accompaniment to increased Cajun self-esteem and the birth of a regional tourist industy.

The final two selections deal directly with the ongoing construction and reconstruction of ethnic identity in contemporary America. Sabina Magliocco's focus is on the Little Italy Festival in Clinton, Indiana, but her points have wide applicability. Italian-American residents use one set of foods and events to reaffirm their own sense of identity, while offering wine, pizza, and other stereotypical "display" foods as a way to make the event financially successful and to share at least some of their Italian experience with outsiders. Ethnic identity, she concludes, operates simultaneously at different levels. Gaye Tuchman and Harry Levine's exploration of the long-standing attachment of New York Jews to Chinese food is a fascinating demonstration of how attention to an

119

apparently trivial matter can yield deep insights into group character. Eating in restaurants helped the newly arrived immigrants from East Europe to feel cosmopolitan. They selected Chinese establishments over others because they felt safe there from anti-Semitism and because the food seemed at once familiar (no mixing of milk and meat) and exotic (eating taboo but delicious pork and shellfish could be rationalized since everything was chopped so fine as to be unrecognizable). Over time the Chinese dining habit became traditional in many families, and now is maintained for its own sake.

10

Introduction: On Ethnic Foodways

Anne R. Kaplan, Marjorie A. Hoover, and Willard B. Moore

"Tell me what you eat, and I will tell you what you are." This oft-quoted maxim of the nineteenth-century philosopher and gastronome Jean Anthelme Brillat-Savarin posits a direct correlation between foodways and identity. Since his delightful volume, *The Physiology of Taste*, first appeared in 1825, Brillat-Savarin's saying has passed from truism to cliche. Nutritionists, historians, sociologists, anthropologists, and folklorists, in exploring the relationship of what one eats and what one is, have quoted, paraphrased, and rearranged his saying. If nothing else, the dictum has provided food for thought; superficial and catchy though it may be, it captures and expresses some underlying truth, almost universally perceived, that the things we eat can say a great deal about us—who we are, where we came from, our current social, cultural, economic, and religious circumstances, and what our aspirations might be.

The term "foodways" nicely captures all of these nuances. Folklorists first began using the word in the 1970s in an effort to discuss traditional behavior that was more than merely preparing a particular recipe at a particular time, behavior that reaches into many aspects of daily life. At a simple church supper, for example, food is the focus of an event that brings people together for social and spiritual interchange. Potluck suppers did not originate for religious purposes, but their symbolic message nicely fits Christian belief: everyone gives a little so that many may eat. The details of the meal are more concrete: what kinds of food are appropriate, who will bring what dishes, what program will be presented, who

Reprinted by permission from *The Minnesota Ethnic Food Book* by Anne R. Kaplan, Marjorie A. Hoover, and Willard B. Moore (St. Paul: Minnesota Historical Society Press, 1986), 1–13. Copyright 1986 by the Minnesota Historical Society.

will perform all the necessary tasks. Members of a church community know the answers to these questions, which have evolved from the traditions of past suppers. In Aitkin, for example, being allowed to bring food to the supper rather than washing dishes afterward is a sign that a girl has come of age. In sum, there is much more to a humble church supper than Jell-O salads and hamburger casseroles. The meal encodes religious and social beliefs as well as hierarchies of age, skill, and status. Foodways are "a whole interrelated system of food conceptualization and evaluation, procurement, distribution, preservation, preparation, consumption, and nutrition shared by all members of a particular society."[1] Ethnic foodways, however, pose a slight problem for this definition.

Contemporary ethnic groups are, in general, much more loosely structured than "a particular society," and membership in them is far from absolute. They are "reference group[s] invoked by people who share a common historical style . . . based on overt features and values, and who, through the process of interaction with others, identify themselves as sharing that style."[2] Ethnicity, then, is basically a function of different culture groups operating within common social contexts, and such interactions are increasingly frequent in American society. We live in a multicultural setting. It is not uncommon to have two sets of grandparents of two different nationalities or even parents of two different ethnic backgrounds. The daughter of a Norwegian-American father and a British-American mother, for example, may identify with either or both of her ethnic traditions. After her marriage to an Italian American, she may learn to cook foods from his family traditions as well. And, in addition, she may also indulge her love of Mexican and Oriental foods. She is of mixed ethnic background, and she is also an American living in Minnesota. All of these factors influence her as she shapes her foodways, choosing items and practices from the traditions and resources available.[3] To put it another way: Ethnic foodways in Minnesota, as elsewhere, operate on two levels. They are a unified system of beliefs, symbols, and actions as described in the definition of foodways above, but they are also part of the larger contexts of American, as well as international, cuisine. No ethnic foods exist in a vacuum, nor are they preserved in a pristine state, uninfluenced by their surroundings.

In fact, it is the multicultural setting that makes ethnic food ethnic. Immigrants sooner or later learn that "Americans" (or members of other ethnic groups in America) do not eat the same things in the same ways as they themselves do. Thus the common food that first-generation settlers considered everyday sustenance gradually takes on a new luster (or stigma, depending on the people and the situation): it is special, it is different, it sets them apart from other groups. In contrast to what surrounding peoples are eating, it has become "traditional" or "ethnic" food. Stories are common about school children and laborers—whose parents or even grandparents had emigrated—discovering to their surprise that their bag lunches differentiated them from their peers. Sandwiches on crusty Italian bread were sometimes enough to mark their bearers as ethnic.[4]

Ethnic foodways are rarely identical to those in the homeland. In the first place, specific ingredients may be unavailable in the new land; substitutions are inevitable. More important, however, are the influences of a new setting, for as food is an integral part of life, so are foodways intrinsic to social and cultural life. As life styles change—both work habits and leisure-time activities—so do foodways. Recipes are modified to accommodate changing time commitments, technology, and ingredients. Occasions for eating traditional foods change; religious or calendar holidays become prime times for eating ethnic food.[5] New foods are incorporated into the everyday diet. Common foods of the immigrant generation are reserved as ethnic treats for special occasions. After decades in America sharp intraethnic demarcations soften. As village or regional loyalties begin to be replaced with national ones, some blending of food traditions occurs.[6] Neapolitan women, for instance, learned to make Calabrian specialties and began to consider themselves—and their foods—Italian. Changes also occur in the Old Country and may be introduced into the ethnic communities by returned visitors. Black families seeking their roots in the Caribbean, for example, bring home recipes for curried goat; Norwegian Americans discover that few people in their ancestral homeland still eat lutefisk. Recent immigrants infuse a knowledge of modern German or Finnish gourmet cookery into the ethnic communities. As a result, ethnic foodways maintain not a direct correspondence but a dynamic relationship with the immigrants' Old World cuisine.

This last point is an important one to remember. Too often we are overwhelmed by the sentimental fallacy that change is an enemy of tradition. This view is basically ahistorical; it focuses on a particular recipe (with or without its social context), removes it from the stream of time, and holds it up as "authentic." Any deviation from this one version is not read as a change, but as a loss of tradition. In reality, however, people—even during previous centuries in the Old World—constantly alter traditions to fit their lives; a static tradition is, most likely, a dead one. Ethnic foodways are far more than surviving relics of Old Country cuisines. A South Slav potica cake, for example—the quick-bread version of a traditional yeasted delicacy—shows how foodways evolve and change with new contexts. By altering the form and preserving the flavor, South Slav women demonstrate their commitment to tradition in the midst of their new status as women who work outside of the home. Precisely because such traditions can be altered to fit circumstances, they are a valuable index of human creativity as well as of the ways people balance cultural continuity with change.

Of all of the ethnic groups included in this volume, nowhere is this delicate balancing act more apparent than among the Hmong. Having lived in Minnesota for barely a decade, at the longest, these people retain much of their traditional culture, including foodways. Eating Hmong food is the norm, rather than a festive highlight of a holiday or other special gathering. In addition, their everyday life is rich in other kinds of customary behavior that relates to food: cooks use homemade knives, cutting boards, and other implements, people speak proverbs or narrate legends to account for certain practices such as eating hot peppers, avoiding certain substances, or offering food to visitors, and families maintain traditional etiquette for serving and eating food. Yet the Hmong daily confront new ways of doing things, and, like the many immigrants before them, they are eager to accept some changes while trying to maintain their cultural integrity.

Watching Hmong ethnicity evolve may give observers a sense of the general process of adaptation in a new setting; whether or not we can deduce from their experience the way it was for the nineteenth- and early twentieth-century immigrants is another matter. For while the other groups included in this book were faced with the notion of America as a melting pot and were encouraged (or forced) to abandon their traditional cultures, the Hmong emigrated in an era when the prevailing ideology encompassed cultural pluralism and ethnic pride. How successful these people will be in directing their own acculturation remains to be seen. At present, however, the Hmong, keeping their traditional culture firmly in mind, stand at a very different point on the continuum of continuity and change from the other ethnic groups discussed in this book.

What are ethnic foodways, and, more specifically, what are ethnic foodways in Minnesota? The creation of food from raw ingredients is a cultural process that varies from individual to individual, group (be it religious, regional, racial, ethnic, or national) to group, and location to location. Various peoples, for example, observe taboos against eating particular items that are considered prime foodstuffs by others; observant Moslems and Jews do not eat pork or any other by-products from pigs. Likewise, ethnic groups follow sometimes strict rules governing the proper ways to process or combine ingredients, thereby transforming them into acceptable food. Again, the Jewish proscription against mixing meat and dairy products—each acceptable when eaten alone—in a single dish or meal can be cited. Another instance is the elaborate techniques of chopping, marinating, or spicing essentially raw meats, such as steak tartare (called "cannibal" by some Minnesotans), sushi, or the Hmong nqaij liab, in order to bring these substances into the realm of what is considered edible by humans. Finally, different religious rites set aside specific fasting times during which participants abstain from certain kinds of food or all foodstuffs for a set period. The point is that such rules and taboos are dictated by cultural beliefs, not biological necessity. And this system of cultural rules and beliefs is the invisible structure upon which is built the distinctive foodways of each ethnic group.[7]

Styles of presentation also characterize certain ethnic traditions, most specifically setting them apart from eating patterns in the United States. Whether they be second- or third-generation descendants of immigrants who generally consider themselves American or recently arrived Hmong refugees, many people contrast their traditional serving styles to a generic "American" one of placing all foods, save dessert, on the table at the same time. When Italian or German Americans enjoy a traditional meal, it is in courses, each presented with new tableware. Russian Jews (and Russians) believe that a dinner is not dinner unless it begins with a soup course—salads are American. Hmong people are adamant about serving rice and vegetable-meat dishes in separate bowls and keeping the foods discrete on individuals' plates.

Taste or flavor is a more tangible factor that distinguishes one ethnic cuisine from another, and this factor, too, is based on cultural (as well as individual) predilection. Researchers have yet to answer the question of why certain villages, nations, or even regions of a continent prefer certain flavors and eschew others. To some degree, geography and climate limit foodstuffs locally available. But exploration, conquests, travel, and trade, sometimes going back to ancient times, have made many nonindigenous ingredients locally available. While scholars study the phenomenon, the popular imagination cherishes stereotypes about ethnic cookery: all Scandinavian food is bland, all Mexican dishes are fiery, Italian food depends on generous amounts of garlic and tomato sauce, and so forth. As the chapters in this book will show, these generalizations, although they may contain a kernel of truth, do not hold true across the board.

Along with favorite ingredients, most groups also have preferred techniques for preparing foods. Southern blacks, for example, traditionally simmer greens and meats for hours, the Hmong often chop and stir-fry their protein-vegetable combinations, while Italians commonly layer crusts or noodles, filling, and sauces. Nevertheless, there are but a finite number of structural possibilities and cooking techniques for "constructing" food; consequently, dishes from various ethnic cultures are bound to resemble each other somewhat. Italian manicotti, Jewish blintzes, Hmong spring rolls, and Mexican enchiladas, like the Anglo-American sandwich, all involve wrapping a starchy jacket around a form of protein. As a novice Jewish cook was advised when trying to visualize how her kreplach should look, "Think of it as a won ton!"[8]

The limited number of forms and cooking processes, combined with common historical, environmental, and cultural experiences, helps account for the similarities in cuisine shared by diverse groups. Despite the historical enmity of the Greeks and Turks, for example, their food-ways bear some resemblance, and the same is true of cultures in the Near and Middle East, within Indochina, and throughout the regions of Europe. In very broad terms, the cookery of the world can be divided into regional cuisines similar in general characteristics but distinctive in detail.

The topic of ethnic foodways in Minnesota raises some perplexing issues. Can a state, a political entity carved out of a geographic region, affect ethnic foodways? Have ethnic Minnesotans and their foods made any impact on the state? While it would be difficult to prove that political boundaries materially influenced foodways, the state's climate and geography, in some cases, caused the immigrants and their descendants to modify or change some practices. Some people emigrated to Minnesota from a completely different geographic zone. South Slavs substituted berries for apricots and other warmth-loving fruits that they were accustomed to growing. Greeks grew grapevines for the leaves, which they stuff to make dolmades, but, like the Italians, bought California grapes for winemaking because the growing season in northern Minnesota was too short for the vines to produce fruit. Hmong people find alternatives to the banana leaves they traditionally used to wrap food, and so forth. Not all changes, however, resulted from necessity rather than choice. Many European immigrants, for example, were delighted by the availability of refined white flour, an upper-class commodity in Europe, and happily replaced darker flours and whole-grain breads with a less health-ful, more prestigious alternative.

Ultimately more important to the shape of ethnic foodways than climate and geography were the socioeconomic conditions people faced in Minnesota. The Ojibway present the most radical example: white settlement caused profound changes in their traditional pattern of life and livelihood as farms, cities, and industry replaced prairies and woodlands. Laws regulated their traditional food-gathering practices such as hunting, ricing, and fishing; the government attempted to turn them into farmers; federal food allotments introduced them to foods like salt pork, beans, and bacon; and Indian agents and other government or church workers taught them to can fruits and wax vegetables. These vast changes are especially ironic, since from the perspective of classic immigration theory, the Ojibway take the role of a "host society" rather than an immigrant group.[9]

In less traumatic ways, members of other ethnic groups shaped their foodways to fit the Minnesota environment. In many instances they showed a good deal of ingenuity in maintaining traditional practices; for example, people as diverse as Greeks, Italians, and Hmong have found places to gather wild greens in urban environments. Members of numerous immigrant groups over the years have planted gardens with seeds carried from their homelands, traded across ethnic lines for particular ingredients, started their own businesses to manufacture, import, or simply merchandise hard-to-find food items. Income seems to have had less effect on traditional foodways than peer pressure, the efforts of social workers and dietitians who sought to "Americanize" immigrants, and prevailing concepts of what foods were prestigious. The Great Depression and subsequent economic crises caused many Americans to adjust their foodways; members of some of Minnesota's ethnic groups claim that hard times brought them back to the simple foods of their ethnic heritages.[10]

Settlement patterns certainly affected the overall shape of ethnic foodways, as many of the people who became neighbors in Minnesota shared their recipes and customs. Residents of the state's iron ranges exemplified this kind of exchange which occurs, to a greater or lesser degree, whenever different nationalities interact. Food columnist Eleanor Ostman summarized the process of sharing that was mentioned by many people interviewed for this book: "It wouldn't be a wedding on the Iron Range without Potica, the [South Slav] walnut-rolled sweet bread, or Sarmas, the [South Slav] meat-stuffed cabbage rolls. Pasties [Cornish and Finnish], Porketta [Italian], Pulla [Finnish]—we all grew up with them no matter our ethnic heritage, because if our families didn't make them, our friends did."[11] Intermarriage often promotes this kind of mingling, when spouses share traditions or when the primary cook learns to prepare items from the spouse's heritage. But so does regular social interaction. Hmong people in the Twin Cities have adopted elements of Lao and Thai cuisine because the ingredients are readily available in Oriental groceries. Germans who live in predominantly Norwegian towns in the Red River Valley have learned to make Norse delicacies.

There is no question, then, that some changes have occurred as a result of Minnesota's multicultural environment. Whether or not the state provides a particularly fruitful setting for ethnic interaction, however, is difficult to gauge. Those familiar with traditional cultures on

Michigan's Upper Peninsula report similar conditions,[12] and it is reasonable to assume that these are widespread. Yet, according to one source, in neighboring Wisconsin, "The border each [ethnic] group established around itself was almost as formidable as an Old World frontier. Commonality of the immigrant experience was usually shared just with landsmen. . . . Gastronomically, such divisions were every bit as rigid. As happens today, new foods were approached with caution."[13] Clearly, the reciprocal relationship of ethnic groups, their eating patterns, and a particular environment such as a state is a topic well worth further investigation.

One thing for certain, however, is the impact that ethnic cooks have had on Minnesota's local markets. Even large chain stores respond to the cooking needs of their patrons in particular neighborhoods, stocking specialty items like fresh mustard, collard, and turnip greens, fish sauce and a variety of Oriental noodles, packaged kosher ingredients and mixes, frozen phyllo leaves, Swedish meatballs and sausages, and so forth. And the state also supports a fair number and variety of ethnic groceries and meat markets which serve patrons from diverse ethnic groups. These stores are rich resources for the scholar as well as the cook; their contents can tell much about neighborhood settlement patterns in addition to ethnic and interethnic shopping habits. The owner of a Mexican grocery in St. Paul, for example, noted that many "Anglo" people, currently enthralled with Mexican food, shop in her store. She also has many Hmong customers whose cuisine does not resemble the Mexican one but who use some of the same ingredients. Similarly, Sicilian Americans shop in Oriental food stores for frozen squid, Finns may go to Jewish delicatessans for smoked salmon, and several specialty groceries on St. Paul's West Side stock Mexican and Lebanese items under one roof.[14]

Most of the institutions that support ethnic life in Minnesota—churches, synagogues, fraternal organizations, and clubs—have at one time or another published cookbooks. These volumes are ostensibly produced as fund raisers or to satisfy those who enjoy a particular ethnic dish but do not know how to prepare it. In a sense cookbooks serve as a public relations device, but more precisely they are a statement about ethnic identity, one of the barometers of the times. The ladies' aid society of a Minneapolis Norwegian church, for example, published a cookbook in 1942. The first eighty pages were devoted to American recipes, many of them typical of depression-era foods: tuna-noodle and hamburger casseroles and Jell-O "surprises." At the back of the book, a mere eleven pages described "Scandinavian Delicacies." Nine years later the tide toward ethnic cooking had begun to rise, and the same group published another edition with the same cover illustration, but the 128 pages carried almost entirely Norwegian recipes.[15]

Ethnic cookbooks help preserve and disseminate recipes, and they present another research source for the student of ethnic foodways. Yet they should be approached with caution. Who uses them? When? Why? How? Many cooks, for example, frequently amend published recipes, their improvements reflecting changing tastes or trends, as well as individual predilection. Ethnic cookbooks and newspaper descriptions of particular holiday foods followed by a recipe convey little of the cultural and even less of the behavioral context of ethnicity or foodways. Cookbooks offer few clues to the significance of a particular dish or its place in traditional life.[16] Furthermore, many cookbooks, because of insufficient space, must ignore regional distinctions or stylistic differences. One lefse recipe, for example, seems to stand for all lefse when, in fact, the bread exists in dozens of variations. And traditional dishes are sometimes adapted with the help of American commercial enterprise. Potato flakes, for instance, may replace freshly peeled potatoes in the lefse recipe, especially if it was developed for a public function, such as a Christmas bazaar, where quantities of bread are needed. In short, published recipes are not always reliable versions of home-cooked ethnic foods, even though they may accurately reflect the shortcuts some cooks take if pressed for time.[17]

Similarly, eating in ethnic restaurants or frequenting events staged for the public gives but a glimpse of true ethnic foodways. In fact, such public meals may alter or blur the proper presentation and meaning of popular foods. Dishes that have a formal, distinct, and functional place within the context of a traditional meal or social occasion are often randomly listed on restaurant menus or laid out informally as part of a mix of delectables on a bazaar table at a county historical society or a country church. Eating in such a setting is a little like visiting a museum full of beautiful tools with no explanatory labels: one appreciates the artifacts but must guess at their meaning or function.

As dietitians and social workers charged with changing immigrant eating habits were quick to discover, familiar foods are preferred for more than their nutritional value.[18] Traditional foodways prove to be intrinsic to the way a particular group views itself and its relation to others, to the natural world, and, often, to a deity. Aside from providing sustenance, foods (with attendant ritual) are also at the core of traditional medical practices, whether for something as serious as removing the evil eye or ensuring good health for mother and unborn child throughout pregnancy and the early postnatal period, or as minor as treating the symptoms of a cold.

But perhaps the most consistently important end to which ethnic foodways are put is a symbolic one. Serving food—any food—is a sign of hospitality and sociability; we can learn a great deal by paying close attention to the kinds of foods offered, the occasion for socializing, and the place where eating occurs. Foodways tell the canny observer about social intimacy and distance, background, and aspirations—in short, the kind of impression one hopes to make, the image one wants to project, and the relationship binding those who gather to eat.[19] When Americans choose to serve their traditional ethnic foods at any occasion, they communicate a message about identity, focusing attention on their membership in a group with a particular background and set of values.

Ethnic foods may be offered at casual or formal gatherings, in public or private settings, to members of the same ethnic group or to "outsiders." And even at a casual, private affair like a family supper, the choice to serve ethnic foods is of symbolic significance; using foodways to project or to teach about one's identity is not confined to feeding a curious public. On an everyday basis, for example, when parents prepare and serve traditional food in the ritually or socially proper manner, they are teaching their children about their heritage at the same time that they are celebrating their own ethnicity and reassuring the larger community of a continuity of tradition. The process of communication and reinforcement is the same, whether the participants are an Ojibway family sharing venison stew, a third-generation Finnish couple eating rutabaga casserole and fish soup, or a recently resettled Hmong family eating pork with hot pepper sauce.

Likewise, at annual religious and secular holidays and on special occasions such as weddings, birth celebrations, and funerals, members of a group reaffirm their identity through the foods they serve and eat. And it is not only individual identity that is celebrated, but each person's membership in a unique group, the members of which share certain cultural traits such as traditional foodways and the knowledge of their appropriate uses and contexts. Thus the foods and foodways of any group help establish a cultural boundary which serves both inclusive and exclusive purposes, uniting those within its bounds and distinguishing that particular group from all others.[20]

The power of foodways to symbolize one's status was not lost on many immigrants or their heirs. While constraints of time and money caused some temporarily to reject traditional foodways, the fear of being marked a "greenhorn" (foreigner) prompted others to try to eat American food, especially in public. Consuming large pieces of meat, such as beef steaks or pork chops, and conspicuously displaying processed, or "store-bought," foods in place of homemade items were signs of success, American style. The soul food movement and the subsequent celebration of American cultural pluralism in the 1970s turned this trend around to some extent, publicly proclaiming pride in heritage as symbolized by foods both distinctive and humble in origin.

Currently, Americans perceive theirs as a pluralistic society, and open expression of ethnicity is appreciated. Even so, not all ethnic foods are deemed appropriate for public notice. Most cultures have certain well-liked foods, such as menudo (tripe soup) among Mexican Americans, greens among blacks, or pasta fagioli (noodles and beans) among Italian Americans, which members think project a derogatory image of themselves, symbolizing poverty, peasant origins, or the willingness to consume foods of doubtful origin. These dishes are reserved for private consumption. After all, many cultures have suffered name-calling and discrimination based upon the foods they allegedly prefer: French "frogs," black "coons," German "krauts," and so forth. These slurs operate on the principle that people who eat food we consider inedible, for whatever subjective reasons peculiar to our culture, are somehow less human than we.[21]

Consequently, members of ethnic communities often make predictably safe choices when occasions call them to present their foodways (and thus themselves) to the public. The foods that are offered as badges of ethnicity, whether at a festival, a religious observance to which outsiders are invited, or an ethnic New Year's celebration, for example, usually maintain a delicate balance: they are "exotic" or distinctive enough to convey an ethnic image, yet they are "tame" enough to appeal to the uninitiated. And, to spare embarrassment at events meant to generate good will, they are often easily handled "finger foods" such as tacos or miniature Greek pitas (pies)—actually appetizers or snack food, and not celebrative fare. Traditional foodways for public consumption convey ethnicity, in reality a complex web of interactions and allegiances, in simplified, favorable, and easily perceived images.

But if ethnic foodways are used to draw boundaries, to separate "us" from "them" (in either a hostile or a supportive manner), they may also be used to bridge the gap between nationalities. Selectively sharing food, as noted, is a basic form of hospitality. Sharing ethnic food is a rudimentary way of giving strangers and friends a glimpse of one's culture while projecting a positive image of one's self and one's group.

Notes

1. Jay A. Anderson, "Scholarship on Contemporary American Folk Foodways," *Ethnologia Europaea* 5 (1971); 57. On church dinners in Aitkin, see interview of staff of KKIN/KKEZ Radio, Aitkin, November 13, 1984.

2. Anya P. Royce, *Ethnic Identity: Strategies of Diversity* (Bloomington, Ind.: Indiana University Press, 1981), 18; Abner Cohen, "The Lesson of Ethnicity," in Abner Cohen, ed., *Urban Ethnicity* (London: Tavistock, 1974), xi.

3. On the ways in which family members may "negotiate" a menu, see Judith Goode, Janet Theophano, and Karen Curtis, "A Framework for the Analysis of Continuity and Change in Shared Sociocultural Rules for Food Use: The Italian-American Pattern," in Linda Keller Brown and Kay Mussell, eds., *Ethnic and Regional Foodways in the United States: The Performance of Group Identity* (Knoxville: University of Tennessee Press, 1984), 79–84.

4. See, for example, interviews of Theresa Inzerillo, Minneapolis, June 7, 1982; Michelina Dreyling, St. Paul, May 10, 1982.

5. In fact, foodways associated with holidays (especially religious observances) or ties of passage are most likely to be maintained in their traditional forms and contexts. Among everyday dishes, traditional baked goods and desserts seem most likely to be preserved.

6. Food often becomes symbolic of regional differences or strife. In an opinion column in *Asian Business and Community News* (St. Paul), November 1985, p. 15, Dac Tong Tuan, a Vietnamese immigrant wrote: "Time only perhaps can erase the discrimination between Northerners and Southerners who belong to the same Vietnamese nation. . . . Southerners gradually learned to eat the bind weed (a kind of vegetable) fried with garlic and Northerners realized that raw bean sprouts are also delicious."

7. The anthropological literature is replete with references from many viewpoints on food taboos, avoidances, and preferences. See, for example, Marvin Harris, *Cows, Pigs, Wars, and Witches: The Riddles of Culture* (New York: Random House, 1974); Mary Douglas, *Purity and Danger: An Analysis of the Concepts of Pollution and Taboo* (London: Routledge and Kegan Paul, 1966) and *Food in the Social Order: Studies of Food and Festivities in Three American Communities* (New York: The Russell Sage Foundation, 1984); Roger Abrahams, "Equal Opportunity Eating: A Structural Excursus on Things of the Mouth," in *Ethnic and Regional Foodways*, ed. Brown and Mussell, 19–36; Frederick J. Simoons, *Eat Not This Flesh: Food Avoidances in the Old World* (Madison: University of Wisconsin Press, 1963). On the nature-culture distinction, see Claude Levi-Strauss, "The Culinary Triangle," *Partisan Review* 33 (1966): 586–95 and *The Raw and the Cooked: Introduction to the Science of Mythology*, vol. 1 (New York: Harper & Row, 1969).

8. Interview of Lisa Schlesinger, St. Paul, November 10, 1981. For a light-hearted treatment, see *Minneapolis Tribune*, April 11, 1982, p. 1K, tellingly titled "It's the same the whole world over (and it's a pancake)."

9. For a description of these changes from an Indian perspective, see Ignatia Broker, *Night Flying Woman: An Ojibway Narrative* (St. Paul: Minnesota Historical Society Press, 1983).

10. For an analysis of a broad range of regional food customs during the Great Depression, see John Charles Camp, " 'America Eats': Toward a Social Definition of American Foods" (Ph.D. diss., University of Pennsylvania, 1978).

11. *St. Paul Pioneer Press*, September 20, 1981, Accent sec., 12.

12. See, for example, interviews of Natalie Gallagher, St. Paul, January 25, 1983, Helen and William Sysimaki, Duluth, August 24, 1983.

13. Harva Hachten, *The Flavor of Wisconsin: An Informal History of Food and Eating In the Badger State, Together with 400 Favorite Recipes* (Madison: State Historical Society of Wisconsin, 1981), 27.

14. Interviews of Maria Silva, St. Paul, May 15, 1984, Eila Eilers, Duluth, August 24, 1983, T. Inzerillo, Minneapolis, June 7, 1982.

15. Ladies' Aid Society of Norwegian Lutheran Memorial Church, *Cookbook of Tested Recipes* (Minneapolis: The Church, 1941, 1950).

16. See Lynn Ireland, "The Compiled Cookbook as Foodways Autobiography," *Western Folklore* 40 (1981): 107–14; Edith Horandner, "The Recipe Book as a Cultural and Socio-Historical Document," in Alexander Fenton and Trefor M. Owen, eds., *Food in Perspective: Proceedings of the Third International Conference on Ethnological Food Research* (Edinburgh, Scotland: John Donald Publishers Ltd., 1977), 119–44.

17. The incorporation of premixed, instant, or convenience foods into traditional ethnic cooking is in step with the use of these foods in American life. Leaving aside judgments of aesthetics or quality, this trend supports the argument that traditional foodways should be regarded as an integral part of everyday life, rather than as a sacrosanct preserve untouched by modernity.

18. See, for example, Bertha M. Wood, *Foods of the Foreign-Born in Relation to Health* (Boston: M. Barrows and Co., 1929).

19. See, for example, two works by Mary Douglas, "Deciphering a Meal," in Clifford Geertz, ed., *Myth, Symbol, and Ritual* (New York: Norton and Co., 1971), 61–82, and "Food as a System of Communication," in Mary Douglas, ed., *In the Active Voice* (London: Routledge and Kegan Paul, 1982), 82–124.

20. A good introduction to this topic is the book edited by Brown and Mussell, *Ethnic and Regional Foodways in the United States.* For a caution against simplistic interpretations of ethnic foodways, see Janet Theophano, "It's Really Tomato Sauce But We Call It Gravy: A Study of Food and Women's Work among Italian-American Families" (Ph.D. diss., University of Pennsylvania, 1982).

21. For more on the phenomenon of labeling a group with reference to a notorious food, see William W. Weaver, *Sauerkraut Yankees: Pennsylvania-German Foods and Foodways* (Philadelphia: University of Pennsylvania Press, 1983).

11

Bierocks

Thomas D. Isern

Jim has speculated in past writings as to what creature might be named the official animal of the Great Plains. Here's a more palatable question: what food might we designate most representative of life on the plains?

I nominate the bierock, or as I sometimes call it, the German-Russian answer to the burrito. The bierock is a piece of sweet dough wrapped around a filling of cabbage, onions, and beef (or whatever else you want to stuff into it) and baked.

The bierock is a characteristic food of Germans from Russia on the southern plains from Texas to Kansas. Germans from Russia in the states from Nebraska north consume the same item, but they call it a runsa.

Both names are figments of German-Russian dialect. "Runsa" is a word for "belly," and so the name presumably recognizes the resemblance of the food to a stomach. "Bierock" is a word evolved from the Russian *pirogi* or *pirozhki,* a name for any food consisting of filling stuffed into dough. This shows that bierocks are not a German food but a Russian food the Germans picked up while living in Russia.

On the Canadian plains, Ukrainian and other Eastern European immigrants make what they call "piroges." These are a soft dough stuffed with potatoes and cheese, boiled, and served with butter, onions, and sour cream. Piroges and bierocks are akin in name and in general concept, but the piroges more closely resemble what German-Russian Mennonites on the southern plains call "verenikas."

Honestly, I never cared much for verenikas. The Mennonites generally fill them with cottage cheese and serve them with a white gravy, and the whole mess seems to me about as exciting as a game of checkers. On

Reprinted by permission from *Plains Folk II: The Romance of the Landscape* by Jim Hoy and Tom Isern (Norman: University of Oklahoma Press, 1990), 80–83.

the other hand, I have developed a liking for the piroges of the north. I can eat a pile of them the way they serve them at the Romanian-Canadian Culture Club of Regina.

There seems to be quite a bit of confusion about bierocks among plains folk. In the first place, people think they are a German dish, but they aren't; they're Russian. And no two cooks agree on how to spell the name of the item, either. In fact a single cookbook by German-Russian women from western Kansas, *Das Essen Unsrer Leute*, spells it six different ways: bierock, bieroch, beerock, bierack, beruch, and beroak.

To get back to the original question: why the bierock as the representative food of the plains? In a great book of the 1950s, *The Great Plains in Transition*, Carl Kraenzel said that the keys to survival on the plains are mobility, flexibility, and reserves. Kraenzel must have loved bierocks. You can carry them anywhere, stuff them with whatever you have on hand, and save the leftovers to reheat later.

The bierock also has intercontinental tradition going for it. It is, after all, a plains food of two continents.

Back for More Bierocks

Here is how to make bierocks, the characteristic food of Germans from Russia on the plains. In the first place, the dough is important. Don't listen to anyone who says you can make bierocks with store-bought, refrigerated bread dough.

First prepare your yeast. Put a couple packages of dry yeast and a tablespoon of sugar into a cup of lukewarm water. Let it stand to dissolve. In another bowl mix three-fourths cup sugar and one tablespoon salt into two cups of warm milk (scalded milk, the old recipes say, but that's not necessary anymore). In still another (big) bowl mix four cups flour, two-thirds cup soft lard, and two eggs. Add the contents of the first two bowls to this one and mix it all up. Let this batter stand and rise for a half-hour or so. What you have here is the *Vorteig*, or predough, which is the key to the whole ethnic tradition of bierock making.

Now add four more cups flour, mix, knead, and put the stuff aside to rise again. Meanwhile, you can get the filling ready. Most people begin by browning some ground beef in a large pot, add chopped onions, and then put in chopped cabbage, cooking until the cabbage is sort of translucent. Seasoning is according to taste, with garlic salt commonly used. The proportion of ingredients in the filling is open for dispute. A real Rooshian wants more cabbage than anything else.

Also a question is how best to roll or spread out the dough to receive the filling. I break off a piece the size of a tennis ball and roll it out. On this I put a large spoonful of filling. Then I pull the edges of the dough together on top and squeeze them together. The trick next is to flip the bierock over onto the baking sheet, so that the edges of the dough are down.

Bake the bierocks at 350 degrees until they are as brown as you want them. Mine come out about the size of a brick, but not quite as hard. Most people make them smaller.

What got me started on this subject of bierocks was when at a grocery here in Emporia I found plastic-wrapped, microwaved bierocks for sale. According to the wrappers they were distributed by Bob and Thelma's Steak House, a good restaurant near Hoisington, Kansas. They were pretty bland, mainly because they contained too little cabbage.

A better commercial product comes from a chain of drive-ins in Nebraska called Runza Drive Inns. This chain, with headquarters in Lincoln but with drive-ins in towns throughout Nebraska and parts of Iowa and Kansas, produces a fairly tasty bierock, which it has trademarked, in the style of the northern plains, as a Runza. The dough is not quite the right sweetness or texture, though.

Various church groups and other community organizations all over the plains sell bierocks at festivals and on special occasions. In my old hometown of Ellinwood, the Lutheran Women's Missionary League sells them each summer at a local festival. I have a copy of the 1984 report of their bierock chairwoman. It says the women worked two days to make 1,189 bierocks containing 150 pounds cabbage, 100 pounds onions, and just $15.23 worth of beef. Evidently the real Rooshians prevailed in the filling mix, I thought at first, but then some of the women involved explained that the $15.23 was the amount for purchased beef and that other beef was donated.

The only public complaint about the sale was that the 1,189 bierocks sold out too fast. The hoarders got to the sale early and bought them up dozens at a time.

12

Cajuns and Crawfish

C. Paige Gutierrez

The crawfish is the dominant food-related ethnic symbol in Acadiana. It is arguable that the crawfish is the most important of all Cajun ethnic symbols today. Its use as a symbol is ubiquitous, and it is acceptable as an ethnic emblem to a wide variety of Cajuns. Revon Reed, a Cajun teacher, writer, and radio personality who has long been active in the Cajun ethnic revival, has predicted that "anthropologists of the future" will classify the crawfish as the symbol of Cajuns in the twentieth century (Reed 1976:109; see also Gutierrez 1984).

Why is the crawfish so popular and effective as an ethnic symbol? What messages does it communicate? The interpretation of the crawfish as symbol can help us understand why Cajun food in general is so important as an expression of ethnic identity.

In contemporary Acadiana, the image of the crawfish is frequently associated with the expression of ethnic/regional consciousness and pride. For example, a popular license plate, bumper sticker, tee shirt, and hat show an upraised fist holding a crawfish, with the accompanying slogan, "Cajun Power." The terms *Cajun, Acadian, Cajun Country,* and *Louisiana* often appear in conjunction with crawfish imagery in tourist-oriented advertisements and on souvenirs. There are crawfish key chains, combs, plates, and plaques; mechanical toy crawfish; seesaw-riding crawfish encased in fluid-filled plastic domes; and locally produced children's books that feature crawfish characters. Available in St. Martin Parish are preserved (real) crawfish attached to plaques or sitting in miniature crawfish nets—the products of a local cottage industry. Advertisements aimed at tourists and convention planners feature crawfish.

Reprinted by permission from *Cajun Foodways* by C. Paige Gutierrez (Jackson: University Press of Mississippi, 1992), 77–82.

Local jewelers sell expensive gold or silver crawfish pendants and earrings, and clothing stores sell crawfish logo shirts.

For years an outdoor mural in downtown Lafayette had as its focus a giant crawfish holding an oil rig in one claw, surrounded by pictures of other items commonly associated with Cajuns—the flag of Acadiana, an Acadian cottage, a horse race. The University of Southwestern Louisiana sponsored a contest for the design of a new icon for the Ragin' Cajuns in the early 1980s. The school did not specifically solicit crawfish imagery, but the winning design portrays a Ragin' Cajun astride a bucking crawfish, and the second prize was awarded to a stylized representation of a crawfish.

The examples of crawfish symbolism described here are modern ones, proliferated by the regional media and mass marketing. There are no indications in historical sources, oral folklore, or oral history that the crawfish was a recognized symbol of ethnicity for Cajuns in earlier times. However, it does appear that Cajuns were associated with the crawfish by both Cajuns and non-Cajuns before the advent of commercialized crawfish iconography. A popular summary of crawfish "legendry," sold locally as a souvenir in the 1970s, states that "when a bayou baby is nine days old, his mother sticks his finger in a crawfish hole, and that makes him a Cajun" (Guirard 1973). In the early 1940s, a similar motif was found in a "taunting jingle flung at Cajun youngsters by Negro children," collected by field workers for the Louisiana Writers' Project of the WPA (Saxon, Dreyer, and Tallant 1945:200):

> Frenchman! Frenchman! Nine days old!
> Wrung his hand off in a crayfish hole.
>
> Frenchman! Frenchman! Nine days old,
> Got his hand broke off in crayfish hole.

A longer version of a similar song, entitled "Cribisse! Cribisse!" ("Crawfish! Crawfish") was collected in French Creole in the 1930s (Whitfield 1939:138). In Whitfield's English translation, it runs:

> Crawfish, crawfish, got no show, baby,
> Crawfish, crawfish, got no show,
> The Frenchman ketch 'im fer to make gumbo, baby.
>
> Get up in the morning you find me gone, baby,
> Get up in the morning you find me gone,
> I'm on my way to the crawfish pond, baby.

Frenchman, Frenchman, only nine days old, baby,
Frenchman, Frenchman, only nine days old,
Broke his arm in a crawfish hole, baby.

Crawfish ain't skeered of a six-mule team, baby,
Crawfish ain't skeered of a six-mule team,
But run from a Frenchman time he see 'im, baby.

Look all 'round a Frenchman's bed, baby,
Look all 'round a Frenchman's bed,
You don' find nothin' but crawfish heads, baby.

One contemporary Cajun ethnic joke told by Cajuns draws on a theme similar to that of verse four above: a mother crawfish calms her off-springs' fears of horses and cows, but tells them to run away quickly when they see a Cajun, because "he'll eat anything."

Such songs and jokes mildly ridicule Cajuns for their excessive love of crawfish and for their unconventional eating habits. These examples associate Cajuns with crawfish, but the association is not a particularly positive one from the Cajun point of view. Elderly residents of Breaux Bridge confirm that in their youths the crawfish was a low-status food— and not a symbol of Cajun pride. There was little tourist demand for them, although traveling gourmets did seek out crawfish at such places as the Hebert Hotel restaurant in Breaux Bridge as early as the 1920s. Local people recall that crawfish were so plentiful that hordes of them migrating across roads commonly created traffic hazards (something that still happens occasionally), and housewives in low-lying areas could scoop up a bucketful for dinner from their own back yards. Crawfish were "poor people's food," provided freely by the swamps and streams.

Cajuns who lived on the edge of the Atchafalaya Basin in the 1930s said that crawfish were "just another variety of fish," and that they became tired of eating them so often; these Cajuns sometimes made financial sacrifices to be able to purchase canned salmon (Jacobi 1937:29–30). Like other aspects of traditional Cajun culture, crawfish eating was ridiculed by twentieth-century newcomers, who frequently did not recognize the animal as an acceptable food item. Cajuns were accused of eating what outsiders perceived as unclean, inedible vermin. Both outsiders and some Cajuns associated crawfish eating with isolated, "backwards," swamp-dwelling Cajuns.

The eating of crawfish, like other aspects of Cajun culture, has since undergone a change in status. Like being Cajun, eating crawfish is no longer something to be ashamed of, and crawfish are no longer "poor people's food." By 1958 the esteem for crawfish had risen to the point that the town of Breaux Bridge could be "honored" by being named the Crawfish Capital of the World. It is noteworthy that while crawfish are praised by the town's historical marker, erected in 1959, Cajuns themselves are not mentioned. The state legislature honored crawfish nine years before it created CODOFIL and named the region Acadiana.

Today the crawfish is an expensive food item, and one that serves as a gourmet food in some contexts. An elderly Breaux Bridge woman says, "Now the big shots eat crawfish, and the poor can't afford to. I wish I had eaten more back then; now I can't afford to buy them." Actually, able-bodied Cajuns with low incomes can still catch crawfish, even if they cannot afford to buy them.

The change in status of the crawfish as food is illustrated by a story told in Breaux Bridge about an old crawfisherman who used to take the long way home with his catch from the Atchafalaya swamp in order to avoid the humiliation of being seen with crawfish by the Lafayette "city folk" picnicking on the levee. Today, he still must take the long way home in order to avoid the city folk, who now deluge him with offers to buy his crawfish.

When and how did the crawfish become a widespread and widely recognized emblem of Cajun ethnicity? Locals say that modern, commercialized crawfish iconography was not common before 1960, and that it became increasingly popular during the 1970s. No one knows who first designed crawfish "Cajun Power" tee shirts and bumper stickers, or who first discovered that plastic combs shaped like lobsters could be ordered from novelty companies with the words "State of Maine" replaced by the words "Cajun Louisiana." However, it is known that local Cajuns designed and produced keepsakes with the crawfish emblem for the 1959 Breaux Bridge Centennial Celebration. These were intended as much for townspeople as for tourists. That year Breaux Bridge merchants distributed wooden nickels with crawfish imprinted on one side, and several other crawfish trinkets were available. A town flag was also created: its centerpiece is a crawfish, surrounded by other symbols of Cajuns and/or the community. At that time, the specific association between crawfish and the Cajun ethnic group—as opposed to the community of Breaux Bridge—was not as overt as it later became. In 1960, the Centennial Celebration was replaced by the Crawfish Festival, which prompted the further proliferation of the crawfish as an emblem in the Breaux Bridge area.

It is understandable that the crawfish should have become a symbol of Breaux Bridge and St. Martin Parish. Throughout south Louisiana, communities sponsor festivals that focus on a local product, usually a food. For example, there is the Rice Festival in Crowley, Yam Festival in

Opelousas, Sugar Festival in New Iberia, Alligator Festival in Franklin, Boudin Festival in Broussard, Oyster Festival in Galliano, Frog Festival in Rayne, Cotton Festival in Ville Platte, and the Shrimp and Petroleum Festival in Morgan City. The crawfish has long been a major product of St. Martin Parish, making it a logical choice as a festival theme for Breaux Bridge.

Today, however, the crawfish has become a symbol for all Cajuns, and not just those who live in major crawfish industry areas. Some of the other festivals' products occasionally serve as Cajun ethnic emblems, but none as often as the crawfish. The Breaux Bridge Crawfish Festival itself is partly responsible for calling attention to the crawfish as a Cajun symbol. The festival has always been immensely popular among Cajuns throughout the region as well as among tourists. Cajuns from elsewhere in Acadiana may first have seen the crawfish used as an emblem at the Breaux Bridge festival, or they may have become aware of it through media attention to the festival—including national media coverage (Esman 1981:92).

The growth of the Crawfish Festival coincided with other developments. Stirrings of a Cajun ethnic revival had already begun by 1960. During the 1950s, Cajun's income, education, and self-esteem were beginning to rise, and in 1955 the bicentennial of the Acadian exile was celebrated in some parts of Acadiana. By 1960 being Cajun was, for some Cajuns at least, an acceptable identity, and one that could be expressed openly through public symbols. The crawfish was one of several available symbols, and the success of the Crawfish Festival focused attention on it (Esman 1981:179–80). In addition, the crawfish was becoming economically significant throughout Acadiana. Crawfishing as an economic enterprise had been a seasonal activity limited chiefly to the Atchafalaya Basin and other swamp areas. In 1959 modern, commercial crawfish farming began, a practice that has allowed greater numbers of Cajuns throughout much of Acadiana to participate in the crawfish industry as farmers, marketers, and restaurant owners. The Breaux Bridge festival contributed to the growth of the industry: after the centennial celebration faced a shortage of crawfish, a local politician helped obtain a state grant to fund crawfish farming in St. Martin Parish. The festival also spurred outsiders' interest in the crawfish as food, and this in turn was an economic boon to the crawfish industry, the restaurant industry, and the regional tourist industry.

The rise in status of the crawfish as food and the modern expansion of the crawfish industry partly explain the crawfish's acceptance as an ethnic emblem, while the existence of the Crawfish Festival and the influence of mass media and mass marketing in Acadiana partly explain its proliferation. However, these factors do not completely explain the widespread acceptance of the crawfish as the symbol of Cajuns. Both the French language and the Coonass image have been offered as competing ethnic symbols. Both, like the crawfish, have undergone change in status and have been proliferated in part through the mass media and mass marketing. Yet each has been found unacceptable by some Cajuns. So why is the crawfish a widely accepted, successful ethnic symbol?

The power of the crawfish as an ethnic symbol is enhanced by its dual role as a food (a part of culture) and an animal (a part of nature). Because it is both, it possesses a broad range and flexibility as an ethnic symbol. It is what anthropologist Victor Turner calls a "multivocalic" symbol, one "susceptible of many meanings" (1969:8). It is also a very practical symbol in the contemporary setting.

References

Esman, Marjorie R. 1981. "The Celebration of Cajun Identity: Ethnic Unity and the Crawfish Festival." Ph.D. dissertation, Tulane University.

Guirard, Leona M. 1973. "Talk about Crayfish." Printed souvenir.

Gutierrez, C. Paige. 1984. "The Social and Symbolic Uses of Ethnic/Regional Foodways: Cajuns and Crawfish in South Louisiana." In *Ethnic and Regional Foodways in the United States: The Performance of Group Identity*, pp. 169–182. Ed. Linda Keller Brown and Kay Mussell. Knoxville: University of Tennessee Press.

Jacobi, Herman J. 1937. *The Catholic Family in Rural Louisiana*. Washington, D.C.: The Catholic University of America Press.

Reed, Revon. 1976. *Lache pas la Patate*. Montreal: Editions Parti Pris.

Saxon, Lyle, Dreyer, Edward, and Tallant, Robert, eds. 1945. *Gumbo Ya-Ya: A Collection of Louisiana Folk Tales*. New York: Bonanza.

Turner, Victor. 1969. "Forms of Symbolic Action: Introduction." In *Proceedings of the 1969 Annual Spring Meeting of the American Ethnological Society*, pp. 3–25. Ed. Robert F. Spencer. Seattle: University of Washington Press.

Whitfield, Irene T. 1939. *Louisiana French Folk Songs*. New York: Dover.

13

Playing with Food: The Negotiation of Identity in the Ethnic Display Event by Italian Americans in Clinton, Indiana

Sabina Magliocco

The tourist visiting Clinton, Indiana, on Labor Day weekend, the period of the Little Italy Festival, is likely to be assailed by the "taste of ethnographic things" (Stoller 1989) in the form of a wide range of foodstuffs. He or she can visit the Wine Garden and Winery and sample a glass of homemade wine; buy breadsticks and salami at the Mercato; see various kinds of pasta machines and espresso coffeemakers on display at the Piccola Casa; participate in a spaghetti- or pizza-eating contest, or perhaps a grape-stomping demonstration; witness the crowning of the Grape Queen; and buy all manner of Italian and non-Italian foods from the concession stands along Water Street. Food is indeed the primary focus of this festival, which can be more properly called an ethnic display event (Keyes-Ivey 1977), a carefully planned performance intended to draw tourists to this small and otherwise ordinary midwestern town.

That food is the focus of such an event should be of no surprise to anyone. Food is such an immediate part of daily life that its communicative powers are often taken for granted, though they have been noted by a number of scholars (Bahloul 1983; Douglas 1971; Kalčik 1984; Lévi-Strauss 1969; Stoller 1989). Foodways are also one of the most important symbols through which ethnic groups in America have maintained their individual identities and communicated them to the world around them (Kalcik 1984: 44; Camp 1989; Humphrey and Humphrey 1988). Food is

Reprinted by permission from *Studies in Italian American Folklore*, edited by Luisa Del Giudice (Logan: Utah State University Press, 1993), 107–26.

145

in fact the most common form of symbolic ethnicity (Gans 1979) present in ethnic display events and multiethnic festivals, which Dorson has
described as the "public" face of American ethnic folklore (Dorson
1981: 110). It is often a powerful symbol in private or "esoteric" ethnic
events as well: baptisms, weddings, funerals, holidays, and family reunions (Dorson 1981: 110). The reasons for this are varied; one is that,
as Klymasz (1973: 133) points out, the loss of the ethnic language or
dialect often prevents the preservation of verbal folklore forms. But
food, with its sensual qualities, is also a powerful reminder of the past
and an ideal vehicle for communication (Stoller 1989: 34). In the American ethnic panorama, it is often the most pronounced "text" of ethnicity.

Following the lead of Jones's, Giuliano's, and Krell's important volume, *Foodways and Eating Habits: Directions for Research* (1981), numerous
folklorists have examined food for its symbolic valence and communicative powers (Camp 1989; Brown and Mussell 1984; Humphrey and Humphrey 1988). In this paper, I will build on this scholarship by examining
food symbolically, reading, as it were, the text in the form of food present in an Italian-theme festival in a multiethnic community. I will argue
that various foods are chosen by the community to display different aspects of Italian American identity to varied audiences. The choice of
certain foods over others for overt display suggests important aspects of
community identity and the dynamics of ethnic representation. I will
examine four different categories of food present at the Little Italy Festival: esoteric foods, present at the private level in each Italian American
home; display foods, typically associated with Italians and presented for
public sale and consumption; rechristened foods, basically American
items, such as soda pop and ham sandwiches, which are given Italian
designations for this occasion; and pseudofoods, such as large wooden
"cheeses," used mostly in games and contests associated with the festival. Each category of food plays a different role in the display of symbolic
ethnicity and the maintenance of ethnic identity. Examination of these
categories yields important insights into the interpretive process of tradition (Handler and Linnekin 1984: 273).

Background Factors of the Little Italy Festival

In order to discuss the performative roles of the various types of food
outlined above, we must first investigate a number of background factors relating to the festival and its history, and the history of the town
itself.

Immigration in Clinton

Clinton, Indiana (pop. 6,000), located on the Wabash River about twelve miles north of Terre Haute, originated as a mining town during the late 1800s. Local mine owners advertised abroad in handbills and posters for mine workers, attracting hordes of Europeans to the community. At first primarily Welsh miners arrived, but eventually many others followed; not only Italians, but Germans, Poles, Hungarians, Serbs, Ukrainians, and Yugoslavians were attracted by the promise of work.[1] By 1920, the coal mines were booming; "every house had a boarder."[2] as more and more immigrants came and later brought their families to Clinton. During the economic depression of the 1930s, the mine operators suffered financial reversals, and many coal miners were out of work. The collapse of the mining industry brought about a decline in Clinton's economy from which it has never fully recovered.

Most of Clinton's Italians came between 1895 and 1920.[3] Unlike other areas of the United States, which saw heavy immigration from the economically devastated areas of Italy's *mezzogiorno*, many Piedmontese, who had had experience working in the coal mines of that region, emigrated to Clinton. A number of others came from the subalpine regions of Trentino-Alto Adige and Friuli-Venezia-Giulia. These northern Italians then intermingled with the Sicilians and Calabresi who arrived later, mostly after 1900.

But the Italian immigrants faced a strange situation: although they all came from the same country,[4] they did not share a common culture or even a language with which to communicate. The various regions of Italy had developed widely different cultures and dialects due to a number of political, social and economic factors.[5] The immigrants, being largely from the peasant class, knew only their local dialects and had no knowledge of literary Italian, which is based on the Tuscan dialect, and in any case had only recently been designated as the official Italian language. Thus they could not communicate effectively with other Italians who spoke in a different dialect. Ernie Gillio told me that when his parents had emigrated to Clinton from near Turin, they could not even understand the Sicilians who became their neighbors.

The worlds of the northerner and the southerner were miles apart in other ways as well. Because of climatic factors, each area of Italy had developed distinctive foodways based on the ingredients cultivated and available locally. The Piedmontese diet was based on corn (maize) and dairy products. Polenta, a cornmeal much seasoned with butter and cheese, was the characteristic food of this region. Wheat was scarce and expensive in the north before mass transportation; thus the Turinese developed the *grissino* or breadstick, a chopstick-thin (in it native form) sliver of flour, water, and salt. Rice, cultivated in the Po valley, was another staple of northern cuisine and turned up in foods such as risotto. Naturally the northern immigrants brought these and other characteristic foods from the north with them to Clinton.

Their southern neighbors, on the other hand, favored the olive-oil and tomato-based cuisine of the South, which has become identified with Italian cooking in this country. Their foods included the familiar specialties of tomato sauce and pizza (Williams 1938). Pasta was common to both areas, but northern forms included flat ribbons made with eggs and pastas filled with meat or cheese, while southern types were characteristically made without eggs and tended to be tubular in shape (Kittler and Sucher 1989: 122).

Even the religious background of the Italian immigrants differed: while all of the immigrants from Sicily and Calabria were Roman Catholic, a number of northerners were Valdesi, a Protestant sect from the Val d'Aosta. In Clinton, these Italians became members of the Presbyterian church. Under the pressure of Anglo-American discrimination, these regional differences eventually blurred somewhat. By the early 1920s, the area around Ninth Street in Clinton was known as "Little Italy." This ethnic enclave had many of the characteristics of ethnic neighborhoods throughout the United States, including its own bakeries supplying Italian bread and *grissini* and markets selling imported Italian foods. Several immigrants opened restaurants in the neighborhood featuring Italian foods. The immigrants developed ways of communicating with each other despite dialect differences, and the first generation born in America spoke primarily English. But the distinctive regional differences which once divided Clinton Italians are still discernible in each family's culinary specialties. When visiting Italian American homes, one is just as likely to eat *polenta alpina, riso al latte, bagna cauda,* and *zabbaione* as lasagna, pizza, and *cassata siciliana.*

History of the Little Italy Festival

Like many ethnic festivals, the Little Italy Festival in Clinton developed for economic reasons after the Italian community on Ninth Street had begun to assimilate and disband. By the mid-1960s, the steady economic decline following the depression and the postwar flight to urban areas had dealt Clinton heavy blows. Most Italians had left the old neighborhood and lived in newly developed areas scattered around the town. Some first- and second-generation Italian Americans had migrated to cities in search of jobs; many had intermarried with other ethnic groups and led lives which were typical of small-town America. The town itself was in economic decline, and a series of newspaper articles in *The Daily Clintonian* suggested that it was in need of a new identity.

It was Bill Wake, then editor of Clinton's daily, who thought of a festival as a way of attracting tourists to Clinton, boosting the town's economy, and providing it with a new identity.[6] Wake patterned his idea after the nearby town of Rockville's Covered Bridge Festival, a highly publicized, nostalgia-oriented event which attracted many tourists from Indianapolis. Wake, who was not Italian American, nevertheless suggested the "Little Italy" theme be the festival's focus for two reasons: the town was known in the area for its Italian restaurants, and the Italian community had long organized a Columbus Day celebration which already attracted some attention. Many events could thus be transplanted from the Columbus Day festival to the Little Italy Festival. Wake and other interested individuals formed the Little Italy Festival Town Board (LIFT); Wake was the first president and Italian American Ernie Gillio, then president of the Lion's Club, became the first vice-president. The board organized the first Little Italy Festival, which was held on Labor Day weekend of 1966.

At first, community reaction to the festival was mixed. Many older Italian immigrants, who had suffered discrimination and worse at the hands of Anglo-Americans, resented the festival. "[It was] like saying, you didn't treat us right when we first came, and now you're trying to capitalize on the fact that we're an Italian community and make some money off it," the daughter of one of the objectors explained. Moreover, as Raspa (1984: 190) has noted, the foodways of Italian Americans have consistently been the focus of stereotypes and *blasons populaires* in American folklore. Italian Americans are often taunted as "spaghetti benders," and certain foodways are perceived as exotic or even disgusting by non-Italians. It is not surprising, therefore, that there was resistance among Italian Americans, who were being asked to celebrate and market for mass consumption the very traits once held up by the dominant Anglo-American culture as examples of "backwardness."

Of no less import were the objections raised by members of other ethnic minorities in Clinton, who felt Italians were being singled out for special attention although they were not in fact the majority of the population. However, in spite of such objections, the festival persisted, and its benefits to the community in terms of financial assistance and community identity won over some of those with hostile attitudes. What made the festival a success was the strategy adopted by the early organizers, which allowed Italian Americans to conform in part to American stereotypes about them, while retaining control over some private aspects of their ethnic identity (see Klymasz 1970: 115). At the same time, the festival was structured to make Italian ethnicity accessible to everyone during its duration, much as St. Patrick's Day does nationally for Irish ethnicity: one has only to wear green to become temporarily Irish. The performance of foodways, through food-related festival attractions, activities, and events, is an integral part of this strategy.

Food-Related Events and Attractions

The display and performance of foodways take place in a number of contexts throughout the Little Italy Festival. Nearly all of these are open to the general public, making one aspect of Italian ethnicity readily accessible to persons of any background. The importance of food as a symbol in this festival is underlined in its first event, which takes place on the Friday preceding Labor Day: the Little Italy Festival Parade. Leading all the floats and cohorts of dignitaries is Joe Mandarino, pushing his fruit and vegetable cart. The cart, loaded with fresh produce, clearly stands for both the immigrants' past (many Italian immigrants, like Joe Mandarino, operated fruit and vegetable stands upon first coming to the United States) and their present: as Raspa indicates, the reliance on fresh vegetables and fruits as ingredients in cooking is an important part of the identity of many Italian Americans (1984: 191). Also present in the parade are the newly elected Grape Queen and her court—grapes and their by-product, wine, being another important leitmotif of Italian identity throughout the festival.

Other food-related events during the festival include spaghetti-and pizza-eating contests (twice in three days), in which contestants from the town and general audience try to eat the largest amount of the designated food within a specified time; and grape-stomping contests (twice in three days), in which contestants step barefoot into large grape-filled vats and crush them in imitation of earlier winemaking techniques. Daily cooking demonstrations, featuring quickly made Italian dishes, are also held on the festival stage. A cheese-rolling contest, substituting large wooden rounds for the cheeses, tests contestants' ability to propel these "cheeses" the longest distance.

In addition to these events, the festival features a number of food-related attractions. Water Street is lined with concession stands selling various kinds of foods; these stands are put up by Clinton restauranteurs, service organizations, and churches to raise money. The Wine Garden and Winery, built in imitation of a German American *biergarten* in Indianapolis's Oktoberfest, demonstrate the process of winemaking and offer gustatory samples. In the area of Ninth Street, the Mercato is set up as a reproduction of the Italian market which once supplied the ethnic enclave with Italian foods; there one can buy breadsticks, pasta, and salami, as well as T-shirts and mugs proclaiming, "Kiss me, I'm Italian" and souvenirs of Clinton. Near the Mercato, the Piccola Casa (Little House) is arranged to depict a typical coal miner's house from the turn of the century. Patchwork quilts and McGuffy readers, nostalgia elements from an Anglo-American past, share space with pasta machines and espresso coffeemakers of various vintages, including a steam espresso maker very recently imported from Italy.

All of these diversions and events are structured to make Italian ethnicity (or a facsimile thereof) readily accessible to all festival participants and tourists. In flavor, however, they are typically American and scarcely resemble the kinds of activities which would take place at an Italian popular festival (Dundes and Falassi 1975; Falassi 1987; Silverman 1975).[7] The spaghetti- and pizza-eating contests, like the grape-stomping competition, seem to reflect the American preoccupation with competition (Stoeltje 1983: 242); the crowning of the Grape Queen emerges as a symbolic inversion of the democratic political system and an expression of an American fascination with royalty. More importantly, each of these events puts the Italian experience in anyone's reach: one does not, after all, have to be of Italian descent to eat fast or win a beauty contest. As Dorothy Gillio (who is Yugoslavian American) put it, "We all have to be Italian that weekend."[8]

In terms of actual food items, their performers, and their intended audiences, however, an interesting pattern appears, which may shed light on the dynamics of ethnic identity and ethnic display in this town. The nature of the text and its message become clear when one separates the food items into four categories and examines each one's makers, intended audience, and presentation context.

Esoteric Foods

These are prepared by group members for comembers and occur most often within the context of family meals and gatherings. While these foods are present at the festival, they are not usually apparent to tourists; they are usually found in private homes where the female head of the household is of Italian descent. Many dishes of a clearly regional origin continue to be popular at family get-togethers. These foods persist in a highly conservative form, showing clear links to the Italian tradition from which they came. The Fenoglios, for instance, reported that they often serve *bagna cauda,* a dip for vegetables made with butter, oil, garlic, and anchovies, on New Year's Eve. This dish is characteristic of the Piedmont region from which John Fenoglio's mother emigrated. Other families also described favorite regional dishes, such as polenta, potato gnocchi (dumplings), and *risi e bisi,* a Venetian dish of rice and peas. While these dishes are not typically associated with Italians by Americans, they nevertheless remain important sensual links to tradition in many Clinton households. Naturally, many Italian American families also enjoy foods Americans commonly associate with Italians, such as lasagna and spaghetti. One young man said, "We always have to have lasagna on Thanksgiving. We have turkey and everything, but that lasagna's got to be on the table, too."[9]

In addition to private gatherings, esoteric foods also turn up in two other festival contexts: cooking demonstrations, and the *Official Little Italy Festival Town Cookbook*, published as a fund-raiser by a local service sorority, Kappa Kappa Kappa. Cooking demonstrations are held three times during the festival weekend on the open-air stage usually reserved for performances of rock bands, folk-dance groups, and singers. Three dishes can thus be prepared at each festival. The cook is usually a volunteer from the court of the Grape Queen—a young girl who enjoys cooking and has prepared the dish before, perhaps with family coaching. As the recipes change each year, there is no typical demonstration dish, but the recipes are culled from local Italian American women or the *Official Little Italy Cookbook*. The recipe I observed was for *bagna cauda*. Interestingly, two versions were made: the original one, with butter, oil, garlic, and anchovies, and a new one favored by younger Italian American cooks, which added tuna and cream. As far as I can tell, this variant is unique to Clinton and represents an innovative form of the type described by Klymasz (1973: 138–39).[10]

The *Cookbook*, we are told in an introduction, was put together by Mrs. Diane C. Waugh, chairperson of Kappa Kappa Kappa, with the help of Miss Irma Pesavento, who collected the recipes from individual Italian cooks and their families. The booklet's audience, like that of the cooking demonstrations, is a mixture of Italian Americans and interested outsiders: after the first Little Italy Festival in 1966, there was an increasing demand for the codification of Italian recipes within the community itself, as well as a surge of interest on the part of outsiders. The book contains a preponderance of recipes with close analogues in regional Italian cooking,[11] as well as certain modifications—one recipe for *zuppa inglese* substitutes cherry-vanilla pudding mix for traditional egg custard (p. 66)—and a few recipes which can best be called "rechristened foods" (which I'll discuss later). The rich array of foods accurately reflects the regional origins of Clinton's Italian immigrants, with about 40 percent coming from the subalpine areas and the rest from Calabria and Sicily. The recipes range from well-known staples of Italian cuisine such as lasagna, pizza, and chicken cacciatore, to such regional specialties as chestnut soup, fried calf brains, roast squab, stewed rabbit, and sausage with chickpeas. A few, like fried potatoes or fruit salad, are found throughout the whole of Italy.

Esoteric foods are often most meaningful to the family members who make and partake of them. Their symbolic value lies in their sensual ties to immigrants' pasts, rather than their ability to reveal anything about the immigrants to outsiders. In preparing traditional foods for family reunions and special occasions, the Italian Americans of Clinton are essentially discoursing among themselves about the nature of their ethnicity. While there are non-Italians who express an interest in traditional food by buying the cookbook or watching the cooking demonstrations, it is fairly safe to say that these regional specialties do not carry the same emotional and affective meanings for them as they do for the immigrants and their families.

Display Foods

For non-Italians and Italians, food is a potent symbol of Italian identity during the festival. But to the average Clinton tourist, polenta, risotto, and stewed rabbit are meaningless as markers of Italian ethnicity. Because of the preponderance of immigrants from the southern part of Italy, the foods which have become most popular (and thus most closely identified with Italians) in America largely come from that area. These include pasta dishes with tomato sauce, pizza, and Italian sausage fried with peppers and onions, a dish also served at festivals in Italy. Espresso coffee and wine, found in both northern and southern Italy, are also associated with Italians. The wine-drinking habits of Italians must have made an especially strong impression on the beer- and whiskey-drinking midwestern population of Clinton.[12]

It is no accident, then, that these foods have been chosen to represent Italians to outsiders at the festival. They turn up in the eating contests, the grape stomping, the wine garden, and in the kinds of items on display at the Mercato and Piccola Casa: pasta in various shapes, pasta-making machines, and espresso coffeemakers. They also predominate in the food booths set up along Water Street, sponsored by Italian restaurants. Strollers can purchase pizza slices; sandwiches with sausage, meatballs, or Italian beef drowned in tomato sauce (the addition of which automatically spells "Italian" in the semiosis of American foodways); and Italian submarine sandwiches with salami and other cold cuts. These foods are readily identifiable as Italian by the average American. While they are not always consumed in Italian American households, they nevertheless bear some relationship to Italian food; they may be said to represent Klymasz's "transitional" layer of ethnic folklore

(Klymasz 1973: 133) in that they combine some features of Italianness with many aspects of American fast food.

The performers of these foodways include both Italians and non-Italians; but in the case of Italians who sell them, it is no longer the individual, or the single family, making a statement about regional and ethnic roots, but rather the seller as a *representative* of Italian American culture communicating identity to non-Italians. That this type of food is mostly for display is borne out by the fact that few Italian Americans in Clinton subsist on it. In choosing to display food items which in fact do not reflect their regional subcultures, but rather the preconceived notions Americans have about Italian food, Clinton's Italians are conforming to American stereotypes and expectations as suggested by Klymasz (1970: 111). This strategy allows them to reserve certain other demonstrations of ethnicity—for instance, the colorful regional foodways which have often been the targets of American disgust—for the private sphere. Thus Clinton Italians can communicate a version of their ethnicity without violating the idea of Italianness present in the dominant Anglo-American culture (see Klymasz 1973: 139).

Rechristened Foods

Among the food concession stands along Water Street, one can find a number of ordinary American foods, such as soda, lemonade, and ham sandwiches, which have been given Italian (or Italian-sounding) names for the occasion. In 1983, for instance, the First United Methodist Church was selling *pasticcetto di prosciutto,* in reality a baked ham and cheese sandwich which bore little similarity to what a *pasticcetto di prosciutto* (cured raw ham in a pastry crust) would have been like in Italy, presuming this combination exists. Another stand bore hand-lettered signs proclaiming:

Tamarindo [*sic*]	$ .60
Lemonatto [*sic*]	$ .60
Gassoso [*sic*]	$ .60
Corn Dogs	$1.00

Closer inspection revealed that the stand sold orange juice, lemonade, and sodas. Clearly what was important was that these ordinary drinks should sound Italian, since there is little correspondence between their festival names and the Italian ones for these beverages.[13]

Further examples of rechristened foods may be found in the *Cookbook.* On page four there is a recipe for *cedano ripiene* [*sic*] (stuffed celery),[14] using celery, cream cheese, and pimento-filled olives—probably a rechristened American recipe, since neither cream cheese nor pimento-stuffed olives are found in Italy, and the celery is too small and narrow to stuff with anything. Interestingly, unlike other recipes, this one does not state an individual cook as its source. It is thus impossible to determine whether its author was an Italian American or simply a non-Italian contributor. A recipe for "cantaloupe Romana" (p. 53) calls for cantaloupe served with ice cream and Marsala wine—a very unusual combination for Rome, where melon is customarily an appetizer. Here, too, the contributor is mysteriously absent.

The point of all this is not to engage in a fruitless quest for authenticity; as numerous scholars have shown, the genuineness of a tradition is of no consequence in terms of its importance to the community as a symbol of identity (Dégh 1981: 130–31; Hobsbawm 1983). Any tradition may be subject to strategic manipulation by its performers when issues such as identity and emic/etic perceptions are at stake (Bendix 1989: 143). Rather, these elements contain important information about the performer of the item of folklore, its intended audience, and the political and social relationship between the two. In the case of the concession stands, the owner/operator was not Italian American, and I would hypothesize that the same is true of the contributors of the two recipes.

Why, then, is the adoption of a pseudo-Italian identity for the foods so important? Why not sell plain "ham sandwiches" or "sodas"? The answer, I think, lies in the nature of the festival itself, in its focus on Italian American ethnicity. Not only do activities and events deliberately put such an ethnic experience at anyone's disposal, but the semiotics of the festival demand that everyone adopt this ethnicity as his or her own. The LIFT board has long tried to discourage traveling food merchants from setting up their stalls along Water Street with the other concession stands; "We want to stay away from that carnival type; it's not supposed to be commercialized," says Ernie Gillio.[15] But this is clearly a contradictory statement, since the main purpose of the festival is in fact commercial.

It is the nonadherence to the Italian theme, rather than the profit motive, which the organizers find disturbing. In recent years, this has caused an increasing rift within the community and has threatened the Little Italy Festival itself.[16] Food peddlers petitioned the LIFT board, claiming that if Italians could sell their national foods, other nationalities ought to be allowed to sell theirs. Reluctantly the board finally gave in to the merchants in 1984, and now part of Water Street is called "International Street" and features American fast food as well as items from other ethnic groups. This has angered many of the local Italian food merchants, who have withdrawn their participation. According to one local resident, "[The festival] is not like it used to be; now there's hardly anything Italian about it."[17] By rechristening ordinary American foods with Italian-sounding names, American merchants are able to maintain the fiction of adhering to the Italian theme of the festival without actually threatening the status quo.

Pseudofood

The final category of food is actually not food at all. It is fake food—in this case, large wooden rounds substituting for cheeses in the cheese-rolling contest. Unlike the other festival contests, the cheese-rolling event bears a direct link to an Italian festival activity: the *tiro al cacio,* a cheese toss popular at festivals in cheese-producing regions throughout Italy. In the typical *tiro al cacio,* contestants toss or roll real cheeses at a mark or goal. The contestant whose cheese comes the closest wins all the other contestants' cheeses. In the traditional Italian context, cheese is real food with important symbolic links to the regional economy and the socioeconomic structure of the community: the *tiro* ostensibly gives poorer people a chance to win large amounts of the region's primary economic commodity in a classic example of the principle of festive redistribution (Solinas 1981: 221–22).[18]

Apparently in the early days, Clinton's Italians also used real cheeses for this event, which was then associated with the Columbus Day celebration; but as time passed, the feeling grew that it was wasteful and impractical to use actual cheeses, and wooden rounds replaced them. The substitution of pseudofood for real food in this activity marked an important turning point for Clinton's Italian Americans: from a subsistence-based economy and a worldview still tied to traditional Italian models, to one based on capitalism and consumption; from a culture closely tied to its Italian peasant roots, to one firmly rooted in the New World.

Because a festival is a transgressive genre (Bakhtin 1968), it is usual to find in it symbolic inversions of the usual social order. Thus in Italian peasant society, where the daily life was often marked by economic privation and hunger, festival was a time of ostentatious consumption of the primary agricultural products—what Gallini (1971) has called "the consumption of the sacred." In a premarket economy, this strategy allowed everyone to enjoy and consume the economic surplus, while at the same time ensuring a roughly even distribution of goods (Solinas 1981: 220). Within this ethos, the use of surplus cheeses for a cheese toss was not waste, but a sacred consumption of the primary economic product in a pastoral society.

The use of food in a game violated an important ethical and economic principle in Italian peasant culture: conservation. Food and play are normally antithetical: "Don't play with your food," Italian children are told at the table. Food—real food, that is—must not be played with because it is sustenance; playing with it dissipates not only its value, but also its symbolic charge. In the Italian peasant worldview, food, particularly bread, is sacred; leftover bread can be grated or made into other food, but should never be thrown away—or, according to one folk belief, one will be forced to pick it up in purgatory. If for some reason it must be thrown away, then it should be burned like other sacred household items, such as palms and olive branches from Palm Sunday.[19] In the festive context, however, playing with food becomes part of Bakhtin's carnivalesque: a deliberate transgression of the norm in an attempt to provide an antidote to everyday conditions; the "momentary, dramatic and carnivalesque antithesis of a harsh and persistent reality" (Lanternari 1981: 137). As such, the sensual qualities of food become extremely important.

Pseudofood is the furthest removed from the actual regional dishes whose smells, tastes, and textures are powerful reminders of the immigrants' ethnic and regional identities. It bears no connection to the community's means of production or to the local land-based economy. It has no characteristic food taste, smell or texture, since it is not meant to be eaten. It is, then, symbolic and highly abstract: food out of context, it is *meant* to be played with, created for use solely within the festive context. It is the very antithesis of food as sacred sustenance in Italian festivals. The substitution of pseudocheese for real cheese in the Clinton festival reflects the shift in the immigrants' economy (and thus also ethos) from subsistence to consumerism, from premarket to postmodern.

In the Clinton Little Italy Festival, food is a commodity not only to be marketed for its nutritional value, but also—and especially—for its symbolic value as a "text" of ethnicity. In this context, the symbolic valence of food is more important than its reality. The participants in the cheese-rolling contest could theoretically use bowling balls, bocce, or frisbees if the object was simply to see who had the greatest skill at rolling things.[20] But because food is the central symbol of the Little Italy Festival, and because cheese is an item that turns up frequently in Italian cuisine, the idea of a cheese-rolling contest fits better with the festival's overall symbolic theme. This is essentially the same rationale we saw operating in the case of rechristened foods, only here it is taken one step further: the food itself is fake.

Pseudofood and rechristened food do not represent shams so much as a playful use of the symbols available in the cultural register. The entire Little Italy Festival is in fact a kind of elaborate "playing with food": the actual foodstuffs, facsimiles thereof, and the various symbolic meanings attached to them by different local groups. If we look at "playing with food" as "deep play" (Geertz 1972), we find that the range of food items and activities express and negotiate different political, economic, and social relationships present in Clinton among Italians, other ethnic groups, and visiting tourists. Through play and the manipulation of food as symbol, these relationships express themselves through the festival. For the immigrants and their family members who return to Clinton for the event, the preparation and consumption of traditional regional foods reinforces a sensual and affective link with old-country experiences. For first-, second-, and third-generation assimilated Italian Americans, festival foods assert and communicate ethnic identity both within the ethnic group and to outsiders. For non-Italians and tourists, the foods and activities at the festival can offer a taste of Italianness without any of the shock or inconvenience of total immersion in a foreign culture. The quantity and range of the foodways are a testament to the complexity of the political universe in which the festival exists and the cultural reality it plays with and embodies.

Notes

Research for this paper was begun in a seminar, Folklore in an Ethnic Context, taught by Linda Dégh at the Indiana University Folklore Institute during the fall of 1983. I am grateful to Regina Bendix and Allessandro Falassi for their suggestions. Many thanks are also due to the people of Clinton who shared their knowledge of the festival with me, especially Martha Costello, Ernie and Dorothy Gillio, and Jack and Margo Fenoglio.

1. Unlike Roseto, Pennsylvania, which was also settled by Welsh miners and later by Italians, Clinton did not experience a mass migration from a single Italian community. On the situation in Roseto, Pennsylvania, see Bianco's classic study in emigration, *The Two Rosetos* (1974).

2. Joe Airola, from the videotape *Clinton, Indiana, Family History,* produced by Duane Busick and Madelaine Wilson, 1979.

3. Ibid.

4. But Italy had existed as a unified nation only since 1861. For a history of Italy, see Mack Smith 1969. Leeds (1974) fully discusses the impact of the unification on northern and southern Italy.

5. For a discussion of the development of Italian regional cultures, see Mack Smith 1969 and Leeds 1974.

6. Interview with Martha Costello, Nov. 13, 1983. Along with Ernie Gillio, Martha Costello, a retired schoolteacher, was one of the first organizers of the Little Italy Festival. Though not Italian herself, she had lived in the Italian neighborhood in childhood and married an Italian. After she was widowed, working on the festival became a way to maintain contact with Italian friends and revitalize the memories of her husband.

7. Most studies of Italian festivals have been conducted by regional ethnographers and are available only in Italian. Some of the most important works include Pitrè 1881; Cocchiara 1963, 1980; De Martino 1948; Toschi 1959; and Gallini 1971. See also the following collections of essays: Bianco and Del Ninno 1981 and Jesi 1977.

8. Interview with Dorothy Gillio, Nov. 13, 1983.

9. Interview with John Fenoglio, Nov. 23, 1983.

10. Alessandro Falassi has pointed out the similarity between this variation and the popular Italian *tonnato*, a tuna-based sauce. *Tonnato*, however, is normally served as a cold sauce for roast veal and not as a hot dip for vegetables. Also it is based on combining tuna with vinegar and oil and is not cooked, while the Clinton concoction requires cooking.

11. My source for information on regional Italian cooking is Boni 1969. Boni, who has written numerous cookbooks, is regarded in Italy as the Fanny Farmer of Italian cooking.

12. Even as late as the 1960s, wine drinking was regarded as suspect in certain midwestern circles. When I was in grade school in Cincinnati, for instance, it came to the attention of my teachers that my parents permitted me to drink wine mixed with water with the evening meal, as well as coffee at breakfast. The school social worker immediately contacted and berated them for stunting my growth and turning me into a juvenile alcoholic.

13. The Italian words are *aranciata* (orangeade), *limonata* (lemonade), and *gassosa* (soda), although today the brand names Sprite and 7-Up have largely displaced the old-fashioned-sounding *gassosa* to designate white cola.

14. Italian *sedano ripieno*.

15. Interview with Ernie Gillio, Nov. 13, 1983.

16. In his article, "*Festa Italiana* in Hartford, Connecticut," Anthony Rauche describes an analogous situation in which resentments on both sides eventually led to the cancellation of the festival. In the case of Clinton, it is possible that the strategy of rechristening foods may deflect some of the conflict.

17. Donna Sawyer, personal communication, Dec. 1988.

18. See Mathias 1981.

19. For an elaboration of this idea, see Counihan 1984.

20. There is in fact a separate bocce tournament, with men's and women's divisions, which takes place during the festival, but because bocce is strictly an Italian sport, no tourists or outsiders participate. This tradition is thus similar to the "traditional Italian foodways" already discussed in the way it functions. For a treatment of the game of bocce and its permutations in the American diaspora, see Mathias 1974.

References

Bahloul, Joëlle. 1983. *Le culte de la table dressée. Rites et traditions de la table juive algérienne.* Paris: Editions Métalié.

Bakhtin, Mikhail. 1968. *Rabelais and His World*. Translated by Hélène Iswolsky. Cambridge: MIT Press.

Bendix, Regina. 1989. "Tourism and Cultural Displays: Inventing Traditions for Whom?" *Journal of American Folklore* 102(404): 131–46.

Bianco, Carla. 1974. *The Two Rosetos*. Bloomington: Indiana University Press.

———. 1981. "Introduction" to *Festa: antropologia e semiotica,* edited by C. Bianco and M. Del Ninno. Florence: Nuova Guaraldi.

Bianco, Carla, and M. Del Ninno, eds. 1981. *Festa: antropologia e semiotica.* Florence: Nuova Guaraldi.

Boni, Ada. 1969. *Italian Regional Cooking*. New York: Bonanza Books.

Brown, Linda Keller, and Kay Mussell, eds. 1984. *Ethnic and Regional Foodways in the United States*. Knoxville: University of Tennessee Press.

Busick, Duane, and Madelaine Wilson. 1979. *Clinton, Indiana, Family History*. Videotape.

Camp, Charles. 1989. *American Foodways*. Little Rock, Ark.: August House.

Cocchiara, Giuseppe. 1963. *Il mondo alla rovescia*. Turin: Boringhieri.

———. 1980. *Il paese di Cuccagna*. Turin: Boringhieri.

Counihan, Carol. 1984. "Food, Culture and Political Economy." Ph.D. dissertation, University of Massachusetts at Amherst.

Danielson, Larry. 1972. "The Ethnic Festival and Cultural Relativism in a Small Midwestern Town." Ph.D. dissertation, Indiana University.

Dégh, Linda. 1981. "The Wine Harvest Festival of Strawberry Farmers." *Etnologia Europaea* 10(2): 114–31.

De Martino, Ernesto. 1948. *Il mondo magico*. Turin: Boringhieri.

Dorson, Richard M. 1981. *Land of the Millrats*. Cambridge: Harvard University Press.

Douglas, Mary. 1971. "Deciphering a Meal." In *Myth, Symbol and Culture,* edited by Clifford Geertz, 61–81. New York: Norton.

Dundes, Alan, and Alessandro Falassi. 1975. *La Terra in Piazza: An Interpretation of the Palio of Siena*. Berkeley: University of California Press.

Falassi, Alessandro. 1987. "Definition and Morphology." In *Time out of Time: Essays on the Festival,* edited by A. Falassi, 1–7. Albuquerque: University of New Mexico Press.

Gallini, Clara. 1971. *Il consumo del sacro: feste lunghe di Sardegna*. Bari: Laterza.

Gans, Herbert. 1979. "Symbolic Ethnicity: The Future of Ethnic Groups and Cultures in America." *Ethnic and Racial Studies* 2(1): 1–19.

Geertz, Clifford. 1972. "Deep Play: Notes on the Balinese Cockfight." *Daedalus* 101: 1–37.

Handler, Richard, and Joyce Linnekin. 1984. "Tradition, Genuine or Spurious?" *Journal of American Folklore* 97(385): 273–90.

Hobsbawm, Eric J. 1983. "Introduction: Inventing Traditions." In *The Invention of Tradition,* edited by Eric Hobsbawm and Terence Ranger, 1–14. Cambridge: Cambridge University Press.

Humphrey, Theodore C., and Lin T. Humphrey. 1988. *We Gather Together: Food and Festival in American Life*. Ann Arbor: UMI Research Press.

Jesi, Furio, ed. 1977. *La festa: antropologia, etnologia, folklore*. Turin: Rosenberg and Sellier.

Jones, Michael Owen, Bruce Giuliano, and Roberta Krell. 1981. *Foodways and Eating Habits: Directions for Research.* Los Angeles: California Folklore Society.

Kalčik, Susan. 1984. "Ethnic Foodways in America: Symbol and Performance of Identity." In *Ethnic and Regional Foodways in the United States,* edited by Linda Keller Brown and Kay Mussell, 37–65. Knoxville: University of Tennessee Press.

Keyes-Ivey, Saundra. 1977. "Ascribed Ethnicity and the Ethnic Display Event." *Western Folklore* 36: 85–107.

Kittler, Pamela G., and Kathryn Sucher. 1989. *Food and Culture in America.* New York: Van Nostrand Reinhold.

Klymasz, Robert B. 1970. "Ukrainian Folklore in Canada: An Immigrant Complex in Transition." Ph.D. dissertation, Indiana University.

———. 1973. "From Immigrant to Ethnic Folklore." *Journal of the Folklore Institute* 10: 131–39.

Lanternari, Vittorio. 1981. "Spreco, ostentazione, competizione economica. Antropolgia del comportamento festivo." In *Festa: antropologia e semiotica,* edited by C. Bianco and M. Del Ninno, 132–50. Florence: Nuova Guaraldi.

Leeds, Christopher. 1974. *The Unification of Italy.* London: Wayland Press.

Lévi-Strauss, Claude. 1969. *The Raw and the Cooked.* New York: Harper and Row.

Mack Smith, Denis. 1969. *Italy: A Modern History.* Ann Arbor: University of Michigan Press.

Mathias, Elizabeth. 1974. "From Folklore to Mass Culture: The Dynamics of Acculturation in the Games of Italian-American Men." Ph.D. dissertation, University of Pennsylvania.

———. 1981. "Italian American Culture and Games: The Minnesota Iron Range and South Philadelphia." In *Play as Context,* edited by Alyce Cheska, 73–92. West Point, N.Y.: Leisure Press.

Pitrè, Giuseppe. 1881. *Spettacoli e feste popolari siciliane.* Palermo: Pedone Lauriel.

———. 1900. *Feste patronali in Sicilia.* Palermo: Clausen.

Raspa, Richard. 1984. "Exotic Foods among Italian-Americans in Mormon Utah: Food as Nostalgic Enactment of Identity." In *Ethnic and Regional Foodways in the United States,* edited by Linda Keller Brown and Kay Mussell, 185–94. Knoxville: University of Tennessee Press.

Rauche, Anthony T. 1988. "*Festa Italiana* in Hartford, Connecticut." In *We Gather Together: Food and Festival in American Life,* edited by Theodore Humphrey and Lin Humphrey, 205–17. Ann Arbor: UMI Research Press.

Silverman, Sydel. 1975. *The Three Bells of Civilization: The Life of an Italian Hill Town,* New York: Columbia University Press.

Solinas, Pier Giorgio. 1981. "Cibo, festa, fame: spartire e dividere." In *Festa: antropologia e semiotica,* edited by C. Bianco and M. Del Ninno, 220–39. Florence: Nuova Guaraldi.

Stoeltje, Beverly J. 1983. "Festival in America." In *Handbook of American Folklore,* edited by Richard M. Dorson, 239–46. Bloomington: Indiana University Press.

Stoller, Paul. 1989. *The Taste of Ethnographic Things: The Senses in Anthropology.* Philadelphia: University of Pennsylvania Press.

Toschi, Paolo. 1959. *Le origini del teatro italiano.* Turin: Boringhieri.

Williams, Phyllis. 1938. *South Italian Folkways in Europe and America.* New Haven: Yale University Press.

14

New York Jews and Chinese Food: The Social Construction of an Ethnic Pattern

Gaye Tuchman and Harry Gene Levine

> *The concept of culture I espouse . . . is essentially a semiotic one. Believing with Max Weber, that man is an animal suspended in webs of significance he himself has spun, I take culture to be those webs, and the analysis of it to be therefore not an experimental science in search of laws but an interpretive one in search of meaning.*
>
> —Clifford Geertz (1973, 5)

Sociologists and historians have long recognized that ethnic culture and identity, especially in the United States, has been created rather than inherited. People, who in their traditional societies identified themselves by region, village, or tribe, came to be defined by others (and to define themselves) in modern America as an ethnic or national group (Sollors 1986, 1989; Glazer and Moynihan 1963).[1] Furthermore, as Glazer and Moynihan (1963) pointed out in *Beyond the Melting Pot,* the process of cultural invention has not stopped with the first generation:

> The ethnic group in American society is not a survival from the age of mass immigration but a new social group. One could not predict from its first arrival what it might become or, indeed, whom it might contain. . . . In the second generation, and even more fully in the third generation, [ethnic groups] are continually recreated by new experiences in America. (p. 5)

One point of Glazer and Moynihan's flawed but perceptive study is that in New York (and a number of other large cities) the melting pot did not

Reprinted by permission from Sage Publications, Inc. for *Journal of Contemporary Ethnography* 22, 3 (October 1993), 382–407.

happen.[2] Rather, successive generations have continually reconstructed their ethnic cultures and identities.

Ethnic groups usually form their customs and practices from elements of their traditional cultures, including language and speech, religion, wedding and funeral ceremonies, home decorations, dress, and food. As a result, specific ethnic cultural patterns often appear to be the "natural," inevitable, or only possible products of the traditional culture. Over time, it becomes harder for both outsiders and participants to recognize the created character of ethnicity.

In this article, we explore the internal logic of ethnic cultural invention by delving into an unusual but by no means unique case: an American ethnic group (or its predominant variant) that has incorporated into its culture a practice and value that is utterly alien—completely beyond the bounds of its traditional culture. We focus on the way that Jews who immigrated from Eastern Europe to New York City, and especially their children and grandchildren, have incorporated Chinese restaurant food into their new Jewish-American culture. Indeed, New York Jews love Chinese restaurant food so much that they have made it a second cuisine.

Diverse observers have called attention to the phenomenon. Jackie Mason is the most recent in a long line of Jewish ("Borscht Belt" hotel) stand-up comedians to have built routines about Jews and Chinese food. *The New York Times* food writer Mimi Sheraton (1990) recently pointed out that "the longstanding love affair Jews have had with Chinese food (particularly the slightly over cooked, mild-flavored Cantonese specialties) was a well-known fact of the restaurant business in Flatbush fifty years ago" (pp. 71–72). In the preface to *Mishpokhe,* a book about Jewish cousins' clubs, Zenner (1980) comments that "Jewish neighborhoods in New York and Chicago are often notable for having a large number of Chinese restaurants" (p. 5). Chinese restauranteurs concur: A successful Chinese restaurant owner on the Upper West Side of Manhattan and a leader of a Chinatown civic organization both told us that the Jewish love of Chinese food was well known among Chinese restauranteurs. One friend who married into a large Jewish family told us his favorite joke: "According to the Jewish calendar, the year is 5749. According to the Chinese calendar, the year is 4687. That means for 1,062 years, the Jews went without Chinese food." The observations capture an important sociological truth: "Eating Chinese" is part of Jewish culture in New York City.[3]

How did Eastern European Jews in New York come to adopt Chinese restaurant food? In their 2,000 years of migration, the Jews had previously adapted to very different culinary styles (Kirschenblatt-Gimblett 1987). But why did they take to Chinese food over any other cuisine?

In part, Jews like Chinese food for the same reasons as given by people all over the world: It is available, delicious, and relatively inexpensive. Chinese restaurants are popular in Korea and Japan, where they are cheaper than the native restaurant food. There are Chinese-run restaurants in Bombay, Sydney, London, Paris, and Havana. As 6-year old "Ethan" says, "The Chinese are good cookers." The Chinese have, in fact, developed a brilliant cuisine—an outstanding cultural invention replete with regional variation. Quality, price, and proximity are some of the reasons why Chinese food became so important to New York Jews. But good-tasting, nearby, and economical food appeals to anyone who eats out.

To understand the long relationship of New York Jews to Chinese food, we traced its history, interviewed many people, and explored New York neighborhoods. We discuss our methods in the appendix. Without an appreciation of the "webs of significance" that New York Jews have used to interpret Chinese food, their passion for this fare seems incomprehensible.[4] Like other enduring cultural patterns, the Jewish attachment to Chinese food has been caused by many things—it has been "overdetermined" (to use Freud's apt term). However surprising, it is also intelligible.

The Meanings of Chinese Food for New York Jews

Our explanation of the attachment of New York Jews to Chinese food is rooted in the anthropological and sociological understanding that people assign great meaning and importance to cuisine and foodways. Everyone must eat, but the meanings of what, where, how, when, and with whom they eat are cultural inventions. In America, the food of one's ethnic group symbolizes tradition and community. As Everett Hughes reminded (class notes 1963; see Weber 1958, 408 on Hindus; Weber 1963, 254 on Jews), commensality is a strong indicator of social affiliation.

Over the years, New York Jews have found in Chinese restaurant food a flexible open-ended symbol, a kind of blank screen on which they have projected a series of themes relating to their identity as modern Jews and as New Yorkers. These themes were not inherent in the food itself, nor did they arise from Chinese Americans' view of their own cuisine. Rather, Jewish New Yorkers (and, to some extent, other Americans as well) linked these cultural issues with eating in Chinese restaurants. Three themes predominate. First, Jews have construed Chinese restaurant food as cosmopolitan, urbane, and sophisticated. Eating in Chinese restaurants signifies that one is not a provincial or parochial Eastern

European Jew, not a "greenhorn" or hick. Second, Chinese food is un-kosher and therefore non-Jewish. But because of the specific ways that it is prepared and served, Chinese food is found to be less threatening and more attractive than other non-Jewish or *treyf* food. Chinese food was safe treyf. In addition, the low position of the Chinese in American society also made Jews feel safe and comfortable in Chinese restaurants. Third, by the second generation, Jews identified eating this kind of non-Jewish food—Chinese food—as something that modern American Jews, and especially New York Jews, did together. "Eating Chinese" had be-come a New York Jewish custom, an aspect of group identity.

Chinese, Italians, and Jews in Lower Manhattan: 1870s through 1930s

Jews encountered Chinese food in the streets of lower Manhattan. Can-tonese Chinese, Eastern European Jews, and Southern Italians all came to New York at about the same time—between 1880 and 1920—and set-tled on the Lower East Side where their neighborhoods abutted one another. By 1910, about 1 million Eastern European Jews and 500,000 Italians lived in New York. The Jews constituted over one quarter of the city's population and the Italians about one sixth. There were many fewer Chinese—about 7,000 by 1900 (Chen 1980; Tsai 1986; Glazer and Moynihan 1963).

Most of the Chinese came to New York from California after the 1880s when the Chinese exclusion acts, anti-Chinese riots, and other forms of racism forced immigrant Chinese to look for ways of making a living that did not place them in direct competition with Whites (Lyman 1974). Many Chinese workers turned to restaurants. The growing num-ber of restaurants needed to attract more non-Chinese customers in order to stay in business, and cooks tailored their dishes and menus for Americans (see Chen 1980; Kwong 1987; Light and Wong 1975). In lower Manhattan, immigrant Jews opened delicatessens for other Jews, and Italians ran restaurants for other Italians (see, e.g., Rischin 1962). But Chinese restaurants welcomed everyone. As a result, even in the 1890s both Jews and Italians usually felt more at home in Chinese restau-rants than they did in each other's eateries.

Any immigrant family *could* eat at Chinese restaurants. But the experi-ences of our informants support the conclusion that as a group Eastern European Jews did so more often than other immigrants who came to New York at roughly the same time. Jews certainly ate more Chinese food than did the next largest group of immigrants, Southern Italians. The very poorest Jews and Italians rarely, if ever, ate out, but first- and second-generation Jews did so more often than did Italians of the same social class. When Italians did dine out, they usually went to Italian restaurants.

Jews and Italians took to restaurants differently because they came from different cultures, had different experiences before immigrating, and came to America for different reasons. Many Italians intended to work here for only a while. By 1920, more had returned to Italy than remained in the United States (Glazer and Moynihan 1963). Jews, however, had lived in various European countries as increasingly unwelcome and segregated strangers.[5] They had fled discrimination and pogroms as well as poverty. Most of them believed they had no choice but to make their home here. In addition, because a higher proportion of Jews than Italians had lived in cities before immigrating, they were more likely to be literate in at least one language (Steinberg 1981). As a result, the Jews were not only more motivated to explore and adapt to their new urban environment, they also possessed more skills with which to do so.

Jews also appear to have been less attached to their food specialties than Italians were to theirs. Our Italian American informants ate and praised Italian food more than our Jewish informants ate and praised Eastern European Jewish food. The Jewish informants also tended to denigrate their ethnic restaurant food more than the Italian Americans did theirs. Some people we interviewed suggested that Jewish Americans actually may have had more gastronomical reason than Italian Americans to look beyond their own ethnic restaurants. Compared to Italian restaurant food, they observed, Eastern European Jewish restaurant food seems undeveloped. American Jews have never evolved what we might call a fancy tablecloth style of restaurant serving Eastern European food. The gourmet delicatessen with formica tables—New York's Carnegie Deli, for example—likely represents the pinnacle of the American Jewish ethnic restaurant. The growing number of Continental-style kosher restaurants in the New York area also testifies to the willingness of Eastern European Jews to abandon their traditional cuisine (see Kleinman 1989).

Today, many Jews show more enthusiasm for Chinese restaurant food than for Eastern-European-style Jewish food. Women and men now in their late 60s and 70s stressed that they did not want to eat delicatessen very often because, as one 67-year-old secretary put it, "That we could eat at home." Frequently, they choose to eat at a Chinese restaurant. Two third-generation Jews spontaneously told us the same thing: "The first restaurant I ever went to was Chinese." We never found an Italian American who said that.

Jews looking for nearby, inexpensive restaurants could have patronized the Italians' places, but they faced obstacles. First, like Jewish delis,

Italian restaurants did not as a rule seek out the patronage of people from other ethnic groups. Second, because of competition for jobs, the anti-Semitic teachings of 19th-century Catholicism, Jewish distrust of European gentiles, and parental fears of intermarriage, Jews and Italians tended to be wary of each other. Third, Southern Italian neighborhoods and restaurants frequently displayed Christian images. The crucifixes and pictures of Jesus, Mary, and the saints certainly would have made Jews feel uneasy. However foreign Chinese restaurants might be, the decorations were *non-Christian*: They did not raise the issue of Jews' marginal position in a Christian society. As a result, for at least the first three decades of the 20th century, immigrant Jews and their children felt far more comfortable in Chinese restaurants than they did in Italian ones.[6]

Safe *Treyf*

The Eastern European Jews did not immigrate as one people. They thought of themselves as Russian Jews, Polish Jews, Hungarian Jews, or Rumanian Jews. After fleeing Eastern Europe and arriving in the United States, many of these diverse Jews and their children also continued to flee from the parochialism of the *shtetl* and ghetto cultures they had brought with them. Jewish immigrants, and especially their children and grandchildren, were open to new secular and cultural experiences. Many were anxious to prove that they could behave in "un-Jewish" ways (Cohen 1984; Sklar 1955).

The late British critic Raymond Williams (1977) pointed out that a culture spawns the terms of its own rejection. Rebels can disavow the strictures of a food-oriented culture by eating forbidden food. But a food-oriented rebellion cannot be accomplished with just any forbidden substance. It cannot be food that looks so like prohibited fare that it automatically triggers revulsion, nor can it be food that requires some expertise to eat. (One must be taught how to dissect a lobster.)

Wherever religious Jews had lived, kosher food was an elaboration of three dietary regulations derived from Exodus, Leviticus, and Deuteronomy: Do not eat "unclean" animals and fish; do not inhumanely slaughter animals; and do not mix milk and meat. Eastern European Jews, whether religious or not, had been powerfully socialized in their dietary customs. As a result, many immigrant, second-, and even third-generation Jews in America found it difficult to break away from ancient taboos, especially the bans against mixing meat with milk and against eating pork and shellfish. Jews yearning to be cosmopolitan might have dined anywhere in New York, but the restaurant food of other European groups did not mesh easily with the Jews' deeply ingrained culinary aesthetics.

At first glance, Chinese food also seems an unlikely choice for Eastern European Jews: Chinese cooking *does* incorporate pork, shrimp, lobster, and other forbidden items. Nonetheless, because of three distinctive characteristics of Chinese cuisine, Chinese food was actually unusually well suited for use by New York Jews seeking to demonstrate independence from the orthodoxies of traditional Eastern European Judaism. Chinese food was safe treyf.

As people we spoke with were quick to point out, Chinese cooking disguises the tabooed ingredients by cutting, chopping, and mincing them. Ancient Chinese texts refer to cooking itself as *ko p'eng*—"to cut and cook" (Chang 1977). Chinese food could be adopted by rebellious Jews because the forbidden substances were so disguised that dishes did not reflexively repulse and so undermine their ability to rebel.

Many of the Jews we interviewed appreciated this disguise. Several reported what was certainly a very common experience. They loved to eat egg rolls in Chinese restaurants because the pork and seafood tasted delicious but were so minced that they could pretend these ingredients were not there (see Nemeroff and Rozin 1987). One middle-aged man said that when he thought he had pork in his mouth he instantly got a headache, but when he swallowed it the headache just as quickly disappeared. A woman in her 40s recalled dining regularly as a child with her sister, mother, and grandmother: The girls ate spare ribs and sweet and sour pork, mother did not eat pork, and grandma pretended not to know treyf was on the table. One woman even reported that in the 1950s her aunt had three sets of dishes: one set for dairy meals, another for meat meals (as is traditional in kosher homes), and paper plates and plastic cutlery exclusively for take-out Chinese food.

Also, Chinese cooking was unusually well suited to Jewish tastes because, like Jewish cooking, it does not mix milk and meat. Indeed, unlike virtually any other cuisine available in America, Chinese cooking does not use any milk products. As anthropologist Marvin Harris (1985) pointed out, the Chinese, along with many other peoples from Asia, found milk repulsive. Thus some Chinese exchange students boasted of their acclimation to American culture by noting they had learned to eat ice cream.

Additionally, Chinese cuisine had gastronomical resonance for Jews. Both cultures favored chicken recipes and had, as Mimi Sheraton notes, a preference for dishes seasoned with garlic, celery, and onions. The Cantonese restaurants frequently overcooked the vegetables somewhat—just the way Eastern European Jews liked them. Jews could order sweet and sour dishes, vaguely reminiscent of their own sweet and sour tongue. They could order the ubiquitous Jewish cure-all—chicken soup—with either rice or *kreplach* (wontons). Jews were not beer or cocktail drinkers, and their religion had taught them to view wine as sacramental. But Eastern European Jews were used to drinking tea without milk, and Chinese restaurants immediately placed a steaming pot on the table. When drinking tea in Chinese restaurants, some Jews followed their traditional patterns: After the meal they requested a fresh pot and drank tea with lots of sugar.

Anti-Chinese racism also facilitated Jewish adoption of Chinese restaurants. In the process of adapting themselves to New York and American culture, some Jews absorbed disdain for the Chinese. People who were labeled "kikes" and "sheenies" learned to refer to Chinese Americans as "Chinks." Two of our informants, whose mothers used to say "Let's go eat at Chinks," did not discover until adolescence or later that "Chinks" was a disparaging and contemptuous term. They had thought that it simply referred to a kind of restaurant. A few people even insisted that their parents, who had learned their English on the streets, had not known that Chinks was a racist epithet.

Philip Roth (1969) used Alex Portnoy to talk about the sometimes strange psychological consequences of living at the interstices of American racial and ethnic stratification. Portnoy suggested that eating in Chinese restaurants enabled his family to deny their lowly status in an anti-Semitic society by participating in the prejudice against an even more lowly group. Recall the monologue:

> Why we can eat pig on Pell Street and not at home is because . . . frankly I still haven't got the whole thing figured out, but at the time I believed that it has largely to do with the fact that the elderly man who owns the place and whom amongst ourselves we call "Shmendrick," isn't somebody whose opinion of us we have cause to worry about. Yes, the only people in the world whom it seems to me the Jews are not afraid of are the Chinese. Because one, the way they speak English makes my father sound like Lord Chesterfield; two, the insides of their heads are just so much fried rice anyway; and three, to them we are not Jews but white—and maybe even Anglo Saxon. No wonder they can't intimidate us. To them we're just some big-nosed variety of WASP. (p. 90)

We think Roth is right: American racism also helped Jews feel safe in Chinese restaurants. And once there, they sometimes behaved very badly. One doctor we interviewed recalled a childhood incident where her uncle (then in his mid-30s) repeatedly mimicked the Chinese waiter's accent to his face. Jewish Borscht Belt comedians and their fans also made insulting jokes about Chinese restaurants and accents—especially about the Chinese difficulty with the "r" sound, including the ubiquitous line about ordering "flied lice."

This sort of contempt was by no means universal, as indicated by the doctor's embarrassment at her uncle's behavior. Most of the people we interviewed (not a random sample) grew up in families that regarded it as unacceptable to ever make derogatory or racist comments about the Chinese. Some said that as children they had never heard the Chinese referred to as Chinks, even in passing. But lots of Jews (and other ethnic New Yorkers) clearly did hear the Chinese referred to that way. And Jewish comedians, such as Buddy Hackett, even told their Chinese accent jokes on national television.

In short, the character of the cuisine, the low position of the Chinese in American society, and perhaps other factors, such as the formality of Chinese manners, made Chinese restaurants and their food feel safe for Jews.

Becoming Cosmopolitan

Jews felt secure in Chinese restaurants, but they were also drawn to these places for nonculinary reasons. Of all the peoples whom immigrant Jews and their children met, of all the foods they encountered in America, the Chinese were the most foreign, the most "un-Jewish." Yet Jews defined this particular foreignness not as forbidding but as appealing, attractive, and desirable. They viewed Chinese restaurants and food as exotic and cosmopolitan and therefore as good. Indeed, many Jews saw eating in Chinese restaurants as an antidote for Jewish parochialism, for the exclusive and overweening emphasis on the culture of the Jews as it had been.

People now in their 70s as well as those in their 40s repeatedly used the word "sophisticated" to describe their early feelings about Chinese food. Many of these Jews felt that eating in this distinctively "un-Jewish" way showed that they were at least somewhat sophisticated, urbane New Yorkers. A number of the New York Jews we interviewed recalled their childhood awe in Chinese restaurants. As one man reared in Queens said, "I felt about Chinese restaurants the same way I did about the Metropolitan Museum of Art—they were the two most strange and fascinating places my parents took me to, and I loved them both." The restaurants used exotic decorations, unusual wallpaper or paintings, lanterns, plates with foreign designs, and chopsticks. The Chinese waiters spoke a strange-sounding tongue and were of a different race. The entrees bore fantastic names: chow mein, moo goo gai pan, egg foo yung, wonton soup. If, as cosmopolitans claimed, experiencing exotic food was broadening, then Chinese food was as far out as a would-be cultural explorer could get.

Jews are not the only people who have associated Chinese food with sophistication and escape from provincialism. One man reared in a small town outside of Seattle, Washington recalled that in the 1950s when his high school friends wanted to show that they were "artsy" or sophisticated, they would go to Seattle to a Chinese restaurant and then perhaps to a foreign movie with subtitles. In a monologue on his "A Prairie Home Companion" radio show, Garrison Keiller told of his beloved high school teacher who once visited New York City, an unusual vacation for someone from Lake Wobegon. The man returned with a playbill from a Broadway show and a huge, red menu from a Chinese restaurant covered with that extraordinary Chinese writing. The playbill and especially the menu symbolized for young Keiller the sophistication and adventure available in the world beyond his little town.

Many Americans and New Yorkers found in Chinese food a symbol of cosmopolitanism. But no other 20th-century ethnic group in New York valued cosmopolitanism as highly as did Jews, nor made it such an important part of group identity. The sociologists Steven M. Cohen and Samuel Heilman have pointed out that as Jews withdrew from traditional Eastern European Judaism, they created a modern Judaism that embraced and emphasized cosmopolitan and universalistic values. Especially in the second and third generations, Jews—a people without a national home—staked their new modern identity on cosmopolitanism: on being at home in the world (Cohen 1984; Heilman and Cohen 1989; also see Sklar 1955; Liebman 1973). Along with attendance at theaters, concerts, museums, and universities, Jews regarded eating at Chinese restaurants as a sign that they possessed the sophistication and urbanity so central to both modern society and to modern Jewish culture—and, as many respondents spontaneously pointed out, it was also more fun than many of these other activities.

Forging a New York Jewish Culture at the Chinese Restaurant

At Chinese restaurants, New York Jews frequently savored the exotic in the midst of their own community. The oldest New York Jews we interviewed reported that even as children they usually found (or believed) that their neighborhood Chinese restaurants were filled with other Jews. One 67-year-old woman said of the Chinese restaurants of her Brooklyn youth: "Everybody there was Jewish."

Whether going to Chinese restaurants with family or friends, some Jews used Chinese food to make themselves over as self-styled cosmopolitan Americans. However, in the very act of rejecting Eastern European Jewishness, Jews who went to Chinese restaurants together were helping to define Chinese food as an essential element in the lifestyle of modernized New York Jews. As they declared their independence from traditional Jewish culture and affirmed their identity as sophisticated New Yorkers, they also forged a new, urban, Jewish culture. This New York Jewish culture included elements from traditional Eastern European culture, such as an emphasis on family meals, intense dinner table conversation, love of an abundant table ("eat, eat"), and appreciation of a real bargain. It also included new items, such as a fondness for the Brooklyn Dodgers (the underdogs of baseball) and for Chinese food. Along with other factors, including the anti-Semitism in American society, Chinese restaurant food helped to turn the children and grandchildren of the jumble of immigrant Jews from many countries into New York Jews. Because the majority of Eastern European Jews lived in New York until at least the 1950s (Steven M. Cohen, personal communication), the New York way of being Jewish greatly influenced Jewish culture in America.

Many of the people we interviewed recalled with enthusiasm that in Chinese restaurants ordering was half the fun. The communal character of Chinese restaurant food, where every dish is shared, has allowed Jews to indulge their love of discussion and debate. Even when picking one from column A and two from column B on the menu, Jews conferred and dickered over what to order. A Protestant man from the Midwest married to a Jewish New Yorker reported that when he first went to Chinese restaurants with his New York Jewish friends he discovered that they discussed the menu "with an enthusiasm which eluded me."

According to the people we interviewed, if ordering was half the fun, the other half was eating. In Chinese restaurants, Jews ate off their own plates, they ate off the serving plates, and they ate off their friends' plates. They shared special tidbits. Although Jews might have eaten this way sometimes at home, in Chinese restaurants they did this regularly. A good meal, many said, required companions.

Our informants pointed out that Chinese food was not simply inexpensive, it was a bargain. One person we interviewed, still a great bargain hunter, recalled with some astonishment that in the 1930s her family regularly ate in a Brooklyn restaurant for 25 cents a person, "plus a nickel tip." A steak dinner cost at least four or five times as much. Our respondents said that as college students and young workers they had found that eating Chinese, especially in Chinatown, made for a cheap date and an interesting evening. It also demonstrated a sophisticated palate, a sense of worldliness, and good financial sense.

New York Jews now between the ages of 40 and 70 found that Chinese restauranteurs had followed them to uptown neighborhoods, the boroughs, and the suburbs. By the 1950s, Cantonese Chinese restaurants had become a New York Jewish family tradition. They welcomed children and even babies, and the menus sometimes explained that wonton soup was "chicken soup with kreplach." The column A and column B choices were called "family dinners"; the larger the group, the more dishes one could taste. On Sunday nights the restaurants in middle-class Jewish neighborhoods often had a waiting line. In some wealthy Jewish neighborhoods, such as sections of Great Neck, Chinese restaurants also had a line on the maid's night off. Chinese restaurants were so common in Jewish neighborhoods that sometimes Chinese American families went there for Chinese food. Sociologist Clarence Lo reports that his parents were scientists who, in the early 1940s, immigrated from China to Philadelphia. His family usually ate at Chinese restaurants in Jewish neighborhoods "because that's where the good restaurants were."

For immigrants and most first-generation Jews, Chinese restaurants were new experiences. However, our middle-aged and third-generation informants viewed them differently. When these Jews talked about Chinese restaurants they usually told us about their parents and family outings. They added that as adults eating Chinese food, they found that their present experiences resonated with a fondly remembered past. For them, Chinese food had become fused with their family experiences and their own social life—part of what it meant to be a New York Jew. As Mimi Sheraton (1990) put it, describing Cantonese cooking, "These dishes, with their meltingly tender vegetables and soothing garlic overtones, are for me what Federico Fellini once described as 'the soft and gentle flavors of the past' " (p. 71).

Jews, Chinese, and the Shaping of New York Culture

In most cities in the world, Chinese restaurants occupy a small specialized niche. In New York they are everywhere. A large industry has grown up to furnish Chinese restaurants and take-out places with their specialized cooking ingredients and utensils, including plates, chopsticks, fortune cookies, and menus.

Certainly, New York Jews have eaten so much Chinese food because Chinese entrepreneurs and workers have established so many well-run restaurants. Peter Kwong (1987) points out in *The New Chinatown* that in 1980 some 450 Chinese restaurants crowded into lower Manhattan's Chinatown—even more than in San Francisco's Chinatown—and there are at least 1,000 more in the rest of the New York area. New York is the Chinese food capital of the United States.

But the reverse is true as well: Chinese restaurants flourished in New York because the large Jewish population provided a reliable base of customers who liked to eat out, who had the money to do so, and who wanted to eat in Chinese restaurants. As a result, New York City probably has more Chinese restaurants than any non-Chinese city in the world. Chinese food seems fashionable in New York, something that almost everyone eats sometimes. "Eating Chinese" is a New York thing to do. New residents quickly become familiar with Chinese restaurants and cuisine. The neighborhoods of Italians, Greeks, Lebanese, Germans, Puerto Ricans, Cubans, Dominicans, African Americans, and Japanese—to name but a few—all have Chinese restaurants in addition to their own ethnic ones.

In part, the recent increase in the number of Chinese restaurants in non-Jewish neighborhoods has resulted from the increased migration of the Chinese to New York. Manhattan's Chinatown has long been one of the most densely populated areas of New York. The increasing concentration of residents has prompted Chinatown to expand into Little Italy. But today, Queens and Brooklyn also have little Chinatowns, mainly in areas abutting the subway lines that pass through Manhattan's Chinatown. However, in almost every non-Jewish ethnic neighborhood, the group's own restaurants outnumber the Chinese places. In most Jewish neighborhoods, Chinese restaurants outnumber Jewish delis. In most non-Chinese ethnic neighborhoods, the Chinese restaurants tend to be small and modest or simply store fronts selling only take-out food. But neighborhoods with many Jews (or Chinese or Koreans) possess more Chinese restaurants and more large and fancy ones.

Chinese restaurants have never stopped expanding and innovating. Chinese restaurants offered "take out" long before MacDonald's, Pizza King, and Colonel Sanders' Kentucky Fried Chicken. In the 1950s and 1960s, as Jews prospered in the postwar boom, many Chinese restaurants began to deliver. After a hard day's work or on a hot night, a wet night, or a cold, snowy evening, families could eat delicious Chinese food without going farther than the front door. Chinese restaurants had few competitors in this enterprise; none served meals as good. Only since the 1980s have other New York restaurants offered high-quality delivered or even take-out food—but most of it remains more expensive than Chinese food. Even the strictly kosher restaurants now advertise take-out food.

Since the 1970s, a new influx of immigrants have arrived bringing the spicy cuisines of the North, and as a result, new restaurants have sprung up serving Hunan and Szechuan food. Younger second-and third-generation Jews have taken to them en masse. One friend refers to a 30-block stretch of Broadway on Manhattan's upper west side as the Szechuan

Valley. Chinese restaurants have even altered their interior design to keep up with changing fashion. In the 1940s and 1950s, Chinese restaurants featured exotic decorations and plush, sculpted booths. Contemporary Szechuan and Hunan houses often have a sleek minimalist style more in line with the aesthetic preferences of educated middle-class New Yorkers (a group that still includes many Jews). These places, with their international design style, are today as sophisticated and cosmopolitan as the older ones were in their time.

Jews Who Do Not Eat Chinese Food

Some Jews are no longer as attached to Chinese food as they had once been. A few Jews now in their 40s told us that eating Chinese food had such strong associations with Jewishness that they avoided Chinese restaurants. However, the largest group of Jews who have abandoned their intense involvement with Chinese food live in retirement communities in Florida. Many of these women and men, faced with the boredom and pleasures of perpetual vacation, regard the evening meal as the highlight of the day. Even those who still "eat Chinese" dine much less often at Chinese restaurants (or Jewish delis) than at other eateries. Instead, they frequent restaurants offering "Early Bird Specials"—soup or salad, a main course, dessert, and a beverage for under $8.00 if you are seated before 5:00 or 5:30 p.m. Chatting in and around swimming pools, they exchange information about a topic that interests them all: the bargain restaurants they have found and when the line to be seated forms. As they are happy to explain to their visiting children, "With such prices, who needs to cook?" Already secure in their identity as American Jews, establishing new identities for themselves as retired and as Floridians, and living in an area where Chinese restaurants are not as common as in the New York metropolitan area or as much of a bargain as the "Early Bird Specials," they might well ask, "Who needs Chinese food?"

Some Jews had never taken to Chinese restaurants, especially German-American Jews. In the late 19th century, German-American Jews in New York lived uptown, away from the immigrant Jewish and Chinese neighborhoods, and they tried to distance themselves from the Eastern Europeans. Many other German-American Jews lived in the Midwest and South and had not settled even temporarily in what was to become the American capital of Eastern European Jews. The German Jews who came to America before and after World War II remained strongly attached to German culture and food. However, when they moved into the same neighborhoods as the Eastern European Jews, they learned to eat Chinese food—at least sometimes. A colleague whose family immigrated in the 1930s told us that her staunchly German Jewish mother frequently ate at Chinese restaurants on Sunday night as did her neighbors. But after 50 years in New York, this woman still eats only bland chicken chow mein.

Recent Jewish immigrants from the Soviet Union and Israel have followed the patterns of the German Jews and of other recent immigrants from all ethnic groups. Israelis and Russians have each concentrated in specific neighborhoods in Brooklyn and Queens, where they patronize restaurants serving their own ethnic foods: Middle Eastern specialties and Russian cuisine. However, these new Jewish ethnics are also learning to eat Chinese food sometimes.

For those Eastern European Jews and their descendants living away from the Northeast coast, Chinese food has usually not been as important, often because it is harder to get. But the love of Chinese food remains strong for at least some Jews in large cities, such as Chicago, and especially for Jews who moved away after a generation or two in New York. Former New Yorkers often complaint that their new communities lack adequate Chinese restaurants. But many of these ex-New Yorkers do eat Chinese restaurant food when it is available: The powerful symbolic meanings still hold.

"The Soft and Gentle Flavors of the Past"

New York Jews did not develop their web of cultural meanings out of thin air. The values and habits that Eastern European Jews brought with them channeled change and invention along specific axes. As Giddens (1948) reminds us, social meanings are recursive. Historically constructed meanings become the raw materials for new cultural creation. However, long-standing webs of significance also set limits on what an immigrant or ethnic group can use to construct new collective activities and forms of identity. The tastes and smells of childhood are among our most powerfully evocative memories. They spur memory (Ackerman 1990). They provide biographical continuity. For middle-aged Jews, childhood memory is captured, for example, by the comforting smell of the chicken soup their mothers prepared to celebrate a holiday or expel an illness. To a perhaps surprising extent, Chinese food has also provided that biographical continuity for generations of New York Jews. Chinese food, especially Cantonese cooking (with its absence of milk and its use of chicken, chicken stock, eggs, garlic, celery, onions, sweet and sour dishes, and tea) resonated with Eastern European Jewish home cooking. More than any other restaurant food available, Chinese food was attractive to Jews in part because it was familiar and did not instinctively repel. It was what we have called safe treyf. Jews were also attached to Chinese food because they perceived it as sophisticated, non-Christian, and a bargain. In subsequent generations, these associations then became overlaid with memories of family meals in Chinese restaurants (where, after 1950, New York Jewish families ate far more often than they did in Jewish restaurants). In different ways, for different reasons, for four generations of New York Jews, Chinese restaurant food has continued to be part of what Federico Fellini called "the soft and gentle flavors of the past."

Especially in large urban areas, ethnic and national culture is clearly mutable but not easily meltable. Sometimes, when people dress similarly and talk the same language, the differences are hidden or harder to see. Sometimes, as Zbrowoski (1952) showed in his study of the way that different ethnic groups respond to pain, the cultural traits might not even be recognized by the participants themselves. In the case of the Jewish adoption of Chinese food, the different patterns might be discussed in jokes and anecdotes. Nevertheless, however subtle or submerged, constructed cultural differences remain Durkheimian social facts, enduring and real in their consequences, yet malleable to reinterpretation by future generations.

It might seem contradictory to emphasize both the relative unmeltability of ethnic cultures—the tenacity of ethnic culture—and the changing and socially constructed character of ethnicity and nationality, but the contradiction is only apparent. Ethnic culture is tenacious precisely because it is so mutable (Craig Reinarman, personal communication). People change and create their cultures, but they do so in particular ways, frequently along already well carved grooves, establishing comfortable (if surprising) blends of old and new. In effect, all ethnic groups find their own versions of safe treyf.

Since the early 19th century, many observers have pointed out the homogenizing effects of modern society. Yet whatever its unifying tendencies, modernization contains strong tendencies toward cultural differentiation. These include both multiculturalism and the cultural pastiche now fashionably termed "postmodernism." Today in the United States, Eastern Europe, and Africa, to choose three obvious examples, cultural differences remain central in shaping such everyday "small" life experiences as eating as well as such large political practices as forming governments. In large cities in the United States, especially those now undergoing intense multiracial and multiethnic immigration, many groups might find it impossible *not* to construct a group identity. They could likely be institutionally and symbolically captured in new ethnic ghettos.

Knowledgeable observers and even participants might not be able to predict the materials from which today's immigrant groups will forge their new cultural combinations—how, for instance, Mexican Americans, Puerto Ricans, Cuban Americans, Dominicans, Costa Ricans, and all the other peoples today labeled "Hispanic Americans" will create a common identity and culture (see Rumbaut 1991). One can only be sure that the because of discrimination in the United States (including being lumped together by Anglos) and out of their own various cultural traditionals (and "flavors"), the descendants of Latin American immigrants will together construct new "webs of significance" with their own internal logic. These, too, might appear as strange as the Jewish passion for Chinese food.

Appendix: Research Methods

Social scientists' discussions of methods usually focus exclusively on techniques used to identify and test hypotheses. We are including as well certain shared characteristics of our individual backgrounds and sociological orientations that helped turn our lifelong delight in Chinese food into a research problem that informed our approach. As Krieger (1991) suggested, we have found in conducting research in general, and especially in this project, that our visceral reactions to questions and data are often empirically relevant and theoretically revelatory. We believe, therefore, that briefly mentioning key biographical factors is both appropriate and useful in understanding the development of this project.

We were both first schooled in the sociology of culture by European emigré intellectuals and American-born ethnographers when we were undergraduates at Brandeis University in the mid-1960s. Our teachers (and the intellectual spirit of Brandeis at the time) immersed us in a broad, critical, anthropological, historical, and theoretical understanding of society and culture. Brandeis had been established in 1948, in the shadow of the Holocaust, primarily by American Jews, as a modern, secular, nondenominational university. It was also a place where faculty and students talked openly and frequently about the meaning and experience of being Jewish in a modern secular world.

More than 20 years later, as colleagues at the City University of New York, we found ourselves exchanging jokes and anecdotes about the Jewish attachment to Chinese food. Our first conversations drew on our different New York Jewish backgrounds: One of us was reared in a religious family, the other in a secular home. The more we talked (alone and with our colleagues), the more we realized that our shared delight in humor and gossip could not account for our fascination with the

topic. Chats, we insist, are not idle. Although we had individually re-
searched very different empirical topics, the embrace of Chinese restaurant food by New York Jews raised a central sociological (theoretical and
methodological) issue for us both: the importance of meanings, interpretations and symbols in culture and lived experience. We had inadver-
tently come upon a subtle but concrete example of the social
construction of ethnic culture and identity—and we had lived in the
middle of that phenomenon for most of our lives.

In previous writings, we had each combined historical and ethnographic research. Therefore, we marked the formal beginning of our
joint project by researching the intersecting histories of Jewish, Chinese,
and American cultures and foods. Much of this detailed historical research was edited out of this article many drafts ago, but it provided
most of our major hypotheses and hunches as well as the frame we used
to organize and make sense of our data.

For over a year we interviewed friends, relatives, and acquaintances
about their experiences eating in restaurants and particularly their experiences with Chinese restaurants and food. Our selection of informants was often opportunistic. For instance, at social events we turned
conversations to Chinese food and interviewed people about their experiences and backgrounds. After hearing what people had to say about
Chinese food, we would ask them their backgrounds. When we felt that
some groups whose experiences we believed relevant to our project were
underrepresented, we consciously sought informants from that group.
All told, counting informal chats, nearly 100 people told us about their
experiences with Chinese food.

We sought to interview different categories of Jews and non-Jews who
might have had different sorts of experiences with Chinese restaurants.
Jewish informants included men and women reared in families with different sorts of attachments to Jewish identity (religious, ethnic, or political); people whose ancestors had migrated from all areas of Europe and
from other continents; and people who grew up in the 1920s, '30s, '40s,
and '50s in different areas of the country and who, as children, had
belonged to different social classes. Our oldest Jewish informant was 82,
our youngest, 6. Because outsiders and newcomers to a culture might
see more than would insiders (Mannheim 1952; but see Merton 1972),
we interviewed non-Jews, especially those who had married Jews or those
with many Jewish friends. We spoke with a number of Chinese Americans, Italian Americans, and Irish Americans. We interviewed Jews and
non-Jews from many parts of the United States. Nearly all of our informants are middle or upper-middle class now. We stopped recording people's stories when our past experience with ethnographic research
indicated that we had reached the saturation point. That is, we stopped

taking informal notes when people relayed experiences comparable to ones we had already heard.

What we wanted to know also determined who we interviewed and when (see Glaser and Strauss 1967). For instance, when German Jews explained that fondness for Chinese food was specific to the descendants of Eastern Europeans and convinced us that the German and Austrian Jewish experience was simply different, we concentrated on speaking with people of Western European descent. When colleagues raised questions about the restaurant habits of Italian Americans, we interviewed members of that ethnic group. At one point, we hypothesized that Jews who had lived or passed through China might have introduced other Jews to Chinese food. We rejected this possibility after interviewing Jews who had lived in China (or whose parents had).

When we conducted interviews, we also explored New York metropolitan area neighborhoods, counted Chinese restaurants in neighborhoods that New Yorkers defined as being different in terms of class and ethnicity, and ate at Chinese restaurants in neighborhoods outside of our daily rounds, including *glat kosher* Chinese restaurants in Queens and Manhattan and restaurants in the new Queens Little Asia, Afro-American neighborhoods, and working-class Hispanic neighborhoods. Wherever we went, we collected menus.

We focused primarily on New York Jews, particularly those from families whose members immigrated from Eastern Europe at the end of the 19th century and in the first two decades of the 20th century. Jews living away from the East Coast have not usually developed the same degree of attachment to Chinese food, often because it is not so readily available. But what we have found holds for at least some Jews in such large cities as Chicago and especially for those who moved away after a generation or two in New York.

Notes

We dedicate this article to the Brandeis Sociology Department of the 1960s. Its faculty and students taught us to think big about everything, including seemingly small things. Our colleagues Steven M. Cohen and Samuel Heilman, outstanding sociologists of American Jewry, offered us continuing advice and encouragement. We also presented an early draft of our findings to colleagues and students in sociology and history; their comments were invaluable. We also acknowledge the pizzeria across the street from our Queens College offices. We worked out many of our ideas at La Pineta and determined senior authorship by a coin tossed there. Address correspondence to Gaye Tuchman, Department of Sociology, U-68, University of Connecticut, Storrs, CT 06269.

1. The examples are legion: People from Sicily, Naples, Rome, and Milan

became Italian Americans; Navaho, Iroquois, and Cherokee became Native Americans; the descendants of Africans brought as slaves became African Americans; Cantonese, Taiwanese, and Fukienese became Chinese Americans; and Egyptians, Saudis, and Lebanese became Arab Americans. People have forged ethnic identities and cultures for many reasons: in response to discrimination and racism; because language, religion, or similar experiences enabled them to establish bonds of community and culture; and because, in America, shared economic and political interests dwarfed past differences.

2. Glazer and Moynihan's (1963) *Beyond the Melting Pot* has been properly criticized for its lack of attention to enduring and institutional racism and to the structural character of contemporary urban poverty (see Valentine 1968). However, among the book's clear strengths is its unblinking acceptance of the inescapable cultural pluralism of American cities. From its title onward, *Beyond the Melting Pot* straightforwardly promotes what in today's terms would be called a multicultural understanding of American society.

3. Even the strictly kosher can eat Chinese food. For the past few years, Chinese restaurants have constituted about a third of the strictly kosher restaurants serving meat that advertised in "The Dining Guide" of New York's *The Jewish Press*.

4. We believe that an analysis of webs of significance requires both ethnographic and historical research. As Park and Burgess (1921) wrote so long ago, "History and sociology . . . are concerned with man as a person participating with his fellows in a common fund of social traditions and cultural ideas. History seeks to find out what actually happened and how it all came about. Sociology . . . seeks to explain, on the basis of a study of other instances, the nature of the process involved" (p. 11). By providing those other instances, historical research can facilitate an understanding of process. For a more contemporary analysis of the relationship between history and sociology, see Giddens (1984).

5. For a structural analysis of European Jews as the "classical example" of the stranger, see Simmel (1950, 402–8).

6. We do not wish to give the impression that in the early 20th century most Jewish immigrants ate in Chinese restaurants. To reiterate, most immigrants were quite poor, rarely ate out, and when they did they were more likely to go to a Jewish eatery (Rischin 1962). However, based on our interviews and historical research, we are confident that some Jews frequented Chinese restaurants *before* the 1930s, were more likely to go to Chinese restaurants than to the eateries of other non-Jewish ethnic groups, and were more likely to go to Chinese restaurants than were other immigrants at the time.

References

Ackerman, D. 1990. *A natural history of the senses.* New York: Random House.
Chang, K. C., ed. 1977. *Food in Chinese culture.* New Haven, CT: Yale University Press.
Chen, J. 1980. *The Chinese of America.* San Francisco: Harper & Row.

Cohen, S. M. 1984. *American modernity and Jewish identity.* New York: Tavistock.

Douglas, M. T. 1966. *Purity and danger: An analysis of concepts of pollution and taboo.* New York: Praeger.

Geertz, C. 1973. *The interpretation of cultures.* New York: Basic Books.

Giddens, A. 1984. *The constitution of society: Outline of the theory of structuration.* Berkeley: University of California Press.

Glaser, B., and A. Strauss. 1967. *The discovery of grounded theory: Strategies for qualitative research.* Chicago: Aldine.

Glazer, N., and D. P. Moynihan. 1963. *Beyond the melting pot.* Cambridge: MIT Press.

Harris, M. 1985. *Good to eat: Riddles of food and culture.* New York: Simon & Schuster.

Heilman, S., and S. M. Cohen. 1989. *Cosmopolitans and parochials: Modern Orthodox Jews in America.* Chicago: University of Chicago Press.

Kirschenblatt-Gimblett, B. 1987. Recipes for creating community: The Jewish charity cookbook in America. *Jewish Folklore and Ethnology Review* 9 (1): 8–12.

Kleinman, D. 1989. Kosher cooking: Goodbye derma, hello sushi. *The New York Times,* September 27: C1, C6.

Krieger, Susan. 1991. *Social science and the self.* New Brunswick, NJ: Rutgers University Press.

Kwong, P. 1987. *The new Chinatown.* New York: Hill & Wang.

Liebman, C. S. 1973. *The ambivalent Jew.* Philadelphia: Jewish Publication Society.

Light, I., and C. C. Wong. 1975. Protest or work: Dilemmas of the tourist industry in American Chinatowns. *American Journal of Sociology* 80:1342–68.

Lyman, Stanford M. 1974. *Chinese Americans.* New York: Random House.

Mannheim, K. 1952. *Essays on the sociology of knowledge,* edited by P. Kecskemeti. London: Routledge & Kegan Paul.

Merton, R. K. 1972. Insiders and outsiders: A chapter in the sociology of knowledge. *American Journal of Sociology* 78 (1): 9–47.

Nemeroff, C., and P. Rozin. 1987. Sympathetic magic in kosher practice and belief at the limits of the laws of kashrut. *Jewish Folklore and Ethnology Review* 9 (1): 31–32.

Park, Robert, and Ernest Burgess. 1921. *Introduction to the science of sociology.* Chicago: University of Chicago Press.

Rischin, M. 1962. *The promised city: New York's Jews, 1870–1914.* Cambridge, MA: Harvard University Press.

Roth, P. 1969. *Portnoy's complaint.* New York: Random House.© 1969 Random House.

Rumbaut, R. 1991. Passages to America: Perspectives on the new immigration. In *America at century's end,* edited by Alan Wolfe, 208–44. Berkeley: University of California Press.

Sheraton, Mimi. 1990. A Jewish yen for Chinese. *The New York Times Magazine,* September 23: 71,72 Copyright © 1990 by The New York Times Company Reprinted by permission.

Simmel, G. 1950. The stranger. In *The sociology of Georg Simmel,* translated and edited by Kurt H. Wolff, 402–8. Glencoe, IL: Free Press.

184 G. Tuchman & H. G. Levine

80

Sklar, M. 1955. *Conservative Judaism: An American religious movement.* New York: Schocken.

Sollors, W. 1986. *Beyond ethnicity: Consent and dissent in American culture.* New York: Oxford University Press.

———. ed. 1989. *The invention of ethnicity.* New York: Oxford University Press.

Steinberg, S. 1981. *The ethnic myth: Race, ethnicity, and class in America.* New York: Atheneum.

Tsai, S. H. 1986. *The Chinese experience in America.* Bloomington: University of Indiana Press.

Valentine, C. A. 1968. *Culture and poverty.* Chicago: University of Chicago Press.

Weber, Max. 1958. *From Max Weber: Essays in sociology,* edited by Hans Gerth and C. Wright Mills. New York: Oxford University Press.

———. 1963. *Essays in the sociology of religion,* translated by Ephraim Fischoff. Boston: Beacon.

Williams, R. 1977. *Marxism and literature.* New York: Oxford University Press.

Zbrowoski, M. 1952. Cultural components in response to pain. *Journal of Social Issues* 8 (4): 16–30.

Zenner, Walter P. 1980. Preface to the paperback edition. In *Mishpokhe,* by William E. Mitchell, 3–6. Hawthorne, NY: Aldine.

Section Three

Eating Out

Before World War II restaurants were a minor part of the American eating scene. Their dollar sales volume equaled only about a fifth of that spent in grocery stores, and the foods they served differed but slightly from those consumed at home. These characteristics began to change by 1950, and the popularity of restaurants has increased ever since. "Eating out" today is both a necessity for those too busy to cook and a diversion for those seeking inexpensive ways to have exotic experiences.

The readings in this section explore the pattern and meaning of the rapidly evolving restaurant culture. They begin with a historical overview, Charles Kovacik's survey of South Carolina restaurants since 1930. General establishments serving indigenous dishes (including barbecue) yielded ground first to drive-ins during the 1950s, then to fast-food chains in the 1960s and 1970s, and most recently to ethnic establishments. In the process, he argues, South Carolina has become more like the rest of the nation.

The other four readings discuss specific types of restaurants. The first, John Milbauer's survey of unpretentious, local eateries in eastern Oklahoma, shows the considerable potential of such studies for revealing transition zones between regional cultures and degrees of isolation from national fads. Joe Manzo's paper explores another traditional type of restaurant, the diner. These stainless-steel models of efficiency originally catered to factory workers, but their continuing success is largely a product of high levels of personal interaction between customers and staff. Diners, Manzo argues, are a treat for the soul as well as the body.

Fast-food restaurants, the most ubiquitous on the American landscape, are more often the subject of insults than serious study. Michael Roark, however, asks one of the basic questions, whether each of their types (burger, pizza, et al.) is distributed evenly across the country. Predictably, perhaps, he finds that only the West fits this norm. Finally, Wilbur Zelinsky takes on the richly varied and booming field of ethnic restaurants. He reports a higher incidence of this fare in the northeastern and western sections of the country than in the Midwest and the South. Chinese, Italian, and Mexican food dominate the field while Western European specialties are rare, but the reasons behind these predilections remain obscure.

15

Eating Out in South Carolina's Cities: The Last Fifty Years

Charles Kovacik

The South has always been identified as a distinctive region, but economic development and population growth since World War II have altered the Southern lifestyle and landscape dramatically. Change has been so striking, especially in metropolitan areas, that social scientists and others have debated the issue of cultural convergence between the South and the rest of the nation. While there is no support for the notion that convergence has been complete, some argue that the region's identity is threatened. Others maintain that the South has maintained its regional identity because cultural dissimilarities persist despite recent changes associated with economic development, and yet another claims that basic cultural differences between the North and the South are minimal.[1]

Food often is listed as one of the most distinctive Southern cultural traits along with accent, religion, music, literature, and localism.[2] Despite its frequent mention and its significance to the cultural convergence controversy, however, there are no studies concerning recent economic development in the South and its affect on food consumption. This is not surprising since social scientists have long neglected the study of foodways in America despite what Zelinsky claims are their "profound social, cultural, and economic implications."[3] Geographers recently have completed several studies concerning restaurants, but none has a specific regional focus and only Jakle's has been concerned with change through time.[4] This study examines the growth of the restaurant industry and change in restaurant types in three South Carolina

Reprinted by permission from *North American Culture* 4, 1 (1988), 53–64.

cities since the 1930s. The purpose is to determine if general patterns of restaurant dining reflect the social and economic transformation that has taken place over the last half century and how food preferences, as reflected in restaurant types, have changed.

Data

There is no convenient source that provides historical data concerning restaurant types or food preference. The *Census of Retail Trade* includes information concerning the economic and spatial characteristics of eating and drinking establishments, but types cannot be determined. Trade journals, such as *Restaurant Hospitality* and *Restaurant Business,* periodically publish survey data for metropolitan areas, but restaurant types are very broadly classified and the temporal dimension is limited. City directories provide suitable information, but they are not comprehensive and often do not cover entire metropolitan areas.

Information for this study was gathered from the Columbia, Charleston, and Greenville Telephone Directory Yellow Pages dating from the 1930s to 1984.[5] Telephone directories usually serve entire metropolitan areas, and coverage is relatively comprehensive since the yellow pages provide an inexpensive but effective means of advertising. Certainly not all restaurants within a given metropolitan area are listed in its directory. Pillsbury, for example, found that between 10 and 20 percent of the listings in the Atlanta directory were inaccurate with respect to their existence or type.[6] Some small or very exclusive restaurants may not appear in the yellow pages because a fee must be paid to be listed, or an establishment may choose not to advertise. Also, telephone directories normally do not include restaurants which are ancillary to some other function such as those in hospitals, private clubs, office buildings, universities, and food stores.

Perhaps the major shortcoming of telephone directories is that there is not enough information to classify all listed establishments by type of food served. Five types, however, easily were identified: barbecue, drive-in, seafood, ethnic and chain. Ethnic restaurants were further classified as Italian, Chinese, Mexican, French, Greek, and German. The ethnic classification does not mean that these restaurants necessarily are owned and operated by people of a specific ethnic group. It does mean, however, that these establishments serve food that is ethnic in character and differs from local fare. The majority of eating places, however, are listed by name only or by name followed by the generic term "restaurant." Classification of some of these was possible, and they usually were chain or ethnic restaurants. Determination of chain operations was based on checking the names against listings in the *1984 Directory of Chain Restaurant Operators,* and ethnic restaurants were identified by examining box-ads included in the directories.[7] Those which could not be classified were placed in a category called "others." Since establishments in this category did not choose to identify a specific type of cuisine in their name, or advertise one in a box-ad, it is assumed they offered a menu consisting of standard American or local foods. This category also includes restaurants that were advertised as a cafe, lunchroom, cafeteria, grill, coffee shop, tea room, or diner.

Restaurant Dining and Change

The restaurant has become an increasingly more significant element in the American lifestyle and landscape as rising personal income, increased urbanization and suburbanization, the changing role of women in the labor force, the development of franchising, and the relatively low cost of chain restaurant meals have all contributed to explosive growth in the restaurant industry.[8] Not only has eating-out become more commonplace, but food consumption patterns have changed as millions of Americans have been exposed to a greater variety of foods because of experiences during World War II, the Korean War, Vietnam, and a boom in American overseas tourism.[9]

One means of tracing the growing significance of eating meals away from home is to examine the relationship between consumer expenditures at food stores with those at restaurants (Table 1). Between 1929

TABLE 1
Food Store and Restaurant Sales,
United States and South Carolina: 1929–1982

	United States				South Carolina		
Food Stores	Restaurants ($ millions)		%		Food Stores	Restaurants ($ millions)	%
1929	10837	2125	20				
1939	10165	2135	21				
1948	30966	6468	21		274	40	15
1958	49022	11038	23		444	72	16
1967	70251	18879	27		741	140	19
1977	158444	55670	35		2022	559	28
1982	240520	93158	39		3096	1040	34

Source: U.S. Census of Business, 1948-1967 and U.S. Census of Retail Trade, 1972-1982.

and 1982, restaurant sales in the United States expanded at a rate more than twice that of food store sales. Restaurant sales as a proportion of food store sales, however, grew from only 20 to 21 percent between 1929 and 1948, indicating that restaurant dining was not common for most Americans. Eating-out became more popular in post-war America as restaurant sales grew from 21 to 27 percent of food store sales between 1948 and 1967. As changes in American society became more widespread, particularly the increase in the number of working women, the restaurant industry boomed and sales soared to 39 percent of food store sales in 1982.

The significance of the restaurant in America varies over time and through space. Frequent dining out in the South, for example, is a relatively recent experience and corresponds to basic economic and social changes that have their roots in the New Deal policies of the Roosevelt administration and intensified after World War II. South Carolina, like other southeastern Sunbelt states, experienced considerable post-war economic development and population growth. Urban areas experienced the greatest change as the State moved away from its traditional rural agrarian way of life toward a more urban industrial orientation. Its total population, for example, grew by 47 percent between 1950 and 1980. But, its urban population more than doubled and nonagricultural employment increased by 2 1/2 times. Perhaps most importantly, per capita income rose from about 60 percent of the 1950 national average to 77 percent in 1980. Rural population increased only slightly, however, and the number of farms fell from nearly 150,000 in 1945 to fewer than 25,000 in 1982.[10]

The number of restaurants and restaurant sales mirror these basic changes. Restaurants in Charleston, Columbia, and Greenville demonstrated little numerical growth between 1930 and 1940, a large increase during the next decade, and substantial growth during the 1960s, 1970s, and early 1980s (Table 2). As late as 1967, restaurant sales accounted for only 19 percent of food store sales, significantly behind the 27 percent for the nation as a whole. Between 1967 and 1982, however, restaurant sales in South Carolina increased more than sevenfold and more closely approximated the national average. This growth indicates that dining-out has become more significant as the present-day South Carolina lifestyle more closely resembles that of the rest of the United States than it did prior to World War II.

Meat, Meal, and Molasses: 1930 & 1940

Restaurants in Charleston, Columbia, and Greenville reflected the cultural and economic milieu of the South and South Carolina in 1930 and

TABLE 2
Restaurant Types in Three
South Carolina Cities: 1930–1984

	1930[a]	1940[a]	1950	1960	1970	1984
Barbecue	2	8	21	17	19	32
Seafood	1	2	8	10	41	91
Drive-In			37	96	52	29
Ethnic	3	3	19	17	37	176
Italian	1	1	10	11	22	54
Chinese	1		6	3	5	56
Mexican	1	1	3	1	5	31
French				1	2	15
Greek					1	11
German					1	7
Other		1		1	1	2
Chain		1	1	10	146	405
Others	74	133	347	373	464	525
Total	80	147	433	523	743[b]	1183[b]

Source: Data collected from the Charleston, Columbia, and Greenville Telephone Directory Yellow Pages.

[a]1930 and 1940 telephone directories were unavailable for each of the three cities. Data reported for 1930 were collected from the 1934 Charleston, 1930 Columbia, and 1933 Greenville Telephone Directories. Data reported for 1940 were collected from the 1941 Charleston, 1940 Columbia, and 1937 Greenville Telephone Directories.

[b]Columns do not sum to total because chain restaurants include establishments counted in barbecue, seafood, and ethnic categories.

1940. Cotton dominated the economy and way of life to such a degree that Rupert Vance argued, in an almost deterministic fashion, that the lifestyle of the region's people was related to "the seasonal cycle of the cotton plant."[11] He also claimed that the food habits of the majority of southerners were "among the most obvious of the material culture traits associated with cotton." The basic diet consisted of salt fat pork, cornbread, and molasses or what was called the "three M" diet—meat, meal, and molasses.[12]

There were few restaurants in the South prior to World War II even though restaurant food was relatively inexpensive.[13] Still, few people in the South's depressed economy could afford even the cheap meals offered at the few restaurants that did exist. Southerners, therefore, ate most all their meals at home, and eating-out was not common before the 1940s.[14] This paucity of restaurants was reflected in the telephone directory yellow pages for the three cities since only 80 were listed in 1930 and 147 in 1940.

Over 90 percent of the restaurants were classified as "others," and the majority were cafes or lunchrooms. Without access to a suitable sample of menus, it is difficult to determine restaurant fare during this time but Taylor noted that the diet of city dwellers differed only slightly from those who lived on farms.[15] More than likely, restaurants in this category served foods that did not stray far from the basics of the "three M" diet typical of the dominant rural population. Southerners customarily ate the day's big meal at midday and called it dinner, in contrast to most other parts of the country.[16] It consisted of a main course, three or four vegetables, bread, and a drink. The main course was usually some form of pork or fried chicken and the vegetables were some combination of white beans, pintos, black-eyed peas, crowders, butter beans (limas), green beans, hominy, cabbage, turnip greens, white potatoes, stewed tomatoes, or candied yams.[17] Cornbread and either a soft drink or iced tea also were served.

The eating place with the strongest Southern identity is the barbecue restaurant. In South Carolina and other Deep South states, barbecue means pork. The traditional method of cooking the pork is to roast it slowly in pits over wood coals, but many establishments recently have converted to gas or electric cookers. The meat is always basted with a piquant sauce either while it is cooking or prior to serving. Sauces vary markedly from place to place and are prepared from time-honored and often secret recipes. The meat is served with a myriad of side dishes all of which are based on local custom. They amounted to just over 2 percent of all advertised restaurants in 1930 and about 5 percent in 1940. While their significance diminished as an urban restaurant type after 1940, they continue to be important in the culinary tradition of the region.

The vast majority of restaurants in the three cities served traditional foods in 1940 since 96 percent of them were either barbecues or classified in the "others" category. Ethnic and seafood restaurants provided some variety in restaurant dining, but both were uncommon in 1930 and 1940 with one notable exception—Charleston. Zelinsky states that even in the 1980s there are few ethnic restaurants in the South relative to the rest of the United States, and that this may be related to the region's insignificant foreign-born population, relative poverty, and general tardiness in adopting cultural innovations.[18] In addition, he claims a region's receptivity to ethnic cuisines is related to such factors as general socio-economic status, cultural sophistication, education levels, and tourist activity.[19] Charleston was the most culturally sophisticated South Carolina city since it was an important colonial and antebellum city and long served as the cultural, intellectual, and financial center of the state. It undoubtedly was the most cosmopolitan because it was a port and attracted peoples with diverse cultural backgrounds. Whatever the reason, Charleston's telephone directories included advertisements for a Chinese, Italian, and Mexican restaurant in 1930 and 1940. It also had the only seafood restaurant in 1930, and this category increased to two in 1940 when another was opened in Columbia.

Post-War Developments: 1950 & 1960

The New Deal policies of the 1930s began to impact the economy and way of life in post-war South Carolina as the economic dependence on agriculture diminished. An increase of 77 percent in nonagricultural employment, for example, was accompanied by a doubling of the state's urban population between 1940 and 1960. The urban population grew from 24 percent to 41 percent during this period. In addition, per capita income rose from 38 percent of the national average in 1930 to 62 percent in 1960.[20]

These changes, especially the growing urbanism and rising prosperity, were significant to the restaurant industry. The number of restaurants advertised in the telephone directories of the three cities nearly tripled between 1940 and 1960, a rate that exceeded even the growth of the urban population. This large increase in restaurant numbers included some change in restaurant types. Most notable was the appearance of the drive-in and chain restaurant plus additional ethnic and seafood restaurants.

Drive-ins first appeared in the United States in the 1920s and paralleled the growth of the automobile industry.[21] In South Carolina, probably because of its depressed economy, drive-ins did not become popular until the post-war period. Their number increased significantly, and drive-ins accounted for over 18 percent of all restaurants in the three cities by 1960. Foods, normally served by carhops, usually were of the short-order variety and sandwiches, primarily the hamburger, reigned supreme.

Chain restaurants—such as White Castle, the A & W Root Beer stands, and Howard Johnson restaurants—which appeared as early as the 1920s in other parts of the United States also were late to develop in South Carolina.[22] Only one, the Toddle House at Columbia, was listed in the 1940 and 1950 telephone directories. Their number increased to ten by 1960 and included four Howard Johnson restaurants, three Toddle House restaurants, two A & W Root Beer stands, and a Morrison's Cafeteria. These early chains accounted for only about two percent of the urban restaurants in 1960 and served familiar standard American or local foods.

Racial segregation, a distinctive element of the cultural geography of
the South, was apparent in South Carolina's urban restaurant scene in
1950 and 1960. Blacks, who were denied service in restaurants that catered to whites prior to the Civil Rights Act of 1964, patronized restaurants advertised as "colored restaurants" in the telephone directories.
There were eighteen in 1950 and only ten in 1960. This does not mean
that these were the only restaurants which served blacks exclusively.
Some of those counted in the "others" category more than likely served
only black customers. These advertisements, however, may indicate that
urban blacks also were beginning to experience a growing prosperity
and that a black middle class was emerging.

While the number of ethnic restaurants increased from three to seventeen between 1940 and 1960, their proportion of total restaurants
remained small at only about 2 percent. Italian cuisine was the most
popular with eleven establishments, far outnumbering the three Chinese restaurants which ranked second. Charleston had ten ethnic restaurants in 1960 and continued to rank first among the three cities. It
also offered the greatest variety of ethnic cuisines with six Italian and
one each serving Chinese, Mexican, French and Kosher. Columbia had
five ethnic restaurants, four Italian and one Chinese, while Greenville
had one Italian and one Chinese restaurant. This contradicts Zelinsky's
generalization, supported by Pillsbury, that the Chinese restaurant may
have been "the pioneer species" of ethnic restaurants in most metropolitan areas.[23] When South Carolinians experimented with ethnic cuisines,
they were most likely to choose Italian. Seafood restaurants remained a
minor type in 1960 and comprised less than 2 percent of all restaurants.
Furthermore, there did not seem to be a significant demand for seafood
away from the coast since nine of the ten restaurants were in Charleston.

The greatest growth in restaurant numbers occurred in the "others"
category and, when combined with barbecue restaurants, those which
served traditional foods accounted for at least three-fourths of all restaurants in 1960. The paucity of ethnic and seafood restaurants indicates a
relatively minor acceptance of these foods, and that food preferences in
South Carolina had not undergone any fundamental change even
though the sizeable increase in restaurant numbers meant that more
meals than ever were consumed away from home. The vast majority of
the new urban residents were from rural South Carolina and Taylor
noted that while urban life forced some changes on Southerners, their
rural habits resisted change and southern food tended to remain distinctive.[24] Furthermore, Hooker claimed that even after World War II the
South continued to cling to its established food habits. He listed pork,
cornbread, grits, molasses, and a variety of vegetables such as turnips,
collards, mustard and poke greens, and field peas boiled in fatback as
mainstays. Soft drinks and tea, drunk year-round in the South, were pop-

ular beverages.[25] The establishment of the drive-in, however, does reveal that some of modern America's foodways were being assimilated. In addition, the limited development of the chain restaurant indicates that South Carolina had entered the national marketing system of standardized restaurant foods and restaurant landscapes.

Homogenization: 1970 & 1984

Developments of the immediate post-war period fueled the economy, the pace of change intensified, and the way of life in South Carolina became more like the rest of the country than ever before. The state's population grew by 20 percent between 1970 and 1980 which exceeded the national growth rate of 11 percent. Important to this growth was the rise in nonagricultural employment. It more than doubled, and 70 percent of the new jobs between 1960 and 1980 were in service-producing activities. Growth was most significant in the metropolitan areas, accounting for 60 percent of the total population, and suburbs flourished. Minicities, including factories, subdivisions, regional shopping malls, strip development, and office malls, materialized in the suburban fringe. For most South Carolinians these changes were accompanied by a steady rise in their standard of living as per capita income reached 77 percent of the 1980 national average.[26]

Changes in the restaurant industry matched and even exceeded these developments. Increased employment among both men and women, more disposable income, and the large urban-suburban population combined to create a greater market and demand for restaurants. The number of restaurants in the three cities exploded between 1970 and 1984 with an increase of nearly 60 percent which more than doubled the metropolitan population growth of 24 percent for the 1970–1980 period. Not only was there a tremendous increase in restaurant numbers, but there was a significant change in restaurant types, which indicates that food preferences had undergone a transformation.

The most notable change was the emergence of the chain restaurant. Franchise operations flourished after 1960, increasing to 20 percent of all restaurants in 1970 and to 34 percent by 1984. Chain restaurants became popular because of fast service, low cost, standardization of product, and an increasing reliance on the automobile as South Carolinians adopted a more urban-suburban lifestyle. While individual chains are associated with standardized and limited menus, these restaurants collectively offer an almost bewildering variety of foods and new products are constantly being introduced as they struggle to maintain or improve their market share. Hamburgers and chicken are the most popular fast-food fare but steaks, seafood, health foods, trendy upscale foods invariably served in stores with brass and fern decor, and a growing diversity of ethnic foods have been franchised.

Chain restaurants, therefore, have had a significant impact on food preferences. With their convenience, individual uniformity, national advertising campaigns, and acceptance as safe places to eat, chain operations encouraged a greater willingness among South Carolinians to experiment with foods alien to their traditions. Many foods commonplace in urban South Carolina today were limited to those with a sophisticated palate only a few years ago. The change came thanks to the franchises and such offerings as pasta Alfredo, fajitas, and croissants.

Along with the rise of franchise operations was a proportional decline in restaurants that served traditional foods. Establishments classified as "others" and barbecues increased in absolute numbers but proportionally declined from about 75 percent of the total to 47 percent since 1960. The recent movement of chain restaurants into central city locations and their inclusion of breakfast menus created severe competition for traditional restaurant types. Drive-through windows and the locational strategies of franchise stores, along major traffic arteries, also affected drive-in restaurants. The number of drive-ins steadily declined from 96 in 1960 to 29 in 1984. The decline in drive-ins and such traditional restaurant types as the cafe, lunchroom, and grill has been so great that they have become, in some instances, fashionable places to eat.

The best evidence of the change in food preferences, however, is the surge in ethnic restaurants. A comparatively minor type through 1970, led by the growing popularity of Italian cuisine, ethnic restaurants quintupled by 1984. Although Zelinsky did not include chain restaurants in his study of ethnic cuisines, and gourmets disdain these establishments, franchised ethnic foods introduced legions of South Carolinians to nontraditional foods. The Pizza Hut chain, for example, no doubt influenced the general acceptance of ethnic foods in South Carolina since it periodically offered several different Italian entrees besides pizza.[27] Because chain restaurants were perceived as safe places to eat, customers likely experimented with other menu items. Similarly, most South Carolinians ate their first Mexican food at a franchise store. These experiences undoubtedly furthered culinary exploration at independently owned restaurants and with other ethnic cuisines.

Chinese restaurants benefited most from this growing enthusiasm for ethnic cuisine. The five restaurants in 1970 indicate that Chinese food was not widely consumed in South Carolina, but growth since has been spectacular. Chinese surpassed Italian as the leading ethnic restaurant type with 58 stores in 1984. Factors such as low cost, the entrepreneurial skills of the Chinese, and the military experience in East Asia undoubtedly accounted for some of this growth.[28] But this tardy and mercurial growth in South Carolina was probably more the result of a recently developed market for nontraditional foods. French, Greek, and German restaurants were less popular but add significantly to the variety of foods available in South Carolina cities.

Seafood restaurants also reflect a change in food preferences among South Carolinians. While a relatively minor type as late as 1960, they accounted for 8 percent of all restaurants in 1984. Not only did the number of seafood restaurants increase, but they gained a wider distribution throughout the state. Nine of the ten establishments were situated in Charleston as late as 1960 and none existed in Greenville. In 1984, however, more than one-half were outside the coastal city.

Conclusion

The increase in restaurant numbers and sales in South Carolina corresponds to the transformation of the state's economy and lifestyle. Restaurant dining was much more common for other Americans than it was for South Carolinians before World War II and even into the 1960s. As the state moved away from its traditional agricultural way of life and depressed economy toward a more prosperous urban industrial orientation, eating-out became more popular. By the early 1980s, restaurant dining was almost as commonplace in South Carolina as it was in the nation. Also, the change in restaurant types illustrates that food preferences are more similar to mainstream America than ever before. The rise of the drive-in in South Carolina after World War II signalled the acceptance of some of modern America's foodways. But, it was not until the 1970s and early 1980s with the widespread establishment of chain, ethnic, and even seafood restaurants that food preferences changed significantly among South Carolinians. There is little question that the restaurant has become a more prominent feature in the cityscapes of South Carolina and that dining out, as well as eating a greater variety of foods, has become part of the South Carolinian lifestyle. In both respects, South Carolina is more like the rest of the United States today than it was fifty years ago.

Notes

1. For two good accounts concerning the threat to southern identity see: Rupert Vance, "The Sociological Implications of Southern Regionalism," *Jour-*

nal of Southern History, 26 (February, 1960), pp. 44–56 in John Shelton Reed and Daniel Joseph Singal (eds.), *Regionalism and the South: Selected Papers of Rupert Vance* (Chapel Hill: The University of North Carolina Press, 1982), pp. 208–10 and John Egerton, *The Americanization of Dixie: The Southernization of America* (New York: Harper's Magazine Press, 1974). Perhaps the most cited work concerning the uniqueness of the South is John Shelton Reed, *The Enduring South: Subcultural Persistence in Mass Society* (Lexington, MA: D.C. Heath, 1972). A selection of studies by Reed pertaining to southern identity include "Below the Smith and Wesson Line: Reflections on Southern Violence," in *Perspectives on the American South,* Vol. 1, edited by Merle Black and John Shelton Reed. New York: Gordon and Breach Science Publishers, 1981, pp. 9–22; *One South: An Ethnic Approach to Regional Culture* (Baton Rouge: Louisiana State University Press, 1982); and *Southern Folk, Plain and Fancy: Native White Social Types.* Mercer University Lamar Memorial Lectures. No. 29 (Athens: The University of Georgia Press, 1986).

2. Norval D. Glenn and J.L. Simmons, "Are Regional Cultural Differences Diminishing?" *Public Opinion Quarterly,* 31 (Summer 1967), p. 193; John Shelton Reed, "The Same Old Stand," in *Why the South Will Survive,* edited by Clyde N. Wilson. Athens: The University of Georgia Press, 1981, p. 20; William C. Havard, "The Distinctive South: Fading or Reviving?" Ibid., p. 36.

3. Wilbur Zelinsky, "The Roving Palate; North America's Ethnic Restaurant Cuisines," *Geoforum,* 16(1) (1985), p. 51.

4. John A. Jakle, "Roadside Restaurants and Place-Product-Packaging," *Journal of Cultural Geography,* 3 (Fall/Winter, 1982), pp. 76–93; Michael Roark, "Fast Foods: American Food Regions," *North American Culture,* 2 (1) (1985), pp. 24–36; Zelinsky, footnote 3, pp. 51–72; and Richard Pillsbury, "From Hamburger Alley to Hedgerose Heights: Toward a Model of Restaurant Location Dynamics," *The Professional Geographer,* 39 (August, 1987), pp. 326–44.

5. Some local libraries archive old directories, but their collections often are not chronologically complete. Data for this study was gathered from eighteen telephone directories. Directories for each of the three cities were available for the years 1950, 1960, 1970, and 1984. But, directories for 1930 and 1940 were found only for Columbia. The 1934 and 1941 directories provided data for Charleston, and data for Greenville were gathered from 1933 and 1937 directories.

6. Pillsbury, footnote 4, p. 327.

7. *The 1984 Directory of Chain Restaurant Operators* (New York: Business Guides Inc., 1984).

8. D. Daryl Wyckoff and W. Earl Sasser, *The Chain Restaurant Industry* (Lexington, MA, Lexington Books, 1978), p. xxxi.

9. Richard J. Hooker, *Food and Drink in America: A History* (Indianapolis: The Bobbs-Merrill Company, Inc., 1981), p. 336.

10. Charles F. Kovacik and John J. Winberry, *South Carolina: A Geography* (Boulder, CO: Westview Press, 1987), pp. 133–34, 159–61, and 181–82.

11. Rupert Vance, "Cotton Culture and Social Life and Institutions of the South," *Publications of the American Sociological Society,* 23 (1929), pp. 51–59 in Reed and Singal, footnote 1, p. 20.

12. Vance, footnote 11, pp. 21–22.

13. John Egerton, *Southern Food: At Home, on the Road, in History* (New York: Alfred A. Knopf, 1987), p. 31

14. Joe Gray Taylor, *Eating, Drinking, and Visiting in the South: An Informal History* (Baton Rouge: Louisiana State University Press, 1982), p. 126 and Egerton, footnote 13, p. 31.

15. Taylor, footnote 14, pp. 125–26.

16. Egerton, footnote 13, p. 35.

17. Egerton, footnote 13, p. 67–68.

18. Zelinsky, footnote 3, pp. 59–60.

19. Zelinsky, footnote 3, p. 68.

20. U.S. Bureau of Labor Statistics, *Employment and Earnings, States and Areas, 1939–1978.* Bulletin 1370–13 (Washington, DC: 1979), p. 589 and U.S. Bureau of the Census, *Historical Statistics of the United States, Colonial Times to 1970.* Part 1 (Washington, DC: 1975), pp. 34, 245.

21. Hooker, footnote 9, p. 327 and Jakle, footnote 4, p. 77.

22. Hooker, footnote 9, p. 354.

23. Zelinsky, footnote 3, p. 71 and Pillsbury, footnote 4, p. 333.

24. Taylor, footnote 14, p. 149.

25. Hooker, footnote 9, pp. 338–42.

26. Kovacik and Winberry, footnote 10, pp. 134–37, 181–92, and 203–4.

27. Pizzerias, chain or independent, were not counted as ethnic restaurants because of their limited menus. But, establishments that featured pizza and offered other Italian entrees were included as ethnic restaurants.

28. Zelinsky, footnote 3, pp. 60–64 and Pillsbury, footnote 4, p. 332.

16

The Geography of Food in Eastern Oklahoma: A Small Restaurant Study

John A. Milbauer

Geographers have long studied the phenomena that give character to the regions of the world. Food certainly adds to the personality of a place; what would Mexico be like without tortillas, Italy without pasta, or East Asia without rice? Until recently, American geographers have devoted little attention to the eating and drinking habits of their country. Lately, however, this indifference has been eroding. Included among the topics recently studied by geographers are rice consumption, regional preferences of fresh produce, fast-food eateries, the location of ethnic eating places, restaurant location dynamics, and restaurant history (Shortridge and Shortridge 1983, 1988; Roark 1985; Zelinsky 1985; Pillsbury 1987; Kovacik 1988). Still largely uninvestigated are the menus of indigenous neighborhood-type eating places that cater to culture-bound communities (Zelinsky 1985). What follows is an attempt to fill that void.

Eastern Oklahoma (Figure 1) is a culturally conservative land of small towns and rural landscapes. The population consists of an Anglo majority and a sizeable Native American component, mostly Cherokee north of the Arkansas River and Choctaw to the south of it. Other minorities are few, with the exception of a significant black element in the southern part of the region. Some authorities have recognized eastern Oklahoma as part of the South (Vance 1932; Gastil 1975), more specifically the predominantly white Upland South (Zelinsky 1973; Jordan 1982; Noble 1984). Extreme southern Oklahoma, additionally, has been included in the Lowland South (Zelinsky 1973), historically a land of plan-

Reprinted by permission from *North American Culture* 6, 1 (1990), 37–52.

Figure 1

tations and numerous blacks. This locale is referred to as "Little Dixie" by scholars and residents alike (Goodman 1977; Zdorkowski and Carney 1985). The inhabitants of eastern Oklahoma perceive their region as transitional between the South, the Southwest, and the Middle West (Zelinsky 1980; Shortridge 1987).

Food is part of the overall cultural baggage of a people. Culture also includes speech, religion, architecture, and many other phenomena. This study was undertaken to ascertain the extent to which the diet of eastern Oklahoma, as revealed by small eateries, reflects the culture of the region, and how it fits into a broader cultural context. Since the inhabitants of eastern Oklahoma are first and foremost loyal Americans, just how prevalent are "American" foods and beverages? Are Southern foods popular in this peripherally Southern land? If the residents of eastern Oklahoma consider their home to be transitionally Southwestern, do they demand that region's Mexican and Texas-Mexican foods in their local cafes? Are other ethnic cuisines present? Are faddish foods and dietary trends finding any acceptance at all among this conservative population?

Methodology consisted of analyzing menus and administrating a questionnaire in 65 randomly selected restaurants in 13 counties in eastern Oklahoma. The questionnaire dealt with items not expressly stated in the menus, such as daily and weekly special plates and seasonal foods. These eateries, located both in towns and on highways, were unpretentious and catered largely to a local clientele. The region has its ethnic, trendy, ostentatious, and fast-food restaurants. I excluded these from the study, however, since my objective was to learn something of indigenous foodways.

American Foods

Nonregional "American" foods, not surprisingly, are ubiquitous in eastern Oklahoma. To be sure, it is not easy to determine just what belongs in this category, since the literature of the nation's alleged eating habits often deals with scarce, regional, and even ethnic dishes. Despite this, the aliments discussed below are recognized as part of our culinary heritage (Stewart 1954; *American Heritage Cookbook*. . . . 1969; Brown 1968; Root and de Rochemont 1976; Levenstein 1988).

Breakfast includes such national favorites as fried eggs, omelets, toast, pancakes, waffles, oatmeal, and dry cereal. Beefsteaks, hamburgers, and frankfurters are served later in the day. The ketchup bottle is ever present, if sometimes hidden from view. Sandwiches abound, including the indigenous peanut-butter-and-jelly variety. Cooks attempt to satisfy the voracious American appetite for potatoes; they appear in baked, mashed, french fried, hash browned, and other forms, including potato chips. Other common vegetables include peas, carrots, and green beans. Salads are popular, and fresh fruit is served in season. Beverages include coffee, tea, milk, soft drinks, and fruit juices. Coffee is clearly the preferred hot drink, in compliance with national tradition. Ice cream and various pies are nearly universal desserts. One can justifiably assert that the above foods and beverages are as American as any, and they are readily obtainable in all parts of the United States.

Southern Foods

The South has long been known for its unique cuisine, which been recognized by many authorities (Vance 1932; Hibben 1946; McGill 1949; Botkin 1949; Cussler and DeGive 1952; Hilliard 1969, 1972; Walter 1971; Hart 1976; Newton 1977; Smith 1942; Kovacik 1988; Shortridge and Shortridge 1989).

Southern cookery is not uncommon in eastern Oklahoma (Table 1). Fried chicken, an old Southern favorite, was served regularly in 89 percent of the establishments visited. Eighty-two percent of the restaurants

TABLE 1

Major Southern Foods and Beverages

Served Regularly in the

Small Restaurants of Eastern Oklahoma

(n-65)

	No.	%		No.	%
pork (all forms)	53	82	black-eyed peas	22	34
fried chicken	5	89	sweet potatoes	2	3
chicken-fried steak	53	82	okra	42	65
barbecue	53	82	salad greens	2	38
catfish	51	78	pecan pie	35	54
corn	37	57	iced tea	62	95
cornbread	31	48	biscuits/white gravy*	46	85
hushpuppies	17	26	hominy grits	2	3
buttermilk	12	18			

SOURCE: Field survey, 1988. Percentages are rounded to the nearest whole number.

*Biscuits and white gravy are largely a breakfast food, and the statistics given here are derived from the 54 restaurants that serve breakfast.

offered pork in various forms, including bacon, pork sausage, pork chops, ham, and hamsteak. By contrast, red-eye gravy, often served with ham in the South, was totally absent. Chicken-fried streak and barbe-cued meat exhibited the same relative frequency as pork. Barbecue in eastern Oklahoma could be either beef or pork, whereas in the Deep South it is usually the latter. Catfish appeared in 78 percent of the re-gion's eateries. It was usually served as a catfish dinner, or as a "fish sandwich"; unidentified fish in eastern Oklahoma is catfish.

Favorite vegetables of the South manifested the following relative oc-currences: fried okra, 65 percent; corn, 57 percent; and black-eyed peas, 34 percent. Sweet potatoes, a favorite of the South, appeared in only two restaurants. Salad greens (the leaves of mustard, turnip, pokeweed, and similar plants boiled in pork fat with seasoning) were available in 38 percent of the area's eateries. Hominy grits were prepared on a regular basis in two restaurants, one in Leflore County and the other in McCur-tain County. In addition, nine restaurants occasionally served the item. Still others received requests for hominy grits, although they did not offer them. Eastern Oklahoma apparently lies immediately beyond the "grits line," which demarcates the Deep South with its abundant hom-iny grits (Marshall 1978).

Nearly half of the eating places visited served cornbread, which was prepared without sugar in conformity with Southern tradition. Hush-puppies, often eaten with catfish, exhibited a relative frequency of 26 percent. Biscuits and white (cream, milk, thickening, sawmill) gravy, popular on Southern breakfast tables, were obtainable in 85 percent of the restaurants that served the morning meals.

Pecan pie is a favorite Southern dessert and is served in more than half of the region's eateries, either all year or during the holiday season only. Cafe proprietors stated it would be more common if its ingredients were less costly. Sweet potato pie, relished in the Deep South, was not encountered.

Most establishments serve iced tea. In eastern Oklahoma iced tea is drunk in equal quantities at all times of day and in all seasons, as it is throughout the South. Buttermilk, traditional in the South, occurs in 18 percent of the study's eateries. None of the restaurants examined served alcoholic beverages, which complies with Oklahoma's Southern tradi-tion of low availability and consumption of intoxicating drink (Smith 1982).

In order to learn if there were any regional preferences for Southern foods within the study area, the section north of the Arkansas River was designated as Northeast Oklahoma, and the area South of the river was referred to as Southeast Oklahoma (Figure 2). Contrasting relative fre-quencies for the two subregions are shown in Table 2.

Cornbread and black-eyed peas are customarily eaten together, and

TABLE 2

**Regional Food Preferences
in Eastern Oklahoma**

	Northeast	Southeast
	(percent)	
salad greens	31	47
hushpuppies	20	33
cornbread	12	77
black-eyed peas	9	63

the two are often served in the same restaurant in this area. Figure 2 graphically illustrates the availability of cornbread and black-eyed peas and the fondness of Southern foods in Southeast Oklahoma, which merits its sobriquet of Little Dixie.

Ethnic Foods

Mexican and Texas-Mexican

Mexican cuisine originated south of the border, but like many ethnic foods in the United States, it has been altered considerably. Texas-Mexican ("Tex-Mex") cuisine, by contrast, has been referred to as a "native foreign food" that developed in Texas with alien (Mexican) inspiration (Root and de Rochemont 1976). No clear distinction exists between the two related traditions, since foods that have been recognized as Texas-Mexican, such as tacos, chiles rellenos, and wheat tortillas (Brown 1968), are considered Mexican in states other than Texas. Chili, apparently a product of Texas and not Mexico (Ramsdell 1959; Brown 1968; Root and de Rochemont 1976), was obtainable in most of the restaurants surveyed (Table 3). It was served "straight" (nothing added), with beans, with corn chips ("chili pie"), on hamburgers and frankfurters, and in other ways. Only two places offered fajitas, a recent Texas-Mexican introduction (Arreola 1987). Foods of these two

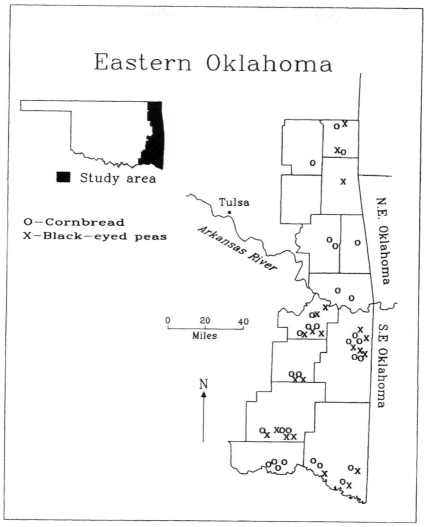

Figure 2

overlapping groups displayed the following frequencies: burritos, 42 percent; pinto beans, 38 percent; "Spanish" omelet, 32 percent; and taco and derivatives (taco salad, taco burger), 28 percent. Also present were tostadas, enchiladas, tamales, chiles rellenos, nachos, jalapeño peppers, chalupas, and tiquitos.

Chili and pinto beans have been present in eastern Oklahoma for

TABLE 3

Mexican and Texas-Mexican Foods

Served Regularly in the

Small Restaurants of Eastern Oklahoma

(n=65)

	No.	%		No.	%
chili (all forms)	62	95	chile relleno	3	5
pinto beans	25	38	nachos	6	9
burrito	27	42	Spanish omelet	21	32
taco (and derivatives)	18	28	Mexican special	9	14
tostada	3	5	fajita	2	3
enchilada	6	9	jalapeño pepper	8	12
tamale	3	5	chalupa	1	2
tiquito	1	2			

SOURCE: Field survey, 1988. Percentages are rounded to the nearest whole number.

some time. The latter, also known as brown beans, are a common substitute for black-eyed peas as an accompaniment with cornbread. The remainder of the food discussed here, according to informants, has been present in eastern Oklahoma only since the 1960s. The recent arrival of Mexican and Texas-Mexican dishes might explain why they are often misspelled on menus (e.g. "Burreto," "rellano," "enchiladae," etc.). Food referred to as Mexican is becoming more common in the area and many restaurants have a separate Mexican section on their menus, while others offer a Mexican special plate or buffet once a week or so.

Other Ethnic Traditions

Foods of at least partial Italian origin are not unknown in the small eateries in eastern Oklahoma. Nine served spaghetti. Pizza appeared in the form of "pizza pocket" in three restaurants, and as a "pizza burger" in one other. Three establishments featured fried zucchini squash, two prepared lasagna, and one offered "Italian steak." Two restaurants served spaghetti and chili, a favorite of Cincinnati, Ohio (Trillin 1974; Lloyd 1983). The Native American contribution to the local fare is meager, which is rather surprising for a region with a large Indian population. Wild onion and eggs, a traditional spring meal of Southeastern Indians, were seasonally obtainable in only two restaurants. Fry bread, popular among various Indian nations (Ulmer and Beck 1951; Welsch 1971; Niethammer 1974; Mankiller 1988), was available only in one restaurant, which also served Navajo tacos. The latter are synonymous with "Indian tacos," and local Native Americans related that they are a recent introduction from the Southwest.

A few other ethnic foods were encountered. Polish sausages and British fish and chips were found in two eating places, while Polish hot dogs, Hungarian goulash, Greek gyros, and multiple-provenience pastrami[1] were offered in one cafe each.

Discussion and Conclusion

If food is merely one aspect of culture, then the fare of eastern Oklahoma's small eateries should be compatible with the overall culture of the region. By and large, this is true.

Most Southern foods and beverages are significant in the region's cafes, especially those of Little Dixie. If some items of Southern cuisine are rare or absent here, this can be ascribed to the region's location at the periphery of the South. In addition to diet, other elements of Southern culture exist in Eastern Oklahoma. In terms of speech, the area has been designated as "Highland Southern," "Mid-Southern," "Plains Southern," and "South Midland" (Guralnik 1970; Wood 1971a, 1971b). Eastern Oklahoma clearly displays a Southern affinity in terms of religion. The area is within Zelinsky's Southern religious region, in which Baptists are strongly dominant and Methodists comprise a large minority (Zelinsky 1961). The Southern folk church building is also present in the locale. The author's study of churches in Northeast Oklahoma revealed that nearly two-thirds of all church structures are of the traditional type common in the South (Milbauer 1988). Eastern Oklahoma, in addition, possesses the Southern folk cemetery (Jeane 1987; Milbauer 1989). Finally, casual observation by the author indicates that folk structures common to the South occur in the region[2] (Kniffen 1965; Glassie 1968; Lewis 1975; Meyer 1975).

The conservative nature of eastern Oklahoma is conspicuous in the region's small restaurants. Patrons expect traditional national or Southern dishes. Native American foods are not popular, possibly due to bigotry. There is little concern for current trends. The recent movement toward low-calorie meals is weak here, since only three eateries served low-calorie plates. Absent from this study were such voguish foods as rice

(Shortridge and Shortridge 1983), quiche, tofu, and sushi. Only two restaurants served fajitas, which are very much in demand from coast to coast (Arreola 1987). Of ethnic foods, only Mexican (and Texas-Mexican) have had moderate acceptance in eastern Oklahoma. Italian food has long been popular in the United States as a whole, but it is rather scarce in the region's cafes. Spaghetti is now naturalized (Jones 1975; Root and de Rochemont 1976; Zelinsky 1985), but only nine of the restaurants visited served it. Pizza might also be considered naturalized, but in its true form it was not found in this study. The author concurs with the Shortridges' assertion that the degree of receptivity of new foods are general cultural indicators (Shortridge and Shortridge 1983)—the unpopularity of new foods and dietary trends in the small restaurants of eastern Oklahoma are indicative of a noninnovative population.

The food and drink of any locale reflect the culture of the region. This is clearly the case in eastern Oklahoma.

Notes

1. Pastrami, first recorded in English 1935–1940, is derived from Yiddish pastrami, which in turn is from Romanian pastrama. The etymology of the word possibly could be traced through modern Greek and Serbo-Croatian ultimately to Turkish pastirma (*Random House Dictionary of the English Language* 1987).

2. Included among the folk structures viewed by the writer in eastern Oklahoma are single pen log dwellings, double pen frame houses, shotgun houses, Southern bungalows, pyramidal-roofed houses, I-houses, and log crib barns.

Acknowledgments

Gratitude is expressed for the financial support of the Faculty Research Committee of Northeastern State University in Tahlequah, Oklahoma. The author is especially indebted to the many waitresses and cafe proprietors who always had time to answer his questions.

References

American Heritage Cookbook and Illustrated History of American Eating and Drinking. 1969. New York: Simon and Schuster, Inc.

Areola, Daniel D. 1987. The Mexican American Cultural Capital. *Geographical Review* 77:17–34.

Botkin, B.A. (ed.). 1949. *A Treasury of Southern Folklore.* New York: Cronon Publishers.

Brown, Dale. 1968. *American Cooking*. New York: Hill & Wang.

Cussler, Margaret and de Give, Mary L. 1952. *'Twixt the Cup and the Lip: Psychological and Socio-Cultural Factors Affecting Food Habits*. New York: Twayne Publishers.

Gastil, Raymond D. 1975. *Cultural Regions of the United States*. Seattle: University of Washington Press.

Glassie, Henry. 1968. *Pattern in the Material Folk Culture of the Eastern United States*. Philadelphia: University of Pennsylvania Press.

Goodman, James M. 1977. Physical Environments of Oklahoma in John W. Morris, (ed.). *Geography of Oklahoma*. Oklahoma City: Oklahoma Historical Society.

Guralnik, David B., (ed.). 1970. Regional Dialects in the United States in *Webster's New World Dictionary*, (Front end papers, 2nd college ed.) Englewood Cliffs, N.J.: Prentice-Hall.

Hart, John Fraser. 1976. *The South*. (2nd ed.). New York: D. Van Nostrand and Company.

Hibben, Shelia. 1946. *American Regional Cookery*. Boston: Little, Brown, and Company.

Hilliard, Sam. 1969. Hog Meat and Cornpone: Food Habits in the Ante-Bellum South. *Proceedings of the American Philosophical Society* 113:1–13.

———. 1972. *Hog Meat and Hoecake: Food Supply in the Old South, 1840–1860*. Carbondale: Southern Illinois University Press.

Jeane, Gregory. 1987. Rural Southern Gravestones: Sacred Artifacts in the Upland South Folk Cemetery. *Markers* 4:55–84.

Jones, Evan. 1975. *American Food: The Gastronomic Story*. New York: E.P. Dutton & Co., Inc.

Jordan, Terry G. 1982. Traditional Rural Culture Regions of the Eastern and Central United States, map in John F. Rooney, Wilbur Zelinsky, Dean Louder, (eds.), *This Remarkable Continent: An Atlas of United States and Canadian Society and Cultures*. College Station: Texas A&M Press.

Kniffen, Fred B. 1965. Folk Housing: Key to Diffusion. *Annals of the Association of American Geographers* 55:549–577.

Kovacik, Charles. 1988. Eating Out in South Carolina's Cities: The Last Fifty Years. *North American Culture* 4(1):53–64.

Levenstein, Harvey. 1988. *Revolution at the Table: The Transformation of the American Diet*. New York: Oxford University Press.

Lewis, Peirce F. 1975. Common Houses, Cultural Spoor. *Landscape* 19:1–21.

Lloyd, Timothy Charles. 1983. The Cincinnati Chili Culinary Complex, in Michael Owen Jones, Bruce Guiliano, and Roberta Krell, (eds.). *Foodways and Eating Habits: Directions for Research*. Los Angeles: California Folklore Society.

McGill, Ralph. 1949. What's Wrong with Southern Cooking? *Saturday Evening Post* 221 (March 26, 1949):38–39;102–103;105.

Mankiller, Wilma. 1988. *The Chief Cooks*. Muskogee, Oklahoma: Hoffman Printing Company.

Marshall, Howard Wight. 1978. What Price Grits? *Pioneer America* 10(2):5–6.

Meyer, Douglas K. 1975. Diffusion of Upland South Folk Housing to the Shawnee Hills of Southern Illinois. *Pioneer America* 7:56–66.

Milbauer, John A. 1988. Rural Churches in Northeastern Oklahoma. *North American Culture* 4(1):41–52.

————. 1989. Southern Folk Traits in the Cemeteries of Northeastern Oklahoma. *Southern Folklore* 46(2):175–185.

Newton, Milton E. 1977. Sliced Tomatoes for Breakfast. *Pioneer America* 9(1):11.

Niethammer, Carolyn. 1974. *American Indian Food and Lore.* New York: Collier
Books.

Noble, Allen G. 1984. *Wood, Brick, and Stone: The North American Settlement Landscape* (2 vols.). Amherst: The University of Massachusetts Press.

Pillsbury, Richard. 1987. From Hamburger Alley to Hedgerose Heights: Toward
a Model of Restaurant Location Dynamics. *Professional Geographer* 39:326–343.

Ramsdell, Charles. 1959. *San Antonio: A Historical and Pictorial Guide.* Austin: University of Texas Press.

Random House Dictionary of the English Language (2nd ed., unabridged). 1987.
New York: Random House.

Roark, Michael. 1985. Fast Foods: American Food Regions. *North American Culture* 2(1):24–36.

Root, Waverly and de Rochemont, Richard. 1976. *Eating in America: A History.*
New York: Morrow.

Shortridge, Barbara G. and James R. 1989. Consumption of Fresh Produce in
the Metropolitan United States. *Geographical Review* 79:79–99.

Shortridge, James R. 1987. Changing Usage of Four American Regional Labels.
Annals of the Association of American Geographers 77:325–336.

————— and Barbara G. 1983. Patterns of American Rice Consumption, 1955 and
1980. *Geographical Review* 73:417–429.

Smith, Christopher J. 1982. *Alcohol Abuse: Geographical Perspectives.* Washington,
D.C.: Association of American Geographers.

Smith, Stephen A. 1984. Food for Thought: Comestible Communication and
Contemporary Southern Culture, in Edith Mayo, (ed.). *American Material Culture: The Shape of Things Around Us.* Bowling Green, Ohio: Bowling Green University Popular Press.

Stewart, George R. 1954. *American Ways of Life.* Garden City: Doubleday & Co.

Trillin, Calvin. 1974. *American Fried: Adventures of a Happy Eater.* Garden City, New
York: Doubleday and Company.

Ulmer, Mary and Beck, Samuel E., (eds.). 1951. *Cherokee Cooklore.* (n.p. Mary and
Goingback Chiltoskey).

Vance, Rupert B. 1932. *Human Geography of the South: A Study of Regional Resources
and Human Adequacy.* Chapel Hill: University of North Carolina Press.

Walter, Eugene. 1971. *American Cooking: Southern Style.* New York: Time-Life
Books.

Welsch, Roger L. 1971. We are What We Eat: Omaha Food As Symbol. *Keystone
Folklore Quarterly* 16:165–170.

Wilson, Eugene V. 1970. The Single Pen Log House in the South. *Pioneer America*
2:21–28.

Wood, Gordon R. 1971a. Dialect Contours in the Southern States, in Harold B.
Allen and Gary N. Underwood, (eds.), *Readings in American Dialectology.* New
York: Meredith Corporation.

————. 1971b. *Vocabulary Change: A Study of Variation in Regional Words in Eight of
the Southern States.* Carbondale: Southern Illinois University Press.

Zdorkowski, R. Todd and Carney, George O. 1985. This Land is My Land: Oklahoma's Changing Vernacular Regions. *Journal of Cultural Geography* 5:97–106.

Zelinsky, Wilbur. 1961. An Approach to the Religious Geography of the United States: Patterns of Church Membership in 1952. *Annals of the Association of American Geographers* 51:139–193.

———. 1973. *The Cultural Geography of The United States.* Englewood Cliffs, N.J.: Prentice Hall.

———. 1980. North America's Vernacular Regions. *Annals of the Association of American Geographers* 70:1–16.

———. 1985. The Roving Palate: North America's Ethnic Restaurant Cuisines. *Geoforum* 16:51–72.

17

From Pushcart to Modular Restaurant: The Diner on the Landscape

Joseph T. Manzo

Introduction and Purpose

Between 1945 and 1965 the shiny, streamlined diner of literature and film ruled the restaurant landscape. Data from three manufacturers indicate diners could be found throughout the country, although the greatest concentration was in the Northeast. Approximately 80% of the diners were Greek owned, and their failure rate was a low 8 to 10% compared to the national average of 70% for restaurants as a whole.[1] Today, the diner of popular image is fading. The demise of the industrial city and the growth of fast-food outlets in the suburbs have demanded new designs and styles from restaurant manufacturers and new management techniques from owners. Thus, still operating dining cars on the contemporary landscape are joined by abandoned dining cars, and modular restaurants bearing the name diner. The purpose of this paper is to explore the historic and contemporary characteristics that accounted for the diner's past success on the landscape and its current status.

Early Diners

The classic diner of popular image which first appeared in the mid 1940s did not spring full blown from the head of some restaurant entre-

Reprinted by permission from *Journal of American Culture* 13, 3 (Fall 1990), 13–21.

preneur. Rather, it was the result of an evolutionary process of design, distribution, and name changes that began in the industrial cities of New England in the late 19th century.[2] These cities, through their working class population, created a demand for quick, cheap food in convenient locations to serve their factories. The result of this demand was the lunch wagon which operated late into the night and answered the need of the factory worker for a cup of coffee and a quick bite or meal between shifts. It also served the "drinking" man on his way home in the wee hours of the morning. With a quick stop at a "dog wagon," so nicknamed because of the success of the hot dog on the menu, a man might also have ordered himself an egg sandwich with a slice of onion, or a boiled egg with a slice of buttered bread. For thirty cents, you could purchase a chicken sandwich; baked beans cost a dime.[3]

The center of diner development shifted in the early 20th century from New England to the greater New York City area. The process was more of a leap than a diffusion, and was encouraged also by the needs of industrial workers and by the growth of the temperance movement.

In these early days, "temperance wagons" prowled the streets of New York offering a nutritious, cheap meal (many times sold below cost) as an alternative to "free lunches" offered at saloons. Operating all night long, the "Owls" (a reference to the late hours they were open) soon attracted a clientele that ranged from the working class to high society. These wagons were clean, the proprietors were honest, and the price and hours of operation meshed with the needs of New Yorkers. With the onset of prohibition the specially built lunch wagons grew in number.[4]

Still in the first quarter of the 20th century the positive image of a wagon custom built for eating was replaced by a negative image through the use of old trolley cars. Since these were cheap to convert into diners they proliferated, many in rough neighborhoods. Such locations, coupled with low intensity lighting, small windows and dark interiors gave off a "dark and dirty" appearance leading the public to conclude that this was not a place for "ladies," much less for families. In fact, a bet on horse racing or the daily number could be placed in many of these cars.[5] Nonetheless, the streetcar diners were an attractive investment as money makers.

Once the wheels came off the cars the importance of location rose dramatically. In his 1928 handbook for prospective owners, diner manufacturing pioneer Jerry O'Mahony wrote, "In hundreds of cities, locations are waiting for some enterprising business man or woman. With automobile tourist traffic and freight hauling as heavy as it is today, there are locations on the main turnpike, near garages or gasoline stations."[6] Beyond the turnpike, locating near areas of continuous business was a must. Even today, the diners, with few exceptions, that are still 24 hour a day operations are located within these kinds of areas.[7]

Another pioneer in the field, Patrick J. Tierney, estimated the size of the threshold population necessary to support a 24-hour diner at five thousand people.[8] He also stressed the notion of focused population. Such locations would be proximal to railroad stations, ferryboat or steamship landing piers, freight stations, factory districts, apartment house districts or suburban traffic lines.[9] The Tierney handbook for prospective customers also states, "Experience has shown . . . the most profitable locations are those where there is 24 hour a day business."[10] In all cases, Tierney and O'Mahony promised help in finding the right location before selling any diner.

From the beginning of the early diner, builders and owners alike always considered themselves innovative and forward looking. Indicative of these perceptions were the name, materials, and styles used. The horse-drawn wagon itself went from "dog wagon" to "owl" to "dining car," and then, in 1908, the first documentable "diner," a name that would become increasingly popular. Materials changed from solid wood exteriors and interiors to steel and marble. Throughout, however, the diner was still an eatery for working-class clientele. It offered an inexpensive meal to the men on break from the local brewery, it had coffee and pie for the women on the second shift from the dress factory, and it was an oasis for the traveling salesman looking for a "home-cooked meal."

The Classic Diner

The diners built in an approximate 20-year period from 1945–65 captured the fancy of artists, authors, movie-makers and the general public.[11] The popularity of the diner seems to have rested on a combination of its outside appearance, food, and the style of management which, when combined, created an ambiance attractive to workaday Americans. The method used in examining the diner from outside to inside centered around a participant-observer approach. I settled on a "diner route" transect across New Jersey into Pennsylvania. First, the diners were photographed and catalogued. Then, hours were logged at fourteen different diners to accommodate differences in location and ownership characteristics. The purpose was to observe diner behavior and atmosphere. The number of hours logged was based on a saturation strategy, that is, until behavior and atmosphere were predictable. Unstructured interviews were also held with customers, management, manufacturers, and former "diner men." Data derived from this approach will be cited throughout as fieldwork.

Outside—The Diner on the Landscape: Past and Present

The model for the classic diner clearly was the railroad dining car. Private railroad cars for the wealthy had become legendary by the 1940s as elegant places with real flowers, carpeting, and stops for fresh strawberries. Steel construction, bullet shape, and wrap-around windows virtually defined "motion technology," symbolizing modern America on the landscape. These railroad cars clearly would be the best possible pushcart, wagon or trolley. Moreover, the price inside still fit the pocketbook of the common man who, like the majority of Americans, was smitten with the idea of the luxury of the "superchief," but could not afford the experience on a regular basis. A "Streamline Moderne" design with Art-Deco ornamentation combined modern materials such as stainless steel and formica in an efficient shape that projected the diner as a post-World War II image of technology and success (Fig. 1).[12]

The modern diner landscape is one in transition. The streamlined car of the popular imagination can still be found, but a new diner/restaurant is appearing on the scene. Many classic cars have, of late, been bricked over or incorporated into larger restaurants as dining rooms;

Figure 1 Streamline Moderne and Art Deco architecture and design give The Diner—Wilkes-Barre, Pennsylvania, its "classic" look.

game rooms are added to suit contemporary tastes. The "new diner" restaurant is linked to the past by its location on a former diner site, proprietorship by a former diner operator, and through the continued use of counter space where regular customers can gather for coffee and conversation (Fig. 2). Simultaneously, there are also attempts to create "new classic" diners as a wave of 50s and 60s nostalgia sweeps the country. The Kullman Dining Car Company has recently built two "new" classics for a corporation in the Washington, D.C. area.[13] The Howard Johnson chain is in the process of establishing a new image for its motel restaurants called "Herbie K's Diner" and a diner-disco has recently been opened in Overland Park, Kansas.[14]

The reason for this transition between the old and new diner landscape is location. The heyday of the diner was the heyday of industrial America. In the northeastern United States almost every large factory had a diner within walking distance of men and women on "break" or between "shifts." As the country moved into its postindustrial phase, factories closed—so did the diners they supported. Secondly, from post-

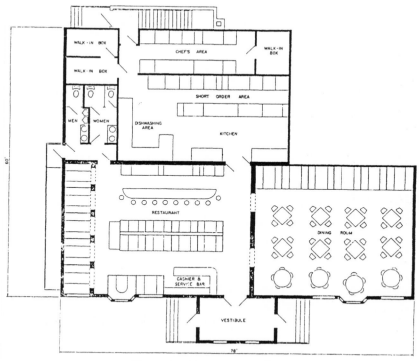

Figure 2 Diner floor plan.

WWII times through the 1960s, the diner was the restaurant to be found on the sparsely populated highways outside of the industrial city. The sparsely populated highways of then are the suburban developments of now. For example, northeastern Pennsylvania and extreme northern New Jersey are now within the commuter range of central New Jersey and Manhattan. Suburban children are more interested in fast-food chains, while parents either cannot identify with the diner or consider it to be part of the "old" neighborhood landscape and not in keeping with their new residence.

My interviews suggest that approximately 1/5 to 1/4 of the post-WWII stainless steel cars remain, primarily because of the quality of their construction. One informant, when asked how he takes care of repairs with so few manufacturers left, responded by saying, "What repairs, this thing was built to last forever."[15] Of those still around, most are on shorter operating hours in the northeastern United States. Within the next decades, as the stainless steel cars deteriorate, all that will remain of the "diner," if anything, is the name on more modern restaurants.

Inside—The Menu, the Chef, the Waitresses and the Boss: Past and Present

The diner would not have been a successful restaurant if it was only pleasing in appearance. The food and personnel contributed considerably to its success. This section outlines the contributions of each of these aspects.

From the beginning, food was an obvious attraction to diner patrons. By the time of the appearance of the classic diner the menu had evolved considerably from the days of the "dog wagon" and its limited offerings. The fare remained inexpensive, was modestly varied, and portions were generous.[16] Any food could be ordered throughout the day, but almost all diners had separate breakfast, lunch and dinner sections on the menu or marquee. Moreover, regular customers had the opportunity to "adjust menu offerings to suit their own tastes." For example, it would not have been unusual to hear a customer ask the cook, "Got any of those potatoes you had yesterday?"[17]

On the contemporary scene diners share the attribute of expanded menus including chicken, steak or duck. They may have a menu with an Italian flavor offering spaghetti, baked sausage or veal parmesan, or they may go Greek with gyros and pita bread. Meatloaf and roast turkey are standard and seafood has become more popular in the last few years.

Those with expanded dining rooms invariably have a salad bar. Prices are still reasonable and portions remain large.

Historically, in the diner business the atmosphere and service in which the food was wrapped was also an important part of the attraction. For example, breakfast was a particularly delightful time in the diner. A cacophony of sounds, smells and sights would start the customer's day. The rattling of cups and the rustling of newspapers mixed with the chatter of customers, snappy-talking waitresses and a manager greeting people provided the backdrop for the diner's food. Add to this scene a cook handling several orders at one time in full view of everyone, the smell of coffee brewing and bacon grilling and a counter lined with executives, construction workers, and truck drivers and you have industrial America starting another busy day.

These ingredients, cook, waitresses and manager, will be examined individually. A key to the success of a diner was the chef who cooked out front. This individual provided a show of culinary artistry for the customers, usually while carrying on a conversation with one or more individuals seated at the counter. It should be noted that the idea of cooking behind the counter and maintaining a successful diner business is not accidental. It is a strategy stressed by early diner manufacturers.[18] The customers could see their food being prepared and become personally acquainted with the workers (often the manager) at the same time. This setup also provided regular customers an opportunity to participate in the operation by offering a little advice, from time to time, on exactly how they may want their food prepared. For example, one customer was overheard asking "Jimmy, cook my burger very well done because my stomach has been acting up here lately."[19] Today, according to diner operators, the short-order chef is a dying occupation and the inability to find them is a threat to business.

Waitresses also interact with the customers in many ways beyond simply taking food orders. This involves general chit-chat about the weather, children, politics, or sports. More often than not the waitress is in charge of this relationship. As one customer related to Ellen Steese, "Eunice always wins . . . if you're in a rush and you tell her, she'll probably tell you to eat somewhere else."[20] Also, there is usually a snappy repartee between the chef, as field boss, and the waitresses. The language may be off-color on occasion but no one seems to mind as long as it's between them. The customer opts to listen in if he or she so desires. It should be noted that these conversations usually involve waitresses with many years experience. Thus, it is not unusual to find diners with older chefs and waitresses. Overall, an ambiance results from the closeness of quarters, the sights and the sounds.

The role of management style is also important. Despite a desire to be a part of the positive "modern" image projected by an upscale restaurant or railroad dining car, the price and style of these places would have made the working-class man and his family feel uncomfortable. Diners were different, however, and this difference was partly the result of skillful management by the boss. Building and keeping a clientele was so important to business that some diner manufacturers stressed "meeting the public" above all other aspects. As a former manufacturer stated, "You could always hire a good cook; being a good manager came first."[21] Most diner owners agree, indicating that the key to their success was not just "in the food, but also in my winning personality."[22] Good managers spent a lot of time "out front" either helping during rush hours or just "kibbitzing" with the customers.

Directly related to the personal style of the owner was and is an ethnic flavor reflective in the diner's realm of the Northeast. Traditionally, much of the humor, in this region, is based on fatherly concern and/or playful denigration of individuals, family or ethnic background. Although an examination of the records of O'Mahony, Swingle, and Mountainview indicates that a variety of European people were involved in the diner business, data indicate that most diner owners, perhaps as high as 80%, were of Greek heritage.[23] The success of the Greek management style seems to have been the result of three reasons: the seriousness which they applied to the business, the added touch of homeyness that developed in diners because family members worked there and the "openness" with which they shared their feelings and philosophy, the latter two being distinctive of southern Europeans. Taken together, individuals of southern European background accounted for approximately 90% of all diner owners.[24] For the many ethnic populations of the industrial Northeast eating at the diner provided an opportunity to dine out in a truly family atmosphere.

Fieldwork in contemporary diners indicates that management styles can be categorized as two basic types: fatherly or feigned Dutch uncle. The fatherly approach may include serving the customer personally and/or with comments such as "You look like you had a rough day" or, particularly to younger customers, "Are you getting enough sleep?"[25] From comments such as these the diner operator may launch into a lecture on the evils of burning the candle at both ends, or he may, in turning to another customer, speak of how hard it is to be young today—"not like the old days."[26] In many instances there will be no charge for either the coffee or the lecture.

The "feigned Dutch uncle" approach also fits the personality of the operator, and it is used primarily with younger and/or well known customers and only rarely in front of families or women customers as many times the boss's language may be full of double entendres and expletives deleted. It is an approach that involves an exchange of bogus insults between the boss and the customer. For example, an owner may be reading the newspaper while a customer is waiting to order. The customer may, in exaggerated form, clear his throat or call for service. The response of the diner owner will be, "I am busy, go someplace else to eat," while at the same time getting up and pouring coffee for the customer.[27] The conversation may go on with further, feigned insults heaped upon the customer. In either case, the manager is a friend to the regular customer.

As Richard Pillsbury noted, some restaurants feed the soul as well as the body.[28] The diner did both. Field interviews with diner "regulars" indicate an affinity for the diner personnel and clientele. For the crowd that gathered after the Saturday dance, the Friday night drive-in or the Tuesday bowling league, the diner was the ideal family setting, a mothering place, if you will. You could eat whatever and whenever you wanted, the management as a family surrogate was always concerned with your needs, and you were never asked to do any chores. The only people who got yelled at, generally in a humorous way, were your "adopted" family members, i.e., busboys, dishwashers, and local characters.[29] In a business run by immigrants with their outgoing but different ways, it was a place where you were accepted for yourself. In the crowded world of the city, with its impersonal nature, noises, and people on the prowl, the diner was a refuge.

Summary and Conclusion

Having been discussed both inside and out, diner aspects can be synthesized into meaningful functions for the public. For the people of the Northeast, diners were clearly meaningful. The classic diner represented a slice of American life. It served an area with a large industrial work force who, looking for a quick, cheap meal, developed a taste for eating out in modern surroundings, particularly in the post-WWII era. Satisfying this demand were innovative diner manufacturers always looking for new menu items, materials and designs that would attract a vast working-class population. Inherent in their designs, until the post-1960s, was motion—from pushcart to wagon, trolley and railroad car. This design was supported with a distinct style of management based on a personal touch and laced with a dash of ethnic flavor. Today, the diner maintains many of its traditions, but is also changing. Its menu is greatly diversified and many diner cars are now bricked or wooded over to meet contemporary taste. About 1/4 of the classic cars are still around. Fortunately then, there may still be a diner on down the road for the traveling salesman, trucker, or vacationing family who cannot find or does not want to find a pair of golden arches.

Notes

Special thanks to Mike Kelker, Swingle Dining Car Company.

1. Although diner ownership was open to all, the Greeks took advantage of the opportunity to a greater degree than did other ethnic groups. The majority of the Greek diner owners were from the island of Karpathos. These generalizations are based on data supplied by the Swingle Dining Car Company for three dining car manufacturers. It should be noted that at its peak the diner industry boasted eighteen manufacturers, most in the greater New York area. These companies were as follows: Swingle, Kulman, D'Raffele, Paramount, Silk City, Montano, Tierney, O'Mahony, Mountainview, Fodero, Musi, Sterling, Valentine, Worcester, Mano, Orange, and Masters, fieldwork, 1987. Today, one manufacturer, David Bernstien, President of Module Mobile Inc., has located in the South. *Atlanta Business Chronicle,* 4 July, 1988; Correspondence, 1988, National Restaurant Association, New York, New York.

2. Richard Gutman and Elliot Kaufman, *The American Diner.* (New York: Harper & Row Publishers, 1979), pp. 2–20.

3. Ibid.

4. Gutman and Kaufman, p. 11; Herman Feldman, *Prohibition: Its Economic and Industrial Aspect.* (New York: D. Appleton and Company, 1930), pp. 96–100; "Mug O'Java: Average Diner Check Is Twenty Cents, But It's Big Business," *The Literary Digest,* May 15, 1937.

5. Fieldwork, 1985–88. This source of information will be listed as fieldwork throughout the remainder of the paper.

6. Jerry O'Mahony, *In Our Line We Lead The World.* (Elizabeth, New Jersey: Jerry O'Mahony Co., Inc., 1928), p. 5.

7. Fieldwork.

8. Patrick J. Tierney, *The Tierney Book of Opportunity.* (New Rochelle, New York: P.J. Tierney Sons, Inc., 1924), p. 16.

9. Tierney, p. 17.

10. Ibid.

11. Robert Penn Warren, "The Patented Gate and The Mean Hamburger" in *Studies In The Short Story* (New York: Holt, Rinehart and Winston, Inc., 1968), pp. 586–596; Carson McCullers, "A Tree, A Rock, A Cloud" in *Studies In The Short Story* (New York: Holt, Rinehart and Winston, Inc., 1968), pp. 76–82; Richard Lester, Dir., "Superman II" (Hollywood, California: Warner Brothers 1980); Mel Brooks, Dir., "Space Balls" (Hollywood, California: MGM, 1987); Barry Levin, Dir., "Diner" (Hollywood, California: MGM, 1982); Barry Levin, Dir., "Tin Men" (Hollywood, California: Touchstone Pictures, 1986).

12. Bill Risenbero, *The Story of Western Architecture* (New York: Charles Scribner's Sons, 1979), p. 235.

13. Fieldwork.

14. Ibid.

15. Ibid.

16. Ibid.

17. Ibid.

18. Ibid.

19. Janice Gable, "Jim McNeely Flipped Over At the Elite of Diners in Region," *The Scrantonian,* 4 July, 1986.

20. Ellen Steese, "Day At The Diner," *The Christian Science Monitor,* 23 June, 1987.

21. Fieldwork.

22. Ibid.

23. Data were derived from the records of Swingle, Mountainview, and O'Mahony dining car companies. These records were supplied by Mike Kelker, vice president of Swingle Dining Car Company, Middlesex, New Jersey.

24. Ibid.

25. Fieldwork.

26. Ibid.

27. Ibid.

28. Richard Pillsbury, "From Hamburger Alley to Hedgerose Heights: Toward a Model of Restaurant Location Dynamics," *The Professional Geographer* Vol. 39 (August, 1987), pp. 326–344.

29. Fieldwork.

18

Fast Foods: American Food Regions

Michael O. Roark

Interest in food consumption is ancient and can be traced back to the classics of Herodotus who described ancient peoples by their primary food intake, such as ichthyophagi, fish eating. He considered such information to be of significant cultural value for understanding a society as have several modern scholars (Mirsky 1981; Anderson and Alleyne 1979). Food has been conceived of as much more than a source of nutrition for it represents cultural taste or symbol (Darby and Mason 1978; Levy 1981). However, few cultural geographers, exceptions being Hilliard and Shortridge, have studied food consumption despite its strong regional character.

How would Herodotus characterize the modern American? An answer must depend on the point in time, since American diets have been undergoing significant change in the last century as folk patterns of life have evolved into modern industrial ones. These changes have been described in national terms for such basic food categories as beef (a significant increase), poultry (an increase), pork (a major decline), dairy products (stable), sugars (an increase), and oils (an increase) (Page and Friend 1978). These changes have involved much more than simple variations in nutrient and energy levels. They have also led to new methods of preparation and new sites of consumption which increasingly are outside of hearth and home.

Fast food restaurants have been significant for many of these changes in American consumption and have been considered to be representative of new lifestyles in the country associated with the changes produced from industrialization (Lohof 1978). As Lohof has stated, not only the technology of fast food production developed but also a power-

Reprinted by permission from *North American Culture* 2, 1 (1985), 24–36.

ful cultural imperative derived from industrialization created the necessity of a quick, fast lunch fitted within the temporal dimensions of the factory lunch break. Fast foods, then, are at the center of a matrix of innovations in American culture of the twentieth century and can be considered to be more representative of contemporary American values than traditional folk foodways such as Cajun crawfish or Texas chili.

Typically, fast foods have been considered to be ubiquitous, representing the standardization of American life. The purpose of this paper is to test this supposed uniformity and to see if regional cultural divisions, which are so profound in American life from political behavior to housetypes, are not also evident in this cultural context.

Methodology

As Shortridge has indicated, a fundamental problem in the study of patterns of food consumption is the lack of data. Most governmental data is presented at the national level or in large-scale units (Shortridge 1983, 417–18). For this study the author used a data source rarely tapped, telephone directory yellow pages (Zelinsky 1980). Obviously, consumption of fast foods reflects their availability in restaurants. Exceptions would include frozen pizza and supermarket hot dogs, but these alternative sources have been in decline while restaurant fast foods have been on the increase (Chamberlain 1984).

The author counted the number of restaurants listed in 88 American metropolitan yellow page directories dated from 1977 to 1982, most of them dated after 1980. The cities in the study were selected to obtain a comprehensive national areal coverage and reflect to some degree a regional representativeness. The five categories of fast food restaurants used in the study, burgers, pizzas, chicken, barbeque, and hot dogs or frankfurters, are not all inclusive. Some fish and Mexican restaurants could also be considered to be fast foods but were excluded because many do not have fast foods.

Percentages of the five food categories were used and not per capita figures in order to allow for comparability. Since the concern in the study was to compare food preferences as expressed through restaurant availability, the relative level of food types was important. Had per capita figures been used they would have introduced serious problems for comparison since the number of fast food restaurants varied considerably for different sizes of metropolitan populations. Percentages of fast food types within each city more clearly reflects the area's taste preferences. Then, for each of the five food categories, the 88 cities were arrayed according to percentages. Lastly, the array of percentages was divided into quartiles which were chosen in order to obtain class comparability, i.e. the same number of cases in each class.

Fast Food Restaurants

An important feature about fast food restaurants in the country is their relative popularity. They account for about a third of the restaurants in America (29.4 percent being the median of the survey sample). Fast foods as a group have strong regional variations (Fig. 1). The two main regional concentrations of fast food restaurants, the industrial Midwestern states of Ohio, Indiana, Michigan, and Illinois and the South from Virginia to Texas, contrast to the relative sparsity of fast foods on the West coast, both the Pacific Northwest and California, and on the Northeastern seaboard or Megalopolis. The highest proportions of fast foods were in Columbus (48.3 percent), Dayton (44.1 percent) and Pittsburgh (40.6 percent) while the lowest cities were Washington, D.C. (7.4 percent), New York City (8.5 percent) and San Francisco (10.7 percent).

Reasons for these variations involve a number of social, economic, and cultural factors. Since fast foods derive from the process of industrialization, as Lohof has indicated, the regions of concentration, the Midwest and South, are not surprising since they have significant levels of manufacturing, particularly in the more traditional, labor intensive forms of manufacturing. Also, the South has been a center of innovation for franchising businesses with Kentucky Fried Chicken and Holiday Inns as two examples. Reasons for the lower levels of fast foods in the Northeast and on the West Coast may derive from the greater interest in health in the West and relative greater purchasing power in these regions.

Burger and Pizza Restaurants

From the survey, burgers and pizzas emerge as the primary American fast foods (Fig. 2). In all of the cities surveyed burger or pizza restaurants were in the dominant category. The number of cities in which burger restaurants were the primary type was about equal to the number in which pizza restaurants were the most significant.

The clearest regional boundary is in the eastern half of the country, between the North and the South, a division which has been traditionally identified as significant for a variety of cultural phenomena in the United States. The West is characterized by diversity with no apparent regional dominance, but with subregional concentration, such as pizza

Michael O. Roark

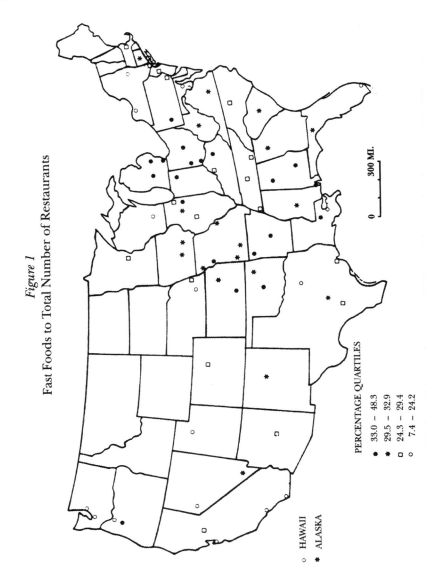

Figure 1
Fast Foods to Total Number of Restaurants

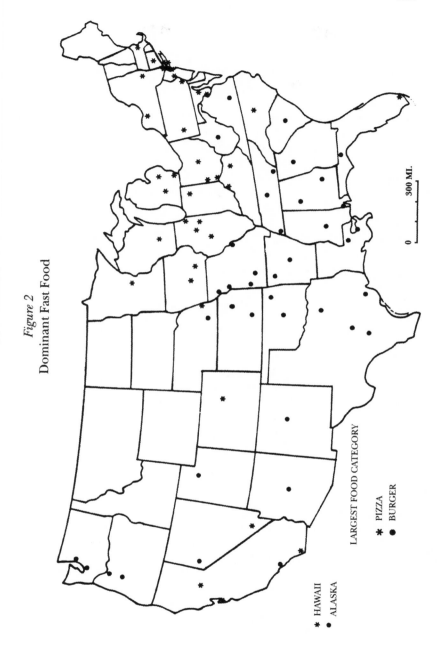

Figure 2
Dominant Fast Food

being the most significant type in the San Francisco-northern California region.

The Northern region where pizza predominates is largely the old American Manufacturing Belt which is peopled by descendants of South and East European immigrants (especially Italians). The preferred type of topping for Northeastern pizza, cheese, rather than the more common meat toppings, is closest to the traditional Italian pizza of Naples or Sicily (Chamberlain 1984, 21). This is not to say that Northeastern pizza is only eaten by people of Sicilian or Neapolitan descent since it must be accepted by a majority of the population to appear as the dominant food type.

Burger preference in the South is more problematic in terms of its origins. In the South fried foods have generally been a larger part of the folk diet and may explain to some degree this preference (Cummings 1940). But pork, not beef, has been considered to be the traditional primary meat type (Hilliard 1972). Yet, recent food studies have shown that Southern tastes have changed along with the rest of the nation. Nationally, beef consumption in the twentieth century has increased continuously while pork consumption has remained constant and in relative decline (Root and de Rochemont 1976, 192–93). A food preference study of white Memphis high school students clearly showed beef products (steak and hamburger) to be among the top foods preferred while pork products were not among the top ten (McCracken 1982).

In more detail, the East Coast Megalopolis area appears as the national core for pizza (Fig. 3). Here, the proportion of pizza restaurants varies in a rather narrow range from 80 percent on Staten Island to 60 percent in Baltimore. An area of relatively high proportions of pizza restaurants extends into the industrial Midwest with examples being Pittsburgh, Pa. (61 percent), Columbus, Ohio (60 percent) and Cincinnati, Ohio (60 percent). Yet not all Midwestern industrial cities, e.g. Fort Wayne, Indiana (46 percent) and Dayton, Ohio (48 percent), had such high percentages. The sphere of pizza preference would incorporate the West and a section of the South, the Atlantic coast and Florida. The extension of pizza preference into the Southern Atlantic states probably is related to the migration of Northeasterners to the area. Cities in the lowest quartile are almost all Southern with the exception of Los Angeles. Cities with the lowest proportion of pizza restaurants are Mobile (15.6 percent), Montgomery (18.6 percent), and Jackson (18.6 percent). Clearly, variability in pizza consumption is significant since the range from the highest to the lowest percentage is about 65 points.

The pattern of burger preference is not a simple reverse image of the pizza map (Fig. 4). It is true that the cities which were in the highest quartile of pizza restaurants (Megalopolis and the industrial Midwest) are in lowest quartile of burger restaurants, but elsewhere there are

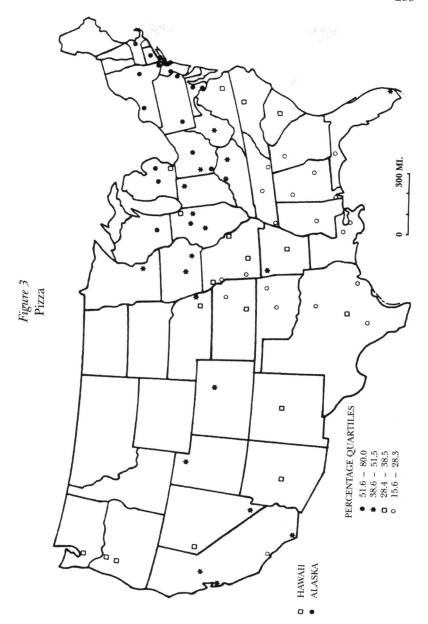

Figure 3
Pizza

PERCENTAGE QUARTILES

● 51.6 – 80.0
✳ 38.6 – 51.5
□ 28.4 – 38.5
○ 15.6 – 28.3

□ HAWAII
● ALASKA

300 MI.

0

Michael O. Roark

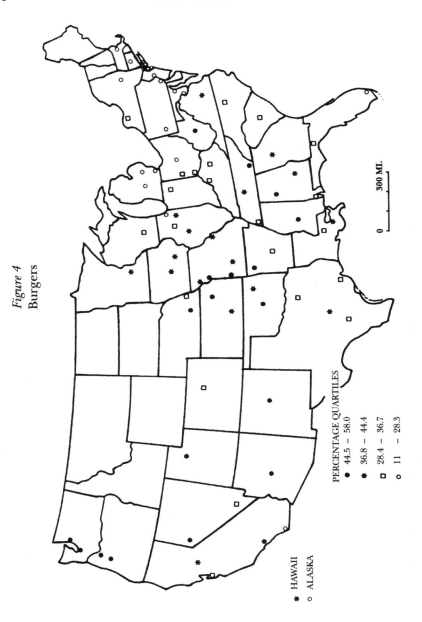

Figure 4
Burgers

PERCENTAGE QUARTILES

● 44.5 – 58.0
✳ 36.8 – 44.4
□ 28.4 – 36.7
○ 11 – 28.3

✳ HAWAII
○ ALASKA

0   300 MI.

important variations. For example, the cities having the highest national proportions are Western, i.e. Olympia (58 percent), Salem (55 percent), and Salt Lake City (50 percent). Another cluster of high proportions is in the Great Plains in such cities as Topeka (52 percent), Kansas City (49 percent), and Oklahoma City (47 percent). The Great Plains concentration may be related to the beef industry in the area. A third cluster of cities with high burger restaurant proportions is in the Gulf Southern states of Alabama and Mississippi and may derive from the apparent twentieth century beef preferences among white Southerners (McCracken 1982, 161). The range for burgers (47 percentage points) is much less than that of pizza, indicating a wider degree of acceptance in the country.

Chicken, Barbeque and Hot Dog Restaurants

The last three fast food types, chicken, barbeque, and hot dogs, are much less significant than burgers or pizza since their combined total is only around 18 percent of America's fast food restaurants. Chicken is the most important of these three types having a national median of 12.1 percent. There is a strong regional concentration in the South, particularly the Deep or Lower South and Texas (Fig. 5). Upper Southern areas such as Kentucky, east Tennessee, Missouri, and northern Arkansas have low to moderate chicken consumption. A strong preference for fried chicken apparently does not occur in Kentucky, despite Colonel Sanders. The highest proportions of chicken restaurants were found in such Deep Southern cities as Baton Rouge (34 percent), New Orleans (33 percent), and Memphis (25 percent). McCracken's food preference survey of Memphis high school students is enlightening in understanding this regional food preference (McCracken 1982). In his study black teenagers preferred chicken to all other foods while for white Memphis teenagers it was number five. Thus, this regional concentration is to some degree a reflection of the concentration of this ethnic group in the South.

This food preference may also account for the relatively high proportions of chicken restaurants in Chicago (17 percent) and Detroit (13 percent). Elsewhere in the North, both in the Northeast and Upper Midwest, there were very low percentages of chicken restaurants, with Des Moines, Iowa, having the lowest percentage in the nation (1.7 percent). Whether this minimal presence derives from ethnic factors in the Upper Midwest, such as Scandinavian and German immigrant descendants, has yet to be established. Possibly, the meat and potatoes stereotypes of these ethnic groups has some validity.

In the West there was again variability with the extremes being in Los

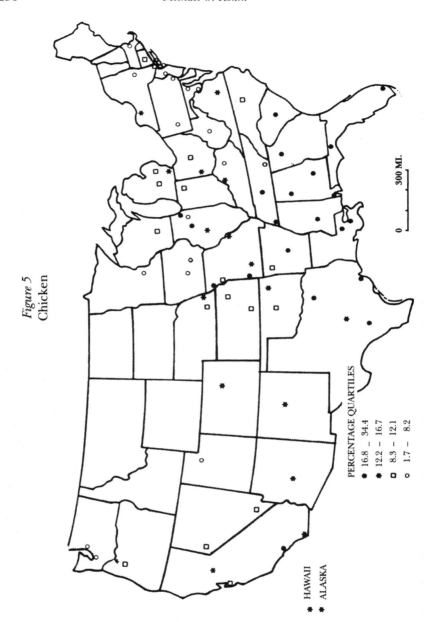

Figure 5
Chicken

PERCENTAGE QUARTILES
- ● 16.8 – 34.4
- ✳ 12.2 – 16.7
- □ 8.3 – 12.1
- ○ 1.7 – 8.2

HAWAII ✳
ALASKA ●

0   300 MI.

Angeles with 20 percent and Salt Lake City with only seven percent. What the impact of the Mexican-American or Asian populations have for the preference of this food type is unknown but could be significant. Salt Lake City's population derived from an original New England component and later additions of Scandinavian and German converts reflects the general Northern lack of interest in the food.

Barbeque is predominantly a Southern fast food with a regional concentration similar to that of chicken (Fig. 6). The highest proportions of barbeque restaurants were in Memphis (25 percent), Chattanooga (20 percent), Tallahassee (19 percent), and Dallas (16 percent). This Southern concentration may have developed from early Spanish contacts in the area since the English word is considered to be derived from the Spanish word, *barbacoa,* coming originally from the Arawak Indians. Another possible influence may have been from Africa and the black slave population. The high proportions of barbeque restaurants in cities outside the South such as Chicago (9 percent) and Los Angeles (11 percent), may have developed from Southern black migrants. Oahu's relatively high proportion of eight percent most likely originates from a Polynesian cultural legacy since contacts with the American South are few. Areas of low proportions include the Northeast, much of the industrial Midwest, and large areas of the West, such as New Mexico, Utah, and the Pacific Northwest. The Western sparsity is somewhat surprising because of a widespread image that barbeque is Western. Apparently, though, barbeque is not generally Western but rather more specific, Southwestern or Texan. Barbeque is one of the most difficult fast foods to find in the nation since the median is only 4.7 percent.

The map of hot dog restaurants does not reflect consumption patterns nearly as well as the previous maps of fast food restaurants because of rarity of restaurants that specialize in the food type (Fig. 7). With a national median of only 1.8 percent, this might be interpreted to mean low consumption throughout the country, but, of course, hot dogs are served widely, especially in burger restaurants. Also, in some parts of the country hot dogs are not sold in a permanently constructed restaurant but by streetside vendors. This is especially the case in the Northeastern Megalopolis. With these factors to consider there appears to be three areas of concentration of hot dog restaurants, the industrial Midwest, the Gulf South, and the West. Cities with the highest percentages are Mobile (17 percent), Tulsa (14 percent), Chicago (12 percent) and Detroit (12 percent).

Conclusion

Fast foods have significant regional variation in the country, contrary to the supposed belief of ubiquity. Many of the historic culture areas, such

Michael O. Roark

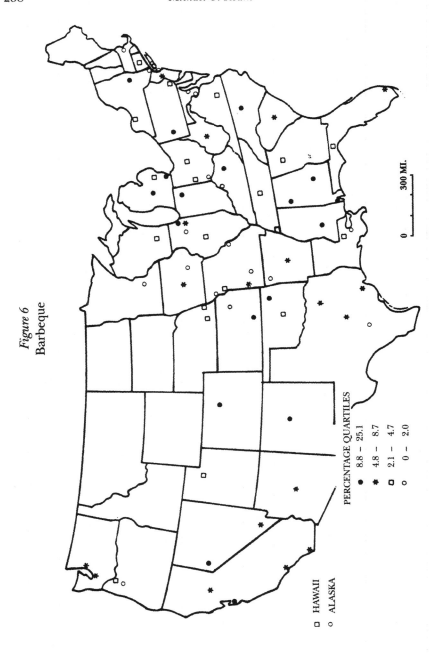

Figure 6
Barbeque

PERCENTAGE QUARTILES

● 8.8 – 25.1
✳ 4.8 – 8.7
□ 2.1 – 4.7
○ 0 – 2.0

□ HAWAII
○ ALASKA

300 MI.

0

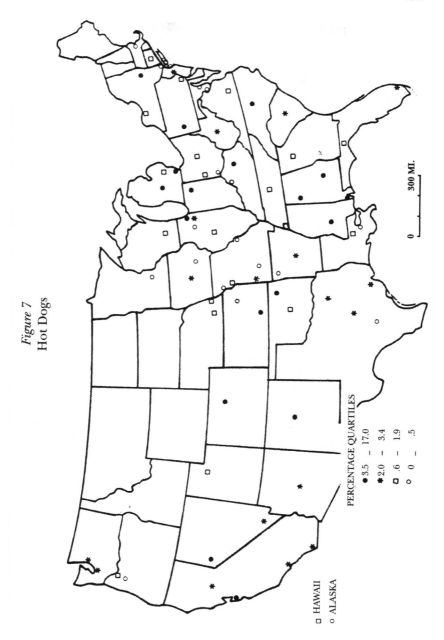

Figure 7
Hot Dogs

PERCENTAGE QUARTILES

● 3.5 – 17.0
✳ 2.0 – 3.4
□ .6 – 1.9
○ 0 – .5

□ HAWAII
○ ALASKA

300 MI.

0

as the North and South in the eastern part of the country, reappear as fundamental break points for this popular cultural phenomenon. The North-South divide was significant for almost all of the food types. The South appears to be the most distinctive food region in the country, especially for chicken and barbeque, while the North is unique for its strong pizza dominance. The West has no clear overall distinctiveness but appears as a set of discrete subregions, lending credence to Meinig's interpretation of several Wests in the West (Meinig 1972).

The most substantial problem in the study was the simple lack of literature on contemporary food trends for ethnic groups in the country. Much more work must be accomplished before there can ever be any definitive statements on American food regions and my explanations must be interpreted in this context. The complex regional interactions of class, life cycles, ethnicity, and marketing strategies have only been sketched for this consumption behavior. Yet, the benefits of continued research in food studies could be immense for cultural understanding and practical application.

References

Anderson, Grace and J. M. Alleyne, "Ethnicity Food Preferences and Habits of Consumption as Factors in Social Interaction," *Canadian Ethnic Studies,* 11(1), 1979, p. 83–87.

Chamberlain, Ross, "National Preferences Shift as Pizza Slices Off the Fairway," *Quick Frozen Foods,* July, 1984, p. 20–27.

Cummings, Richard O., *The American and His Food: A History of Food Habits in the United States,* Chicago: University of Chicago Press, 1940, p. 11–12.

Darby, William and Karl Mason, "Cultural Food Patterns and Nutrition," *Bioscience,* Vol. 28(3), 1978, p. 159.

Hilliard, Sam B., *Hog Meat and Hoecake: Food Supply in the Old South, 1840–1860,* Carbondale: Southern Illinois University Press, 1972.

Levy, Sidney, "Personal Narratives: A Key to Interpreting Consumer Behavior," *Western Folklore,* 40(1), 1981, p. 94–106.

Lohof, Bruce, "Hamburger Stand: Industrialization and the American Fast Food Phenomenon." *Industrial Archaeological Review,* 2(3), 1978, p. 265–276.

McCracken, Robert, "Cultural Differences in Food Preferences and Meanings," *Human Organization,* 41(2), 1982, p. 161–167.

Meinig, D. W., "American Wests: Preface to a Geographical Interpretation." *Annals, Association of American Geographers,* Vol. 62(2), 1972, p. 159–184.

Mirsky, Richard, "Perspectives in the Study of Food Habits," *Western Folklore,* 40(1), 1981, p. 125–133.

Page, Louise and Berta Friend, "The Changing United States Diet," *BioScience.* Vol. 28(3), 1978, p. 192–197.

Root, Waverly and Richard de Rochemont, *Eating in America: A History*, New York: W. Morrow & Co., 1976.

Shortridge, James and Barbara Shortridge, "Patterns of American Rice Consumption 1955 and 1980," *Geographical Review*, 73, 1983, p. 417–429.

Zelinsky, Wilbur, "North America's Vernacular Regions." *Annals, Association of American Geographers*, 70 (1980), p. 1–16.

19

You Are Where You Eat

Wilbur Zelinsky

The diners at ethnic restaurants don't go just for the food. They also hunger for an exotic dining experience. Ethnic restaurants offer an effortless journey to a distant land where the waiter recites a menu of alien delights in charmingly accented English. The patrons of ethnic restaurants are gastronomic tourists.

Ethnic restaurants have become one of the hottest segments of the food service industry over the last decade, and recent changes in immigration patterns can only partially explain the sudden, rapid rise in their diversity and popularity. It's a global trend—ethnic foods are hot in Europe, Japan, Canada, and other countries.

Overall, restaurant traffic in the U.S. increased 10 percent between 1982 and 1986, according to the National Restaurant Association/CREST panel survey. But business increased 26 percent for Italian restaurants during those years, 43 percent for Mexican restaurants, and fully 54 percent for Asian restaurants. Clearly, Americans are on a global eating binge.

But the implications of the trend go far beyond restaurants. A preliminary investigation of the number, type, and distribution of ethnic restaurants in America cities shows that they are leading indicators of an internationalized urban culture.

Reprinted by permission from *American Demographics* 9, 7 (July 1987), 30–33. © 1987 American Demographics.

THE ROVING PALATE

Chinese, Italian, and Mexican cuisines account for almost 70 percent of the ethnic restaurants in North America, but dozens of contenders are emerging.

(ethnic and regional restaurant cuisines in 271 U.S. and Canadian metropolitan areas, 1980*)

	number of metropolitan areas with restaurants serving this cuisine	*number of restaurants serving this cuisine*
European		
Total	267	10,461
Italian	259	5,530
Northern Italian**	46	106
Neapolitan**	12	32
Sicilian**	13	26
French	156	1,408
Continental and International	173	1,139
Greek	137	575
German	144	479
Austrian**	26	40
Bavarian**	25	33
Jewish	81	286
Spanish	58	266
Hungarian	38	123
English	33	94
Scandinavian	36	90
Swedish**	17	44
Danish**	11	13
Irish	30	77
Swiss	35	64
Portuguese	18	58
Polish	21	56
Yugoslav	14	39
Ukrainian	11	36
Russian	17	32
Czechoslovakian	10	30
Mediterranean	17	26
Belgian	10	12
East Asian		
Total	270	9,253
Chinese	270	7,796
Cantonese**	164	871
Szechuan**	152	658
Mandarin**	164	655
Polynesian**	128	412
Hunan**	83	223
Peking**	70	147

Shanghai**	40	75
Northern**	28	41
Hong Kong**	11	14
Japanese	160	1,083
Korean	67	165
Vietnamese	51	146
Filipino	25	63

Latin American

Total	251	5,437
Mexican	250	4,841
Cuban	21	61
West Indian-Caribbean	11	35
Argentinian	13	31
Brazilian	5	14
Peruvian	8	11

North American

Total	137	527
Soul	93	227
Southern	51	96
Creole	44	90
Cajun	23	52
Pennsylvania-German	10	27
French-Canadian	5	17
New England	9	15

South Asian

Total	71	418
Indian	52	251
Pakistani**	8	15
Thai	34	132
Indonesian	11	25

Middle Eastern

Total	87	383
Lebanese	41	68
Armenian	17	53
Arabian	19	36
Moroccan	15	31
Turkish	10	16
Persian	8	15
Israeli	7	14
Other Middle Eastern	54	120

Miscellaneous

Total	17	48
Hawaiian	7	35

*Excludes cuisines served at fewer than 10 restaurants nationwide.
**Included in category totals directly above indentation.
Source: Classified telephone directories for 1979, 1980, 1981.

As Americans have become increasingly educated and well-traveled in the past few decades, more are pursuing a variety of experiences— reaching out to other times and other places, and savoring the exotic thrills of unfamiliar cultures. Ethnic restaurants are a major component of this new lifestyle. Restaurants that cater to it use their divergence from American culture as a marketing tool. More than just places that serve "ethnic" food, they offer patrons vicarious joys, vacations to far-away places without airports or baggage. They are selling the experience of being in another country.

It takes more than ethnic food, then, to make an ethnic restaurant. A Mexican cafe in an all-Mexican section of San Antonio does not qualify, unless it attracts Anglo diners. But a Mexican restaurant in Maine would qualify automatically, as would a Chinese restaurant in a Jewish suburb of Chicago. Likewise, a coffee shop in Macon, Georgia that serves grits and sliced tomatoes with its eggs isn't ethnic to that city's residents. But if an upscale diner in the Northeast called itself "The Macon Diner" and served its eggs that way, it would be celebrating America's regional differences.

Many other kinds of businesses profit from this trend. Supermarket chains are expanding their formerly small "gourmet" sections to include weird and wonderful foreign delicacies, while Italian, Mexican, East Asian, Kosher, and other specialty foods take up large areas of shelf space in many stores. Shops that specialize in arts, crafts, and clothing from one or many areas of the globe are becoming increasingly common as are showings of foreign films. The number of annual festivals in U.S. cities has grown from 1,200 in 1950 to an estimated 3,000 today, according to Pennsylvania State University geographer Catherine Harding—and more than 530 have an ethnic theme.

Hello Central, Give Me Ethnic

In a study of ethnic restaurant cuisines, we analyzed restaurant listings in the 1979 and 1980 Yellow Pages of the 271 largest metropolitan areas in the U.S. and Canada. We also scanned Philadelphia directories at ten-year intervals between 1920 and 1980 to trace the growth of ethnic restaurants' popularity, and analyzed all directories for Pennsylvania to see how the trend extended into smaller towns and rural areas.

According to our subjective definition, a self-consciously ethnic restaurant will show its colors in one of three places: in its name, in its inclusion under an ethnic heading in a special section of the telephone directory, or by listing the specialties of the house in a display ad. The appearance of such "naturalized" items as spaghetti, onion soup, chop suey, tempura, or tamales on an otherwise American menu did not necessarily confer ethnic status on a restaurant. Similarly, pizzerias were not judged ethnic unless they included a full menu of Italian items.

We assigned each restaurant to the appropriate national or regional category within seven larger categories. In order of importance, these were European, East Asian, Latin American, North American, South Asian, Middle Eastern, and miscellaneous.

Surprisingly, a large proportion of places advertise two or more different cuisines, often in addition to an American menu. French and Italian, Spanish and Mexican, and Greek and Middle Eastern are among the more popular combinations, but some are positively mind-boggling, such as the Chicago cafe that characterizes itself as "Kosher & Soul," or this one from Cincinnati: "The Italian restaurant with the Spanish name hosted by the Jewish couple with the Greek partner featuring American steaks, French onion soup, Ecuadorian ceviche and Swiss Fondue."

We identified more than 26,500 ethnic and regional cuisines in the 271 metropolitan areas, more than 10 percent of the total number of restaurants in those places. Our limited data from Pennsylvania indicate

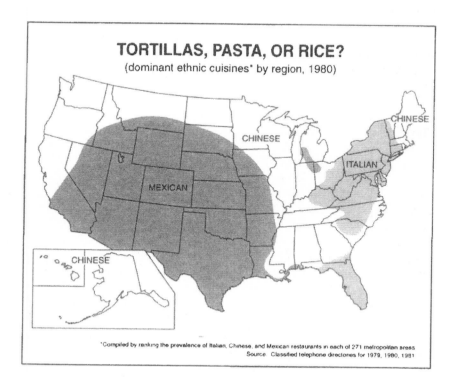

TORTILLAS, PASTA, OR RICE?
(dominant ethnic cuisines* by region, 1980)

*Compiled by ranking the prevalence of Italian, Chinese, and Mexican restaurants in each of 271 metropolitan areas
Source: Classified telephone directories for 1979, 1980, 1981

the rapid growth of the trend and its spread into nonmetropolitan areas. Philadelphia's 253 ethnic restaurants in 1980 were double the number in 1960. We also found a substantial number of ethnic restaurants in Pennsylvania's smaller cities and towns.

New York City has the most ethnic restaurants (3,033), and one metropolitan area (Steubenville-Weirton, Ohio) has none. Do ethnic foods proliferate in America's most populous and ethnically diverse metropolitan areas? To answer this question, we controlled our results for population size, dividing the number of ethnic restaurants by the total number of restaurants in each area. We found definite regional differences in the popularity of ethnic restaurants. If the acceptance of exotic cuisines is a leading indicator of a metropolitan area that has gone international, the process has advanced much further in some North American metropolitan areas than in others.

The Bicoastal Palate

Ethnic restaurants are most common in the Northeast, West, and throughout metropolitan Canada. The greatest concentration occurs in Connecticut and throughout northeastern metropolitan areas. There are fewer ethnic restaurants in the South, the Midwest, or the western reaches of the Middle-Atlantic states. Florida, Texas, and Oklahoma are notable exceptions to this rule.

Many metropolitan areas with large ethnic populations, like Detroit, Cleveland, Gary, Johnstown, Buffalo, and Utica have relatively few ethnic restaurants. But they proliferate in metropolitan areas with large volumes of tourists, such as Washington, Ottawa, New York, Miami, New Orleans, and Las Vegas. Ethnic restaurants also seem to do well in state capitals, college towns, and areas that are growing rapidly.

In general, thrill-seeking North American gourmets look for menus from Eastern and Southern Asia, the Romance lands of Europe, and portions of Latin America. They avoid the cuisines of the United Kingdom, Scandinavia, and Germany, perhaps because they are similar to standard American fare.

With few exceptions, we found no strong relationship between the relative strength of an ethnic cuisine and the distribution of most ethnic groups. Some of the minor cuisines, such as Ukrainian, Polish, Basque, Thai, Afghan, Ethiopian, or Filipino, are restricted to areas with large concentrations of immigrants. But even these—Thai and Ethiopian in particular—can grow rapidly in popularity among general restaurant clientele.

The changing characteristics of immigrants may explain the sudden rise in the diversity of ethnic offerings. In recent years, many of the half-million annual newcomers to these shores have been comparatively affluent and well-educated. Unlike earlier generations of immigrants who had to scramble up the socio-economic ladder painfully and slowly, they arrive with the skills and resources to open their own businesses. And many of the businesses they open are restaurants.

The majority of ethnic restaurants still serve European foods, but Chinese food is by far the most prevalent cuisine. Chinese restaurants accounted for 29 percent of the cuisines tallied in our study, followed by Italian (22 percent), Mexican (20 percent), French (5 percent), Continental (4.5 percent), and Japanese (4 percent) restaurants. These serve the foods that have managed to leap over ethnic and spatial barriers and burrow deeply into the Anglo palates of North America.

Chinese, Italian, and Mexican restaurants accounted for over 70 percent of all ethnic restaurants in this study, and more recent surveys by Gallup and the National Restaurant Association confirm this pattern. Obviously, many of the owners of these restaurants have only a commercial interest in the countries they promote.

Three Big Eaters

To find which cuisine dominates in each region, I ranked the popularity of Chinese, Italian, and Mexican cuisines in each metropolitan area, then compared the rankings. I found that Chinese restaurants are almost universal—they appear in every metropolitan area except Steubenville-Weirton, Ohio—but they do not dominate any one region. Their strongest showing is in Canada, northern California, the Pacific Northwest, and eastern New England.

Italian cuisines are also distributed throughout the continent, but they dominate in the Northeast, especially in a zone that runs from southern New England through New York and into western Pennsylvania. This pattern may reflect the spatial distribution of first- and second-generation Italian Americans. They also dominate in central and southern Florida, indicating that northeasterners who migrated south took their taste for Italian with them.

Mexican restaurants have developed in strength within the past two decades. Mexican food is hurtling northward and eastward at a rapid pace, thanks in part to some aggressive franchisers. By 1990, Mexican restaurants probably will be common in the Southeast and far Northeast where they are still rare today.

Japanese and French restaurants belong to a different social category than the three major cuisines listed above. They attract only well-to-do, sophisticated diners, and they are almost exclusively concentrated in the northern metropolitan areas, San Francisco, Los Angeles, and other metropolitan areas that have large populations of affluent diners.

Studies like this one hint at future opportunities for the restaurant industry. There are few restaurants that serve the marvelous diversity of regional Mexican cuisines, for example, and even fewer that emphasize the exciting cuisines of eastern and southeastern Europe. In 1980, for example, there were no Bulgarian restaurants in metropolitan North America.

This study raises more questions than it answers. Businesses need to know more about the demographic characteristics of ethnic restaurant patrons, their attitudes toward other cultures and other "international" business ventures, and their domestic cooking practices. Which urban neighborhoods are the best places for ethnic restaurants? What role do ethnic cuisines play in the burgeoning fast-food and franchise scene? The unforeseen popularity of Cajun food raises yet another question: How well is the food industry taking advantage of the fascination Americans have with their own regional diversity?

Appendix A

100 QUICKIES—FOODS

Below is a list of food and drinks. Check the appropriate space for each item.

1. I have eaten this food/drink and I like it.
2. I have eaten this food/drink and I don't like it.
3. I have heard of this food/drink but have not eaten it.
4. I don't know this food/drink.

	1	2	3	4
abalone	( )	( )	( )	( )
antipasto	( )	( )	( )	( )
apple pie	( )	( )	( )	( )
artichokes	( )	( )	( )	( )
bagels	( )	( )	( )	( )
barbecued beef	( )	( )	( )	( )
barbecued pork	( )	( )	( )	( )
bierocks	( )	( )	( )	( )
biscuits	( )	( )	( )	( )
blackberries	( )	( )	( )	( )
blintzes	( )	( )	( )	( )
blueberries	( )	( )	( )	( )
boiled peanuts	( )	( )	( )	( )
bratwurst	( )	( )	( )	( )
buttermilk	( )	( )	( )	( )
cabrito	( )	( )	( )	( )
catfish	( )	( )	( )	( )
challah	( )	( )	( )	( )
chestnuts	( )	( )	( )	( )
chitterlings	( )	( )	( )	( )
chowchow	( )	( )	( )	( )
chowder	( )	( )	( )	( )
cider	( )	( )	( )	( )
clams	( )	( )	( )	( )
Coca-Cola	( )	( )	( )	( )

	1	2	3	4
corn on the cob	( )	( )	( )	( )
corned beef	( )	( )	( )	( )
crab cakes	( )	( )	( )	( )
cracklings	( )	( )	( )	( )
crawfish	( )	( )	( )	( )
cream soda	( )	( )	( )	( )
curry	( )	( )	( )	( )
dandelions	( )	( )	( )	( )
Dr. Pepper	( )	( )	( )	( )
eggplant	( )	( )	( )	( )
frappe	( )	( )	( )	( )
French fries	( )	( )	( )	( )
frybread	( )	( )	( )	( )
gooseberries	( )	( )	( )	( )
grits	( )	( )	( )	( )
guacamole	( )	( )	( )	( )
gumbo	( )	( )	( )	( )
gyros	( )	( )	( )	( )
hamburgers	( )	( )	( )	( )
hickory nuts	( )	( )	( )	( )
home brew	( )	( )	( )	( )
hominy	( )	( )	( )	( )
hush puppies	( )	( )	( )	( )
jambalaya	( )	( )	( )	( )
jerky	( )	( )	( )	( )
kidney	( )	( )	( )	( )
knish	( )	( )	( )	( )
lefse	( )	( )	( )	( )
liverwurst	( )	( )	( )	( )
lobster	( )	( )	( )	( )
lox	( )	( )	( )	( )
lutefisk	( )	( )	( )	( )
mussels	( )	( )	( )	( )
mutton	( )	( )	( )	( )
nachos	( )	( )	( )	( )
okra	( )	( )	( )	( )
oysters	( )	( )	( )	( )
pastrami	( )	( )	( )	( )
pasty (not pastry)	( )	( )	( )	( )
persimmons	( )	( )	( )	( )
pigs'feet	( )	( )	( )	( )
piñon nuts	( )	( )	( )	( )

	1	2	3	4
pokeweed	( )	( )	( )	( )
posole	( )	( )	( )	( )
pralines	( )	( )	( )	( )
quahog	( )	( )	( )	( )
ramps	( )	( )	( )	( )
raspberries	( )	( )	( )	( )
red beans and rice	( )	( )	( )	( )
red-eye gravy	( )	( )	( )	( )
rhubarb	( )	( )	( )	( )
ring bologna	( )	( )	( )	( )
Rocky Mt. oysters	( )	( )	( )	( )
sauerkraut	( )	( )	( )	( )
scrapple	( )	( )	( )	( )
scrod	( )	( )	( )	( )
scuppernongs	( )	( )	( )	( )
snails	( )	( )	( )	( )
soft pretzels	( )	( )	( )	( )
sopapillas	( )	( )	( )	( )
spring rolls	( )	( )	( )	( )
squirrel	( )	( )	( )	( )
sushi	( )	( )	( )	( )
sweet-potato pie	( )	( )	( )	( )
tabouli	( )	( )	( )	( )
tacos	( )	( )	( )	( )
tamales	( )	( )	( )	( )
tempura	( )	( )	( )	( )
thuringer	( )	( )	( )	( )
tofu	( )	( )	( )	( )
tortillas	( )	( )	( )	( )
tripe	( )	( )	( )	( )
turnip greens	( )	( )	( )	( )
venison	( )	( )	( )	( )
wild rabbit	( )	( )	( )	( )

Hometown and state _____

Zip code _____ Age _____ Gender _____

100 QUICKIES—RESTAURANTS

Below is a list of restaurants, both past and present. Check the appropriate space for each item.

1. I have eaten at one of these restaurants
2. I have seen one of these restaurants
3. I don't know this restaurant

A & W	( )	( )	( )
Applebee's	( )	( )	( )
Arby's	( )	( )	( )
Arthur Treacher's	( )	( )	( )
Bagel & Bagel	( )	( )	( )
Barbwire's Steak House	( )	( )	( )
Baskin-Robbins	( )	( )	( )
Big Boy	( )	( )	( )
Big Cheese Pizza	( )	( )	( )
Black-Eyed Pea	( )	( )	( )
Blimpie	( )	( )	( )
Bob Evans	( )	( )	( )
Bojangle's	( )	( )	( )
Bonanza	( )	( )	( )
Border Bandito	( )	( )	( )
Boston Chicken	( )	( )	( )
Boston Market	( )	( )	( )
Burger Chef	( )	( )	( )
Burger King	( )	( )	( )
California Pizza Kitchen	( )	( )	( )
Captain D's	( )	( )	( )
Carlos O'Kelly's Mexican	( )	( )	( )
Chi-Chi's	( )	( )	( )
Chick-Fil-A	( )	( )	( )
Chili's	( )	( )	( )
Church's Chicken	( )	( )	( )
Coco's	( )	( )	( )
Country Kitchen	( )	( )	( )
Cracker Barrel	( )	( )	( )
Dairy Queen	( )	( )	( )
Damon's Place for Ribs	( )	( )	( )
Del Taco	( )	( )	( )

David Schul of the University of Kansas contributed the idea for 100 Quickies—Restaurants.

Denny's	( )	( )	( )
Der Wienerschnitzel	( )	( )	( )
Dog 'n' Suds	( )	( )	( )
Domino's Pizza	( )	( )	( )
Dunkin' Donuts	( )	( )	( )
Friendly's	( )	( )	( )
Fuddrucker's	( )	( )	( )
Furr's Cafeteria	( )	( )	( )
Gino's	( )	( )	( )
Godfather's Pizza	( )	( )	( )
Grandy's	( )	( )	( )
Ground Round	( )	( )	( )
Happy Chef	( )	( )	( )
Happy Joe's	( )	( )	( )
Hardee's	( )	( )	( )
Howard Johnson's	( )	( )	( )
Intern'l House of Pancakes	( )	( )	( )
Jack in the Box	( )	( )	( )
KFC	( )	( )	( )
Le Peep	( )	( )	( )
Little Caesar	( )	( )	( )
Long John Silver's	( )	( )	( )
Luby's	( )	( )	( )
Maid-Rite	( )	( )	( )
McDonald's	( )	( )	( )
Mr. Gatti's	( )	( )	( )
Mr. Goodcents Subs	( )	( )	( )
Mr. Steak	( )	( )	( )
Old Chicago	( )	( )	( )
Old Spaghetti Factory	( )	( )	( )
Olive Garden	( )	( )	( )
Outback Steakhouse	( )	( )	( )
Perkins Family Restaurant	( )	( )	( )
Pizza Hut	( )	( )	( )
Pizza Inn	( )	( )	( )
Pizzeria Uno	( )	( )	( )
Po Folks	( )	( )	( )
Popeyes	( )	( )	( )
Rax	( )	( )	( )
Red Lobster	( )	( )	( )
Rio Bravo	( )	( )	( )
Roy Roger's	( )	( )	( )
Ruby Tuesday	( )	( )	( )

Runza	( )	( )	( )
Ruth's Chris Steak House	( )	( )	( )
Schlotzsky's	( )	( )	( )
Shakey's Pizza	( )	( )	( )
Shoney's	( )	( )	( )
Sirloin Stockade	( )	( )	( )
Skyline Chili	( )	( )	( )
Sonic Drive-In	( )	( )	( )
St. Louis Bread Company	( )	( )	( )
Starbucks	( )	( )	( )
Steak and Ale	( )	( )	( )
Steak 'n Shake	( )	( )	( )
Subway	( )	( )	( )
Taco Bell	( )	( )	( )
Taco Grande	( )	( )	( )
Taco John's	( )	( )	( )
Taco Tico	( )	( )	( )
Trader Vic's	( )	( )	( )
Valentino's	( )	( )	( )
Village Inn	( )	( )	( )
Waffle House (yellow)	( )	( )	( )
Waffle House (red/white)	( )	( )	( )
Wendy's	( )	( )	( )
Whataburger	( )	( )	( )
White Castle	( )	( )	( )

Hometown and state _____

Zip code _____ Age _____ Gender _____

Appendix B

Maps of Restaurants

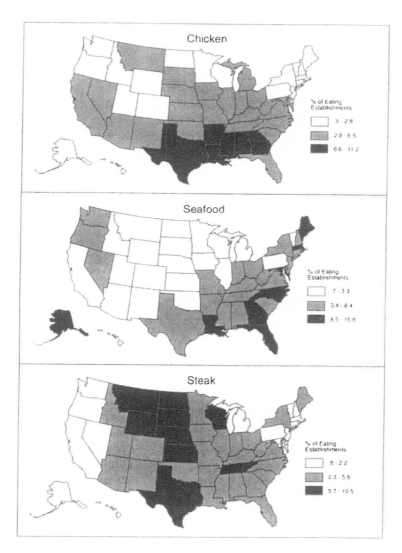

Specialty Restaurants (as identified by restaurant owners). The distributions all conform to regional stereotypes. Source: *1992 Census of Retail Trade,* Subject Series, Table 19. Principal Menu Type or Specialty.

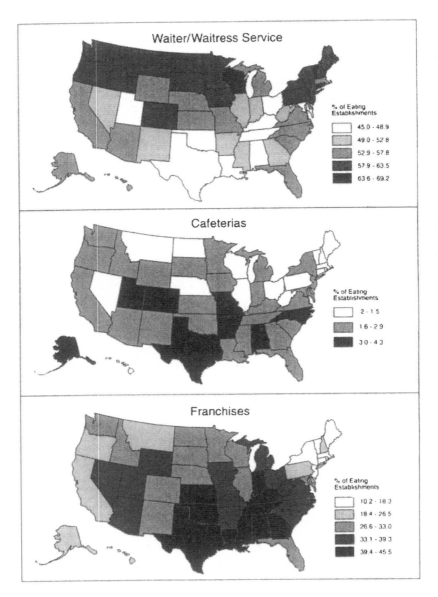

Organizational Styles of Restaurants. Most geographic research on restaurants focuses on types of food sold, but several organizational styles have spatial patterns worthy of attention as well. Franchises includes both restaurants (waiter service) and refreshment places (no waiter service). Sources: *1992 Census of Retail Trade*, Subject Series, Table 18. Primary Type of Food Service. *1992 Census of Retail Trade*, Subject Series, Table 21. Establishments Using a Trade Name Authorized by Franchisor.

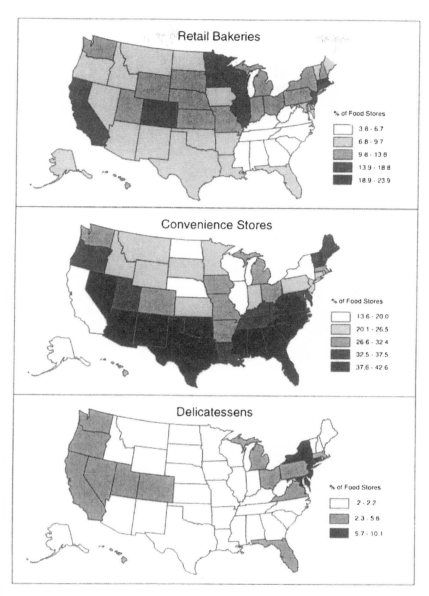

Selected Types of Food Stores. Retail bakeries, convenience stores (including food stores and food/gasoline stores), and delicatessens all exhibit distinctive regional patterns. Delis are easily linked with ethnicity, but the other two distributions are more mysterious. Source: *1992 Census of Retail Trade*, Geographic Area Series, Table 4. Establishments and Sales.

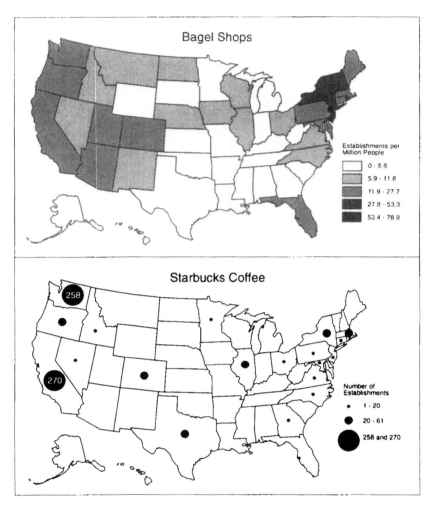

Bagels and Coffee. Bagel popularity has spread unevenly across the country from a hearth in the Northeast. Similarly, Starbucks Coffee has extended its presence in this specialized beverage market beyond its home base on the West Coast. Source of both maps: Big Yellow (http://s17.bigyellow.com), August 1997. The first map is based on use of "bagel(s)" in business name.

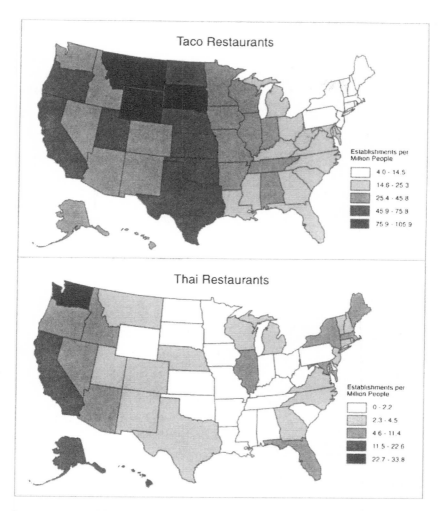

Taco and Thai Restaurants. Tacos are an ethnic fast food that has become well established throughout the western half of the United States. Thai restaurants, in contrast, represent a trendy ethnic cuisine with a decidedly coastal and urban spatial pattern. Source: Big Yellow (http://s17.bigyellow.com), August 1997. The maps are based on the use of "taco" or "Thai" in a restaurant business name.

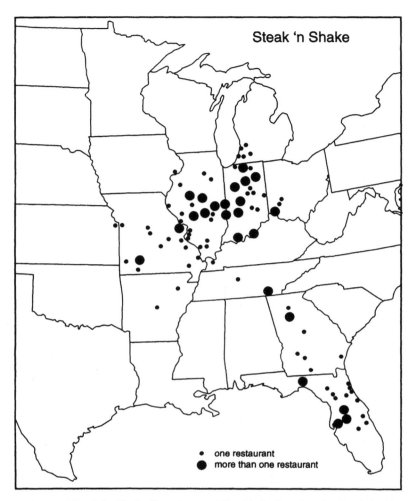

Locations of Steak 'n Shake Restaurants. The birthplace for the Steak 'n Shake restaurant chain was Normal, Illinois, in 1934. Source: Data from the company's Takhomasak® menu, 1996.

Bibliography

Abrahams, Roger. "Equal Opportunity Eating: A Structural Excursus on Things of the Mouth." In *Ethnic and Regional Foodways in the United States: The Performance of Group Identity*, edited by Linda Keller Brown and Kay Mussell, 19–36. Knoxville: University of Tennessee Press, 1984.

Adams, Jane Lilly. "Changes in Southern Food and Table Customs, 1860–1930." Master's thesis, George Peabody College for Teachers, 1981.

Adler, Thomas A. "Bluegrass Music and Meal-Fried Potatoes: Food, Festival, Community." In *"We Gather Together": Food and Festival in American Life*, edited by Theodore C. Humphrey and Lin T. Humphrey, 195–204. Logan: Utah State University Press, 1991.

Airriess, Christopher A., and David L. Clawson. "Vietnamese Market Gardens in New Orleans." *Geographical Review* 84, 1 (January 1994): 16–31.

Albright, Dawn. *Texas Festivals: The Most Complete Guide to Celebrations in the Lone Star State*. El Campo, Texas: Palmetto Press, 1991.

Algren, Nelson. *America Eats*. Iowa City: University of Iowa Press, 1992.

Allen, Terese. *Wisconsin Food Festivals: Good Food, Good Folks and Good Fun at Community Celebrations*. Amherst, Wisconsin: Amherst Press, 1995.

Allured, Janet Lynn. "Families, Food and Folklore: Women's Culture in the Postbellum Ozarks." Ph.D. diss., University of Arkansas, 1988.

American Heritage Editors. *American Heritage Cookbook and Illustrated History of American Eating & Drinking*. New York: American Heritage Publishing Co., 1964.

Anderson, Janet Alm. *Bounty: A Harvest of Food Lore and Country Memories from Utah's Past*. Boulder, Colorado: Pruett Publishing Company, 1990.

———. *A Taste of Kentucky*. Lexington: University Press of Kentucky, 1986.

Anderson, Jay Allen. "Thanksgiving in the U.S.A.: The Meal as Medium and Message." In *Ethnologische Nahrungsforschung: Ethnological Food Research*. Reports from the Second International Symposium for Ethnological Research, 1973. Edited by Nilo Valonen and Juhani Lehtonen, 9–14. Helsinki, Finland, 1975.

Andrews, Jean. *Peppers: The Domesticated Capsicums*. Austin: University of Texas Press, 1984.

Appadurai, Arjun. "How to Make a National Cuisine: Cookbooks in Contemporary India." *Comparative Studies of Society and History* 30, 1 (January 1988): 3–24.

Apte, Mahadev, and Judit Katona-Apte. "Diet and Social Movements in American Society: The Last Two Decades." In *Food in Change: Eating Habits from the Middle Ages to the Present Day*. Fifth International Conference on Ethnological Food Research, 1983. Edited by Alexander Fenton and Eszter Kisbán, 26–33. Edinburgh: John Donald, 1986.

Arnott, Margaret Louise. "Philadelphia Bread Re-assessed." In *Food and Change: Eating Habits from the Middle Ages to the Present Day*. Fifth International Conference on Ethnological Food Research, 1983. Edited by Alexander Fenton and Eszter Kisbán, 24–40. Edinburgh: John Donald, 1986.

———. "A Preference Food: The Philadelphia Soft Pretzel." In *Food in Perspective*. Proceedings of the Third International Conference on Ethnological Food Research, 1977. Edited by Alexander Fenton and Trefor M. Owen, 23–30. Edinburgh: John Donald, 1981.

———. "Thanksgiving Dinner: A Study in Cultural Heritage." In *Ethnologische Nahrungsforschung: Ethnological Food Research*. Reports from the Second International Symposium for Ethnological Food Research, 1973. Edited by Nilo Valonen and Juhani Lehtonen, 15–28. Helsinki, Finland, 1975.

Arreola, Daniel D. "Mexican Restaurants in Tucson." *Journal of Cultural Geography* 3, 2 (Spring–Summer 1983): 108–14.

Austin, Ben S. "The Vanishing Art of Cooking Table Grade Molasses." *Tennessee Folklore Society Bulletin* 55, 3 (1992): 101–7.

Axford, Lavonne Brady. *English Language Cookbooks, 1600–1973*. Detroit: Gale, 1976.

Baker, James W. "Seventeeth-Century English Yeoman Foodways at Plimoth Plantation." In *Foodways in the Northeast*, edited by Peter Benes, 105–13. Boston: Boston University Press, 1984.

Barer-Stein, Thelma. *You Eat What You Are: A Study of Canadian Ethnic Food Traditions*. Toronto: McClelland and Stewart, 1979.

Barry, Dave. "Hold the Bean Sprouts." In *Dave Barry's Bad Habits*, 182–84. New York: Henry Holt & Co., 1985.

Barton, Cathy. " 'It's Nothing But a Big Bowl of Soup!': Kentucky Burgoo and the Burgoo Supper." *Kentucky Folklore Record* 24, 3–4 (July–December 1978): 103–13.

Bass, Mary A., and Lucille M. Wakefield. "Nutrient Intake and Food Patterns of Indians on Standing Rock Reservation." *Journal of the American Dietetic Association* 64, 1 (January 1974): 36–41.

Bass, Mary A., D. W. Owsley, and V. D. McNutt. "Food Preferences and Food Prestige Ratings by Black Women in East Tennessee." *Ecology of Food and Nutrition* 16, 1 (1985): 75–83.

Bass, S. Jonathan. " 'How 'bout a Hand for the Hog': The Enduring Nature of the Swine as a Cultural Symbol in the South." *Southern Cultures* 1, 3 (Spring 1995): 301–20.

Bassett, Thomas J. "Reapings on the Margins: A Century of Community Gardening in America." *Landscape* 25, 2 (1981): 1–8.

Beard, James A. *James Beard's American Cookery*. Boston: Little, Brown and Company, 1972.

Beardsworth, Alan, and Teresa Keil. *Sociology on the Menu: An Invitation to the Study of Food and Society*. New York: Routledge, 1997.

Belasco, Warren J. *Appetite for Change: How the Counterculture Took on the Food Industry*. Ithaca: Cornell University Press, 1993.

———. "Ethnic Fast Foods: The Corporate Melting Pot." *Food and Foodways* 2, 1 (1987): 1–30.

———. "Toward a Culinary Common Denominator: The Rise of Howard Johnson's, 1925–1940." *Journal of American Culture* 2, 3 (Fall 1979): 503–18.

Bell, David, and Gill Valentine. *Consuming Geographies: We Are Where We Eat*. New York: Routledge, 1997.

Benes, Peter, editor. *Foodways in the Northeast*. Dublin Seminar for New England Folklife Annual Proceedings, 1982. Boston: Boston University Press, 1984.

Bennett, John W. "Food and Social Status in a Rural Society." *American Sociological Review* 8, 5 (October 1943): 561–69.

Bennett, John W., Harvey L. Smith, and Herbert Passin. "Food and Culture in Southern Illinois—A Preliminary Report." *American Sociological Review* 7, 5 (October 1942): 645–60.

Bentley, Amy. *Eating for Victory: United States Food Rationing and the Politics of Domesticity during World War II*. Urbana: University of Illinois Press, 1998.

———. "From Culinary Other to Mainstream American: Meanings and Uses of Southwestern Cuisine." *Journal of Southern Folklore* (forthcoming).

———. "Islands of Serenity: Gender, Race, and Ordered Meals during World War II." *Food and Foodways* 6, 2 (1996): 131–56.

Berdichevsky, Norman. "A Cultural Geography of Coffee and Tea Preferences." *Proceedings, Association of American Geographers* 8 (1976): 24–29.

Berolzheimer, Ruth, editor. *The United States Regional Cook Book*. Chicago: Culinary Arts Institute, 1939.

Berry, Wendell. "The Pleasures of Eating." *Antaeus* 68 (Spring 1992): 12–18.

Birkby, Evelyn. *Up a Country Lane Cookbook*. Iowa City: University of Iowa Press, 1993.

Bober, Phyllis Pray. "Lobster: Endangered 'Monarch of Seafoods'." In *Disappearing Foods: Studies in Foods and Dishes at Risk*. Proceedings of the Oxford Symposium on Food and Cookery, 1994. Edited by Harlan Walker, 51–57. Totnes, England: Prospect Books, Ltd., 1995.

Bolsterli, Margaret Jones. "The Very Food We Eat: A Speculation on the Nature of Southern Culture." *Southern Humanities Review* 16, 2 (Spring 1982): 119–27.

Booth, Sally Smith. *Hung, Strung and Potted: A History of Eating Habits in Colonial America*. New York: Clarkson N. Potter, Inc., 1971.

Borrud, Lori G., Patricia C. Pillow, Pamela K. Allen, R. Sue McPherson, Milton Z. Nichaman, and Guy R. Newell. "Food Group Contributions to Nutrient Intake in Whites, Blacks, and Mexican Americans in Texas." *Journal of the American Dietetic Association* 89, 8 (August 1989): 1061–69.

Bossard, James H. S. "Family Table Talk: An Area for Sociological Study." *American Sociological Review* 8, 3 (1943): 295–301.

Boswell, Parley Ann. "Hungry in the Land of Plenty: Food in Hollywood Films." In *Beyond the Stars III: The Material World in American Popular Film*, edited by Paul Loukides and Linda K. Fuller, 7–23. Bowling Green, Ohio: Bowling Green State University Popular Press, 1993.

Bourke, John. "The Folk-Foods of the Rio Grande Valley and of Northern Mexico." *Journal of American Folklore* 8, 28 (January–March 1895): 41–71.

Bova, Juliana. "Eel for Christmas: An Italian Tradition." *Pennsylvania Folklife* 39, 2 (Winter 1989–1990): 82–85.

Bowen, Joanne Vickie. "A Study of Seasonality and Subsistence: Eighteenth-Century Suffield, Connecticut." Ph.D. diss., Brown University, 1990.

Brenton, Barrett Paul. "Hopi Foodways: Biocultural Perspectives on Change and Contradiction." Ph.D. diss., University of Massachusetts, 1994.

Bria, Rosemarie Dorothy. "How Jell-O Molds Society and How Society Molds Jell-O: A Case Study of an American Food Industry Creation." Ed.D. diss., Columbia University Teachers College, 1991.

Bronner, Simon J. "Consuming Things." In *Grasping Things: Folk Material Culture and Mass Society in America*, by Simon J. Bronner, 160–78. Lexington: University Press of Kentucky, 1986.

Bronner, Yvonne, Cathy Burke, and Bernadine J. Joubert. "African-American/ Soul Foodways and Nutrition Counseling." *Topics in Clinical Nutrition* 9, 2 (March 1994): 20–27.

Broussard-Marin, Lydia, and Mary Therese Hynak-Hankinson. "Ethnic Food: The Use of Cajun Cuisine as a Model." *Journal of the American Dietetic Association* 89, 8 (August 1989): 1117–21.

Brown, Cora, Rose Brown, and Bob Brown. *American Cooks: Favorite Recipes from 48 States.* Garden City, New York: Garden City Books, 1940.

Brown, Dale, and the Editors of Time-Life Books. *American Cooking.* Alexandria, Virginia: Time-Life Books, 1968.

Brown, Eleanor Parker. *Culinary Americana: Cookbooks Published in the Cities and Towns of the United States of America during the Years from 1860 through 1960.* New York: Roving Eye Press, 1961.

Brown, Linda Keller, and Kay Mussell, editors. *Ethnic and Regional Foodways in the United States: The Performance of Group Identity.* Knoxville: University of Tennessee Press, 1984.

Brunvand, Jan Harold. "Folk Foods." In *The Study of American Folklore: An Introduction*, by Jan Harold Brunvand, 344–56. New York: W. W. Norton, 1978, second edition.

Bryant, Carol A., Anita Courtney, Barbara A. Markesberg, and Kathleen M. De-Walt. *The Cultural Feast: An Introduction to Food and Society.* St. Paul: West Publishing Company, 1985.

Bureau of the Census. U.S. Department of Commerce. *Agricultural Atlas of the United States.* 1992 Census of Agriculture, vol. 2, part 1. Washington, D.C.: U.S. Government Printing Office, 1995.

Burke, Padraic. "Rolling Carts and Songs of Plenty: The Urban Food Vendor." *Journal of American Culture* 2, 3 (Fall 1979): 480–87.

Butler, Angeline Trombino. "Sauce as Source: Food at the Intersection of Gender, Ethnic, and Labor Ideologies in the Writing of Select Italian American Women." Master's thesis, Bucknell University, 1994.

Butler, Cleora. "Cleora's Culinary Heritage." *American Visions* 8, 4 (August–September 1993): 36–39.

Camp, Charles. *American Foodways: What, When, Why and How We Eat in America.* Little Rock: August House, 1989.

———. "Food in American Culture: A Bibliographic Essay." *Journal of American Culture* 2, 3 (Fall 1979): 559–70.

———. "Foodways." In *The Handbook of American Popular Culture*, vol. 1, edited by M. Thomas Inge, 475–96. Westport, Connecticut: Greenwood Press, 1989.

———. "Foodways." In *American Folklore: An Encyclopedia*, edited by Jan Harold Brunvand, 299–302. New York: Garland Publishing Company, 1996.

———. "Foodways in Everyday Life." *American Quarterly* 34, 3 (Bibliography 1982): 278–89.

Carney, Judith. "Landscapes of Technology Transfer: Rice Cultivation and African Continuities." *Technology and Culture* 37, 1 (January 1996): 5–35.

Carroll, Michael P. "The Logic of Anglo-American Meals." *Journal of American Culture* 5, 3 (Fall 1982): 36–45.

Carson, Barbara G. *Ambitious Appetites: Dining, Behavior, and Patterns of Consumption in Federal Washington.* Washington, D.C.: American Institute of Architects, 1990.

Carstensen, Laurence W., Jr. "The Burger Kingdom: Growth and Diffusion of McDonald's Restaurants in the United States, 1955–1978." *Geographical Perspectives* 58 (Fall 1986): 1–8.

Chalmers, Irena. *The Great American Food Almanac.* New York: Harper & Row, 1986.

Chavez, Noel, Lisa Sha, Victoria Persky, Patricia Langenberg, and Erlinda Pestano-Binghay. "Effect of Length of U.S. Residence on Food Group Intake in Mexican and Puerto Rican Women." *Journal of Nutrition Education* 26, 2 (March–April 1994): 79–86.

Coe, Michael, and Sophie D. Coe. "Mid-Eighteenth-Century Food and Drink on the Massachusetts Frontier." In *Foodways in the Northeast*, edited by Peter Benes, 39–46. Boston: Boston University Press, 1984.

Collin, Richard H. "Gastronomy in American Society: American Writing on Restaurants." In *Commemorating the Past: Celebrations and Retrospection*, edited by Don Harkness, 52–59. Tampa, Florida: American Studies Press, 1987.

Colwin, Laurie. *More Home Cooking: A Writer Returns to the Kitchen.* New York: HarperCollins Publishers, 1993.

Comeaux, Malcolm L. "The Tortilla Industry in Arizona." *North American Culture* 2, 1 (1985): 15–23.

Committee on Food Consumption Patterns, Food and Nutrition Board, National Research Council. "Some Study Design Characteristics." In *Assessing Changing Food Consumption Patterns*, 19–28. Washington, D.C.: National Academy Press, 1981.

Conlin, Joseph R. *Bacon, Beans, and Galantines: Food and Foodways on the Western Mining Frontier.* Reno: University of Nevada Press, 1986.

————. "Grub and Chow: Food, Foodways, Class, and Occupation on the Western Frontier." In *The American West As Seen by Europeans and Americans*, edited by Rob Kroes, 128–38. Amsterdam: Free University Press, 1989.

————. "Old Boy, Did You Get Enough of Pie? A Social History of Food in Logging Camps." *Journal of Forest History* 23, 3 (October 1979): 164–85.

Conroy, David. *The Public Houses: Drink and the Revolution of Authority in Colonial Massachusetts*. Chapel Hill: The University of North Carolina Press, 1995.

Cook, Margaret. *America's Charitable Cooks: A Bibliography of Fund-Raising Cookbooks Published in the United States 1861–1915*. Kent, Ohio: n.p., 1971.

Counihan, Carole M. "Food Rules in the United States: Individualism, Control, and Hierarchy." *Anthropological Quarterly* 65, 2 (April 1992): 55–66.

Counihan, Carole, and Penny Van Esterik. *Food and Culture: A Reader*. New York: Routledge, 1997.

Cox, Jay Ann. "Eating the Other: Ethnicity and the Market for Authentic Mexican Food in Tucson, Arizona." Ph.D. diss., University of Arizona, 1993.

Craigie, Carter Walker. "A Moveable Feast: The Picnic As a Folklife Custom in Chester County, Pennsylvania, 1870–1925." Ph.D. diss., University of Pennsylvania, 1976.

Crandall, Christian S. "The Liking of Foods As a Result of Exposure: Eating Doughnuts in Alaska." *Journal of Social Psychology* 125, 2 (April 1985): 187–94.

Crockett, Susan J., and Diana L. Stuber. "Prestige Value of Foods: Changes over Time." *Ecology of Food and Nutrition* 27, 1 (1992): 51–64.

Cummings, Richard Osborn. *The American and His Food: A History of Food Habits in the United States*. Chicago: University of Chicago Press, 1940.

Curry, Pamela Malcolm, and Robert M. Jiobu. "Big Mac and Caneton à L'Orange: Eating, Icons and Rituals." In *Rituals and Ceremonies in Popular Culture*, edited by Ray B. Browne, 248–57. Bowling Green, Ohio: Bowling Green University Popular Press, 1980.

Curtin, Deane W., and Lisa M. Heldke, editors. *Cooking, Eating, Thinking: Transformative Philosophies of Food*. Bloomington: Indiana University Press, 1992.

Curtis, Karen A. "I Can Never Go Anywhere Empty-Handed: Food Exchange and Reciprocity in an Italian-American Community." Ph.D. diss., Temple University, 1984.

Cussler, Margaret and Mary L. de Give. *Twixt the Cup and the Lip: Psychological and Socio-Cultural Factors Affecting Food Habits*. New York: Twayne Publishers, 1952.

Darby, William J., Clarence G. Salsbury, William J. McGanity, Howard F. Johnson, Edwin B. Bridgforth, and Harold R. Sandstead. "A Study of the Dietary Background and Nutriture of the Navajo Indian." *Journal of Nutrition* 60, Supplement 2 (November 1956): 1–85.

Davidson, Claud M. "Apples in Cow Country: An Alternative Land Use in West Texas." *Focus* 44, 1 (Spring 1994): 23–26.

de Give, Mary Lewis. "Social Interrelationships and Food Habits in the Rural Southwest." Ph.D. diss., Radcliffe College, 1944.

Derven, Daphne L. "Wholesome, Toothsome, and Diverse: Eighteenth-Century Foodways in Deerfield, Massachusetts." In *Foodways in the Northeast*, edited by Peter Benes, 47–63. Boston: Boston University Press, 1984.

Deskins, Barbara Brown. "Spatial Variation in Food Habits among Public High School Students in Ingham and Jackson Counties, Michigan." Ph.D. diss., Michigan State University, 1973.

Deutsch, Ronald M. *The Nuts among the Berries: An Expose of America's Food Fads.* New York: Ballantine Books, 1961.

de Wit, Cary. "Food-Place Associations on American Product Labels." *Geographical Review* 82, 3 (July 1992): 323–30.

Dickins, Dorothy. "Food Preparation of Owner and Cropper Farm Families in the Shortleaf Pine Area of Mississippi." *Social Forces* 22, 1 (October 1943): 56–63.

Dietz, Thomas, Ann Stirling Frisch, Linda Kalof, Paul C. Stern, and Gregory A. Guagnano. "Values and Vegetarianism: An Exploratory Analysis." *Rural Sociology* 60, 3 (Fall 1995): 533–42.

Doerper, John. "Staple Foods of the American West Coast." In *Staple Foods.* Proceedings of the Oxford Symposium on Food and Cookery, 1989. Edited by Harlan Walker, 78–99. London: Prospect Books, Ltd., 1990.

———. "Street Food/Road Food in the Pacific Northwest." In *Public Eating.* Proceedings of the Oxford Symposium on Food and Cookery, 1991. Edited by Harlan Walker, 80–85. London: Prospect Books, Ltd., 1992.

Dolan, Natalie Elizabeth. "Fulton Mill Village Food Habits: Culinary Custom and Culinary Change 1929–1939." Master's thesis, Emory University, 1992.

Doudiet, Ellenore W. "Coastal Maine Cooking: Foods and Equipment from 1760." In *Gastronomy: The Anthropology of Food and Food Habits,* edited by M. L. Arnott, 215–32. The Hague: Mouton Pubs., 1975.

Douglas, Mary. "Deciphering a Meal." *Daedalus* 101, 1 (Winter 1972): 61–81.

Douglas Mary, editor. *Food in the Social Order: Studies of Food and Festivities in Three American Communities.* New York: Russell Sage Foundation, 1984.

Dubisch, Jill. "You Are What You Eat: Religious Aspects of the Health Food Movement." In *Folk Groups and Folklore Genres: A Reader,* edited by Elliott Oring, 124–35. Logan: Utah State University Press, 1989.

Dunier, Mitchell. *Slim's Table: Race, Respectability, and Masculinity.* Chicago: University of Chicago Press, 1992.

Duyff, Roberta L., Diva Sanjur, and Helen Y. Nelson. "Food Behavior and Related Factors of Puerto Rican-American Teenagers." *Journal of Nutrition Education* 7, 3 (July–September 1975): 99–103.

Eckhardt, Linda. *Linda Eckhardt's Great Food Catalog.* New York: Park Lane Press, 1996.

Edison, Carol. "Roast Beef and Pit-Barbecued Lamb: The Role of Food at Two Utah Homecoming Celebrations." In *"We Gather Together": Food and Festival in American Life,* edited by Theodore C. Humphrey and Lin T. Humphrey, 137–52. Logan: Utah State University Press, 1991.

Egerton, John. *Southern Food: At Home, on the Road, in History.* Chapel Hill: University of North Carolina Press, 1993.

Elliott, Daniel R. "Foodways and Economic Systems on the Late California Gold Rush Frontier." Master's thesis, California State University-Chico, 1995.

Engel, Allison. "Ingredients in American Cooking: Recent Trends." *Revue Française D'Études Américaines* 11, 27–28 (February 1986): 147–55.

Epstein, Bart Jacob. "The Quincy Food Market: A Study in Marketing Geography." Ph.D. diss., Clark University, 1956.

Evans, Meryle. "Southern Cooking." In *A Conference on Current Research in Culinary History: Sources, Topics, and Methods*. Proceedings, 1985. Edited by Jillian Strang, Bonnie Brown, and Patricia Kelly, 148–49. Hingham, Massachusetts: Culinary Historians of Boston, 1986.

Fertig, Barbara C. "Hog Killing in Virginia: Work as Celebration." In *"We Gather Together": Food and Festival in American Life*, edited by Theodore C. Humphrey and Lin T. Humphrey, 111–24. Logan: Utah State University Press, 1991.

Fieldhouse, Paul. *Food & Nutrition: Customs and Culture*. Second edition. London: Chapman and Hall, 1995.

Fine, Gary Alan. *Kitchens: The Culture of Restaurant Work*. Berkeley: University of California Press, 1996.

Fisher, Annie May. "Food and Table Customs of the South, 1607–1865." Master's thesis, George Peabody College for Teachers, 1931.

Fjeld, Carla R. and Robert Sommer. "Regional-Seasonal Patterns in Produce Consumption at Farmers' Markets and Supermarkets." *Ecology of Food and Nutrition* 12, 2 (1982): 109–15.

Flack, J. Wesley. "American Microbreweries and Neolocalism: Ale-ing for a Sense of Place." *Journal of Cultural Geography* 16, 2 (Spring–Summer 1996): (forthcoming).

Flexner, Marian W. *Out of Kentucky Kitchens*. Lexington: University Press of Kentucky, 1989.

Fordyce, Eleanor T. "Cookbooks of the 1800s." In *Dining in America 1850–1900*, edited by Kathryn Grover, 85–113. Amherst: University of Massachusetts Press, 1987.

Forêt, Michael James. "A Cookbook View of Cajun Culture." *Journal of Popular Culture* 23, 1 (1989): 23–36.

Foust, Clifford M., and Dale E. Marshall. "Culinary Rhubarb Production in North America: History and Recent Statistics." *HortScience* 26, 11 (November 1991): 1360–63.

Frenkel, Stephen. "A Pound of Kenya, Please or a Single Short Skinny Mocha." *Pacifica: The Association of Pacific Coast Geographers* (Fall 1995): 1, 12–15.

Friedlander, Judith. "Jewish Cooking in the American Melting-Pot." *Revue Française D'Études Américaines*. 11, 27–28 (February 1986): 87–98.

Fussell, Betty. *I Hear America Cooking*. New York: Times Books, 1983.

Geffen, Alice M., and Carole Berglie. *Food Festival: The Guidebook to America's Best Regional Food Celebrations*. Second edition. Woodstock, Vermont: The Countryman Press, 1994.

Georges, Robert A. "You Often Eat What Others Think You Are: Food As an Index of Others' Conception of Who One Is." *Western Folklore* 43, 4 (October 1984): 249–56.

Georgiou, Constance C., and Andrea B. Arquitt. "Regional Differences in Food and Nutrient Intakes of College Women from the United States: Oregon and Oklahoma." *Ecology of Food and Nutrition* 28, 4 (1992): 251–60.

Gibbons, Euell. *Stalking the Wild Asparagus*. New York: David McKay, 1962.

Gillespie, Angus K. "Toward a Method for the Study of Food in American Culture." *Journal of American Culture* 2, 3 (Fall 1979): 393–406.

————. " A Wilderness in the Megalopolis: Foodways in the Pine Barrens of New Jersey." In *Ethnic and Regional Foodways in the United States: The Performance of Group Identity*, edited by Linda Keller Brown and Kay Mussell, 145–68. Knoxville: University of Tennessee Press, 1984.

Gitelson, Joshua. "Populox: The Suburban Cuisine of the 1950s." *Journal of American Culture* 15, 3 (Fall 1992): 73–78.

Gizelis, Gregory. "Foodways Acculturation in the Greek Community of Philadelphia." *Pennsylvania Folklife* 20, 2 (Winter 1970–1971): 9–15.

Golden, Lilly, editor. *A Literary Feast: An Anthology*. New York: Atlantic Monthly Press, 1993.

Goldman, Barbara J., and Katherine L. Clancy. "A Survey of Organic Produce Purchases and Related Attitudes of Food Cooperative Shoppers." *American Journal of Alternative Agriculture* 6, 2 (Summer 1991): 89–96.

Goldstein, Kenneth S. *A Guide for Field Workers in Folklore*. Hatboro, Pennsylvania: Folklore Associates, Inc., 1964. Interviewing on pp. 108–21.

Goode, Judith G., Karen Curtis, and Janet Theophano. "Meal Format, Meal Cycles, and Menu Negotiation in the Maintenance of an Italian-American Community." In *Food in the Social Order*, edited by Mary Douglas, 143–218. New York: Russell Sage Foundation, 1984.

Goode, Judith, Janet Theophano, and Karen Curtis. "A Framework for the Analysis of Continuity and Change in Shared Sociocultural Rules for Food Use: The Italian-American Pattern." In *Ethnic and Regional Foodways in the United States: The Performance of Group Identity*, edited by Linda Keller Brown and Kay Mussell, 66–88. Knoxville: University of Tennessee Press, 1984.

Gordon, Bertram M. "Shifting Tastes and Terms: The Rise of California Cuisine." *Revue Française D'Études Américaines* 11, 27–28 (February 1986): 109–26.

Graham, Joe S. "Mexican-American Traditional Foodways at La Junta de los Rios." *Journal of Big Bend Studies* 2 (January 1990): 1–27.

Griffith, James. " 'We Always Call It "Tucson Eat Yourself" ' : The Role of Food at a Constructed Festival." In *"We Gather Together": Food and Festival in American Life*, edited by Theodore C. Humphrey and Lin T. Humphrey, 219–33. Logan: Utah State University Press, 1991.

Grivetti, Louis E., and Marie B. Paquette. "Nontraditional Ethnic Food Choices among First-Generation Chinese in California." *Journal of Nutrition Education* 10, 3 (July–September 1978): 109–12.

Grover, Kathryn, editor. *Dining in America, 1850–1900*. Amherst: University of Massachusetts Press, 1987.

Gutierrez, C. Paige. *Cajun Foodways*. Jackson: University Press of Mississippi, 1992.

————. "The Social and Symbolic Uses of Ethnic/Regional Foodways: Cajuns and Crawfish in South Louisiana." In *Ethnic and Regional Foodways in the United States: The Performance of Group Identity*, edited by Linda Keller Brown and Kay Mussell, 169–82. Knoxville: University of Tennessee Press, 1984.

Gutowski, John. "American Folklore and the Modern American Community Festival: A Case Study of Turtle Days in Churubusco, Indiana." Ph.D. diss., Indiana University, 1977.

Gvion-Rosenberg, Liora. "Telling the Story of Ethnicity: American Cookbooks, 1850–1990." Ph.D. diss., State University of New York, Stony Brook, 1991.

Hacker, Dorothy B., and Eleanor D. Miller. "Food Patterns of the Southwest. *American Journal of Clinical Nutrition* 7, 2 (March–April 1959): 224–29.

Hall, Irene S., and Calvin S. Hall. "A Study of Disliked and Unfamiliar Foods." *Journal of the American Dietetic Association* 15, 7 (August–September 1939): 540–48.

Hamel, Ruth. "States of Mind." *American Demographics* 14, 4 (April 1992) 40–43.

Hammontree, Patsy G. "Gardening." In *Handbook of American Popular Culture*, edited by M. Thomas Inge, 525–48. Second edition. New York: Greenwood Press, 1989.

Hanke, Robert John. " 'Suddenly a Restaurant Town': An Inquiring into Public Culinary Culture and Communication." Ph.D. diss., University of Pennsylvania, 1987.

Harris, Marvin. "Holy Beef, U.S.A." In *Good to Eat: Riddles of Food and Culture*, by Marvin Harris, 109–29. New York: Simon and Schuster, 1985.

Heisley, Deborah D., Mary Ann McGrath, and John F. Sherry, Jr., "To Everything There Is a Season: A Photoessay of a Farmers' Market." *Journal of American Culture* 14, 3 (Fall 1991): 53–79.

Heldke, Lisa M. "Recipes for Theory Making." In *Cooking, Eating, Thinking: Transformative Philosophies of Food*, edited by Deane W. Curtin and Lisa M. Heldke, 251–65. Bloomington: Indiana University Press, 1992.

Henderson, Floyd M. "Foodways." In *This Remarkable Continent: An Atlas of United States and Canadian Society and Cultures*, edited by John F. Rooney, Wilbur Zelinsky, and Dean Lauder, 225–33. College Station: Texas A&M Press, 1982.

Herrin, Marcia, and Joan Dye Gussow. "Designing a Sustainable Regional Diet." *Journal of Nutrition Education* 21, 6 (December 1989): 270–75.

Hertzler, Ann A. *America's Collectible Cookbooks: The History, the Politics, the Recipes.* Athens: Ohio University Press, 1994.

Hess, John L., and Karen Hess. *The Taste of America.* New York: Grossman Publishers, 1977.

Hess, Karen. *The Carolina Rice Kitchen: The African Connection.* Columbia: University of South Carolina Press, 1992.

Hilliard, Sam. *Hog Meat and Hoecake: Food Supply in the Old South, 1840–1860.* Carbondale: Southern Illinois University Press, 1972.

———. "Hog Meat and Cornpone: Food Habits in the Ante-Bellum South." *Proceedings of the American Philosophical Society* 113, 1 (February 1969): 1–13.

———. "Pork in the Ante-Bellum South: The Geography of Self-Sufficiency." *Annals of the Association of American Geographers* 59, 3 (September 1969): 461–80.

Holzer, Scott. "The Modernization of Southern Foodways: Rural Immigration to the Urban South during World War II." *Food and Foodways* 6, 2 (1996): 93–107.

Hooker, Richard J. *Food and Drink in America: A History.* Indianapolis: The Bobbs-Merrill Company, Inc., 1981.

Hoy, Jim. "Rocky Mountain Oysters." In *Plains Folk: A Commonplace of the Great Plains* by Jim Hoy and Tom Isern, 77–79. Norman: University of Oklahoma Press, 1987.

Hubbell, Sue. " 'Hopping John' Gets the Year Off to a Flying Start." *Smithsonian* 24, 9 (December 1993): 83–88.

Hudgins, Sharon. "Red Dust: Powdered Chiles & Chili Powders." In *Spicing Up the Palate: Sudies of Flavourings-Ancient and Modern.* Proceedings of the Oxford Symposium on Food and Cookery, 1992. Edited by Harlan Walker, 107–20. London: Prospect Books, Ltd., 1993.

———. "Texas Barbecue: A Feast for All Classes." In *Feasting and Fasting.* Proceedings of the Oxford Symposium on Food and Cookery, 1990. Edited by Harlan Walker, 106–19. London: Prospect Books, Ltd., 1991.

Hudgins, Tom. "Burger and Fries: From White Castles to Golden Arches." In *Public Eating.* Proceedings of the Oxford Symposium on Food and Cookery, 1991. Edited by Harlan Walker, 141–49. London: Prospect Books, Ltd., 1992.

———. "Hot Sauces: Fiery Flavorings from the USA." In *Spicing Up the Palate: Studies of Flavourings-Ancient and Modern.* Proceedings of the Oxford Symposium on Food and Cookery, 1992. Edited by Harlan Walker, 121–34. London: Prospect Books, Ltd., 1993.

Hugo, Lawrence R., Jr. "Food Patterns and Their Relations to Urbanism," Ph.D. diss., University of Pittsburgh, 1949.

Humphrey, Lin T. "Small Group Festive Gatherings." *Journal of the Folklore Institute* 16, 3 (September–December 1979): 190–201.

———. "Traditional Foods? Traditional Values?" *Western Folklore* 48, 2 (April 1989): 162–69.

Humphrey, Theodore C. " 'It's a Community Deal Here, You Know': Festive Community Life in Rural Oklahoma." In *"We Gather Together": Food and Festival in American Life,* edited by Theodore C. Humphrey and Lin T. Humphrey, 153–67. Logan: Utah State University Press, 1991.

Humphrey, Theodore C., and Lin T. Humphrey, editors. *"We Gather Together": Food and Festival in American Life.* Logan: Utah State University Press, 1991.

Ikeda, Joanne P., Diane R. Ceja, Richard S. Glass, Janice O. Hardwood, Kimberly A. Lucke, and Jeanette M. Sutherlin. "Food Habits of the Hmong Living in Central California." *Journal of Nutrition Education* 23, 4 (July–August 1991): 168–75.

Ireland, Lynne. "The Compiled Cookbook As Foodways Autobiography." *Western Folklore* 40, 1 (January 1981): 107–14.

Isern, Tom. "Bierocks" and "Back for More Bierocks." In *Plains Folk II: The Romance of the Landscape,* by Jim Hoy and Tom Isern, 80–83. Norman: University of Oklahoma Press, 1990.

Jakle, John A. "Roadside Restaurants and Place-Product-Packaging." *Journal of Cultural Geography* 3, 1 (Fall–Winter 1982): 76–93.

Janiskee, Robert L. "Rural Festivals in South Carolina." *Journal of Cultural Geography* 11, 2 (Spring–Summer 1991): 31–43.

———. "South Carolina's Harvest Festivals: Rural Delights for Day-Tripping Urbanites." *Journal of Cultural Geography* 1, 1 (Fall–Winter 1980): 96–104.

Jerome, Norge W. "Frozen (TV) Dinners—The Staple Emergency Meals of a Changing Modern Society." In *Food in Perspective.* Proceedings of the Third International Conference on Ethnological Food Research, edited by Alexander Fenton and Trefor M. Owen, 145–56. Edinburgh: John Donald, 1981.

———. "Northern Urbanization and Food Consumption Patterns of Southern-Born Negroes." *The American Journal of Clinical Nutrition* 22, 12 (December 1969): 1667–69.

Jerome, Norge W., Randy F. Kandel, and Gretel H. Pelto, editors. *Nutritional Anthropology: Contemporary Approaches to Diet and Culture.* Pleasantville, New York: Redgrave Publishing Co., 1980.

Jett, Stephen. "History of Fruit Tree Raising among the Navajo." *Agricultural History* 51, 4 (October 1977): 681–701.

Joffe, Natalie F. "Food Habits of Selected Subcultures in the United States." In *The Problem of Changing Food Habits: Report of the Committee on Food Habits 1941–1943.* Bulletin 108, 97–103. Washington, D.C.: National Research Council, 1943.

Jones, Diane Veale, and Mary E. Darling. *Ethnic Foodways in Minnesota: Handbook of Food and Wellness across Cultures.* St. Paul: Minnesota Extension Service, University of Minnesota, 1996.

Jones, Evan. *American Food: The Gastronomic Story.* Second edition. New York: E. P. Dutton & Co., Inc., 1975.

———. "Delmonico's." *Antaeus* 68 (Spring 1992): 83–95.

Jones, Michael Owen. "Afterword: Discovering the Symbolism of Food Customs and Events." In *"We Gather Together": Food and Festival in American Life,* edited by Theodore D. Humphrey and Lin T. Humphrey, 235–45. Logan: Utah State University Press, 1991.

Jordan, Susan A. "The Development of an Ethnic Food Frequency for Hispanic Women." Master's thesis, University of Nebraska-Lincoln, 1996.

Jumper, Sidney. "The Fresh Vegetable Industry in the U.S.A.: An Example of Dynamic Interregional Dependency." *Tijdschrift Voor Economische en Sociale Geografie* 60, 5 (September–October 1969): 308–18.

Kaiser, Jo Ellen Green. "Feeding the Hungry Heart: Gender, Food, and War in the Poetry of Edna St. Vincent Millay." *Food and Foodways* 6, 2 (1996): 81–92.

Kalčik, Susan. "Ethnic Foodways in America: Symbol and Performance of Identity." In *Ethnic and Regional Foodways in the United States: The Performance of Group Identity,* edited by Linda Keller Brown and Kay Mussell, 37–65. Knoxville: University of Tennessee Press, 1984.

Kaplan, Anne R. "Ethnic Foodways in Everyday Life: Creativity and Change among Contemporary Minnesotans." Ph.D. diss., University of Pennsylvania, 1984.

———. " 'It's All from One Big Pot': Booya as an Expression of Community." In *"We Gather Together": Food and Festival in American Life,* edited by Theodore D. Humphrey and Lin T. Humphrey, 169–89. Logan: Utah State University Press, 1991.

Kaplan, Anne R., Marjorie A. Hoover, and Willard B. Moore. *The Minnesota Ethnic Food Book.* St. Paul: Minnesota Historical Society Press, 1986.

Kellman, Steven G. "Food Fights in Iowa: The Vegetarian Stranger in Recent Midwest Fiction." *The Virginia Quarterly Review* 71, 3 (Summer 1995): 435–47.

Kelly, James. "Loco Moco: A Folk Dish in the Making." *Social Process in Hawaii* 30 (1983): 59–64.

Kelsey, Mary Wallace. "Beans of the Southwestern United States Indians." In *Staple Foods*. Proceedings of the Oxford Symposium on Food and Cookery, 1989. Edited by Harlan Walker, 119–28. London: Prospect Books, Ltd., 1990.

Kim, Sojin, and R. Mark Livengood. "Ramen Noodles & Spam: Popular Foods, Significant Tastes." *Digest: An Interdisciplinary Study of Food and Foodways* 15 (1995): 2–11.

Kinnucan, Henry, and Benjamin Sexauer. "The Demand for Home-Produced Food by Rural Families." *American Journal of Agricultural Economics* 60, 2 (May 1978): 338–44.

Kirkendall, Judith. "Street Food in Hawaii." In *Public Eating*. Proceedings of the Oxford Symposium on Food and Cookery, 1991. Edited by Harlan Walker, 171–73. London: Prospect Books, Ltd., 1992.

Kirlin, Katherine S., and Thomas M. Kirlin, editors. *Smithsonian Folklife Cookbook*. Washington, D.C.: Smithsonian Institution Press, 1991.

Kittler, Pamela Goyan, and Kathryn P. Sucher. *Food and Culture in America: A Nutrition Handbook*. Second edition. Belmont, California: West/Wadsworth, 1998.

Kleiman, Rhonda H., compiler. *The American Regional Cookery Index*. New York: Neal-Schuman, 1989.

Kolasa, Kathryn Marianne. "Foodways of Selected Mothers and Their Adult Daughters in Upper East Tennessee." Master's thesis, University of Tennessee, 1974.

Kovacik, Charles. "Eating Out in South Carolina's Cities: The Last Fifty Years." *North American Culture* 4, 1 (1988): 53–64.

Kraig, Bruce. "The American Hot Dog: Standardised Taste and Regional Variations." In *Taste*. Proceedings of the Oxford Symposium on Food and Cookery, 1987. Edited by Tom Jaine, 108–13. London: Prospect Books, Ltd., 1988.

Kraut, Alan M. "Ethnic Foodways: The Significance of Food in the Designation of Cultural Boundaries between Immigrant Groups in the U.S., 1840–1921." *Journal of American Culture* 2, 3 (Fall 1979): 409–20.

Kuhnlein, Harriet V., Doris H. Calloway, and Barbara F. Harland. "Composition of Traditional Hopi Foods." *Journal of the American Dietetic Association* 75, 1 (July 1979): 37–41.

Lambert, Walter N. *Kinfolks and Custard Pie: Recollections and Recipes from an East Tennessean*. Knoxville: University of Tennessee Press, 1988.

Langlois, Janet. "Moon Cake in Chinatown, New York City: Continuity and Change." *New York Folklore Quarterly* 28, 2 (June 1972): 83–117.

Laudan, Rachel. *The Food of Paradise: Exploring Hawaii's Culinary Heritage*. Honolulu: University of Hawaii Press, 1996.

———. "Going Today, Gone Tomorrow: The Food or the People?: Hawaii and Loss by Migration." In *Disappearing Foods: Studies in Foods and Drinks at Risk*. Proceedings of the Oxford Symposium on Food and Cookery, 1994. Edited by Harlan Walker, 132–35. Totnes, England: Prospect Books, Ltd., 1995.

Lawson, Annie Hauck. "Foodways of Three Polish-American Families in New York." Ph.D. diss., New York University, 1991.

Lebergott, Stanley. "Food." In *Pursuing Happiness: American Consumers in the Twentieth Century*, by Stanley Lebergott, 77–83. Princeton: Princeton University Press, 1993.

Lederer, Richard. "You Said a Mouthful." *Verbatim: The Language Quarterly* 9, 3 (Winter 1983): 23.

Lentner, Diane L. "Food Choices and Ethnic Backgrounds of Western Pennsylvania Residents: Potential Impact on Nutrition Intervention." Master's thesis, Indiana University of Pennsylvania, 1995.

Levenstein, Harvey. *The Paradox of Plenty: A Social History of Eating in Modern America.* New York: Oxford University Press, 1993.

———. *Revolution at the Table: The Transformation of the American Diet.* New York: Oxford University Press, 1988.

———. "The American Response to Italian Food, 1880–1930." *Food and Foodways* 1, 1 (1985): 1–23.

———. "The New England Kitchen and the Origins of Modern American Eating Habits." *American Quarterly* 32, 4 (Fall 1980): 369–86.

Leverton, Ruth M. "Freshman Food Likes." *Journal of Home Economics* 36, 9 (November 1944): 589–90.

Lewis, George H. "The Maine Lobster as Regional Icon: Competing Images over Time and Social Class." *Food and Foodways* 3, 4 (1989): 303–16.

Lewis, Jane S., and Maria Fe Glaspy. "Food Habits and Nutrient Intakes of Filipino Women in Los Angeles." *Journal of the American Dietetic Association* 67, 2 (August 1975): 122–25.

Linck, Ernestine Sewell, and Joyce Gibson Roach. *Eats: A Folk History of Texas Foods.* Fort Worth: Texas Christian University Press, 1989.

Lincoln, Waldo. *American Cookery Books 1742–1860.* Worcester, Massachusetts: American Antiquarian Society, 1954.

Lloyd, Timothy Charles. "The Cincinnati Chili Culinary Complex." *Western Folklore* 40, 1 (January 1981): 28–40.

———. "Paterson's Hot Texas Wiener Tradition." *Folklife Center News* 17, 2 (Spring 1995): 8–11.

Lockwood, William G., and Yvonne R. Lockwood. "The Cornish Pasty in Northern Michigan." In *Food in Motion: The Migration of Foodstuffs and Cookery Techniques.* Proceedings of the Oxford Symposium on Food and Cookery, 1983. Edited by Alan Davidson, 84–94. Leeds: Prospect Books, Ltd., 1983.

Lockwood, Yvonne R., and William G. Lockwood. "Pasties in Michigan's Upper Peninsula: Foodways, Interethnic Relations, and Regionalism." In *Creative Ethnicity: Symbols and Strategies of Contemporary Ethnic Life*, edited by Stephen Stern and John A. Cicala, 3–20. Logan: Utah State University Press, 1991.

Lovegren, Sylvia. *Fashionable Food: Seven Decades of Food Fads.* New York: Macmillan, 1995.

Lovell, Louva H. "A Day at the JA Chuckwagon in 1936." *Panhandle-Plains Historical Review* 55 (1982): 37–72.

Lovell-Troy, Lawrence. "Kinship Structure and Economic Organization among

Ethnic Groups: Greek Immigrants in the Pizza Business." Ph.D. diss., University of Connecticut, 1979.

Lowenstein, Eleanor. *Bibliography of American Cookery Books 1742–1860.* Third edition. Worcester, Massachusetts: American Antiquarian Society, 1972.

Lu, Shun, and Gary Alan Fine. "The Presentation of Ethnic Authenticity: Chinese Food As a Social Accomplishment." *The Sociological Quarterly* 36, 3 (Summer 1995): 535–53.

Luchetti, Cathy. *Home on the Range: A Culinary History of the American West.* New York: Villard Books, 1993.

Lyle, Katie Letcher. "America's Native Bounty." *Americana* 20, 1 (April 1992): 42–45.

Lyson, T. A., G. W. Gillespie, Jr., and D. Hilchey. "Farmers' Markets and the Local Community: Bridging the Formal and Informal Economy." *American Journal of Alternative Agriculture* 10, 3 (Summer 1995): 108–13.

MacClancy, Jeremy. *Consuming Culture: Why You Eat What You Eat.* New York: Henry Holt & Co., 1993.

Madeira, Karen. "Cultural Meaning and Use of Food: A Selective Bibliography (1973–1987)." In *Cooking by the Book: Food in Literature and Culture,* edited by Mary Anne Schofield, 207–15. Bowling Green, Ohio: Bowling Green State University Popular Press, 1989.

Mader, Gregory. "An Examination of Selected Ethnic Foodways in the Upper Midwest." Master's thesis, South Dakota State University, 1996.

Magliocco, Sabina. "Playing with Food: The Negotiation of Identity in the Ethnic Display Event by Italian Americans in Clinton, Indiana." In *Studies in Italian American Folklore,* edited by Luisa Del Giudice, 107–26. Logan: Utah State University Press, 1993.

Manzo, Joseph T. "The Diner in the South." *Southeastern Geographer* 36, 2 (November 1996): 140–51.

———. "From Pushcart to Modular Restaurant: The Diner on the Landscape." *Journal of American Culture* 13, 3 (Fall 1990): 13–21.

Mariani, John F. "Everybody Likes Italian Food." *American Heritage* 40, 8 (December 1989): 122–31.

Marshall, Howard Wight. "Meat Preservation on the Farm in Missouri's 'Little Dixie'." *Journal of American Folklore* 92, 366 (October–December 1979): 400–17.

———. "What Price Grits?" *Pioneer America* 10, 2 (December 1978): 5–6.

Martin, Abbott C. "Patriotism and Fried Chicken." *Sewanee Review* 37, 1 (January 1929): 34–37.

Martin, Judith A. "If Baseball Can't Save Cities Anymore, What Can a Festival Market Do?" *Journal of Cultural Geography* 5, 1 (Fall–Winter 1984): 33–46.

Matson, Madeline. *Food in Missouri: A Cultural Stew.* Columbia: University of Missouri Press, 1994.

Maurer, Donna and Jeffery Sobal, editors. *Eating Agendas: Food and Nutrition as Social Problems.* Hawthorne, New York: Aldine de Gruyter, 1995.

May, Jon. " 'A Little Taste of Something More Exotic': The Imaginative Geographies of Everyday Life." *Geography* 81, 1 (January 1996): 57–64.

Mayes, Rudolph. "Homemade Hominy: One of America's Oldest Traditions Explained." *Mississippi Folklore Register* 19, 2 (Fall 1985): 103–8.

Mayo, James. *The American Grocery Store: The Business Evolution of an Architectural Space.* Westport, Connecticut: Greenwood Press, 1993.

McCorkle, James L., Jr. "Moving Perishables to Market: Southern Railroads and the Nineteenth-Century Origins of Southern Truck Farming." *Agricultural History* 66, 1 (Winter 1992): 42–62.

McCracken, Robert D. "Cultural Differences in Food Preferences and Meanings." *Human Organization* 41, 2 (Summer 1982): 161–67.

McCulloch-Williams, Martha. *Dishes and Beverages of the Old South.* Knoxville: University of Tennessee Press, 1988.

McIntosh, Elaine N. *American Food Habits in Historical Perspective.* Westport, Connecticut: Praeger, 1995.

McIntosh, William Alex. *Sociologies of Food and Nutrition.* New York: Plenum Publishing Corportation, 1996.

McIntosh, William Alex, and Mary Zey. "Woman as Gatekeepers of Food Consumption: A Sociological Critique." *Food and Foodways* 3, 4 (1989): 317–32.

McKinney, Edgar Duane. "Images, Realities, and Cultural Transformation in the Missouri Ozarks, 1920–1960." Ph.D. diss., University of Missouri, 1990.

McMahon, Sarah F. "A Comfortable Subsistence." Ph.D. diss., Brandeis University, 1982.

———. "Provisions Laid Up for the Family: Toward a History of Diet in New England, 1650–1850." *Historical Methods* 14, 1 (Winter 1981): 4–21.

———. "Sources and Documents: The Study of Diet and Foodways in Colonial America." In *A Conference on Current Research in Culinary History: Sources, Topics, and Methods.* Proceedings, 1985. Edited by Jillian Strang, Bonnie Brown, and Patricia Kelly, 130–37. Hingham, Massachusetts: Culinary Historians of Boston, 1986.

McPhee, John. *Oranges.* New York: Farrar, Straus and Giroux, 1966.

Meloy, Ellen. "Carp Seviche and Jerked Squirrel." *Utne Reader* 60 (November–December 1993): 69–73.

Mendelson, Anne. "Paradise Lost: The Decline of the Apple and the American Agrarian Ideal." In *Our Sustainable Table,* edited by Robert Clark, 53–68. San Francisco: North Point Press, 1990.

Messer, Ellen. "Anthropological Perspectives on Diet." *Annual Review of Anthropology* 13 (1984): 205–49.

Meyers, Angela, editor. *A Cook's Tour of Mississippi.* Jackson: Mississippi Publishers Corporation, 1980.

Milbauer, John A. "The Geography of Food in Eastern Oklahoma: A Small Restaurant Study." *North American Culture* 6, 1 (1990): 37–52.

Mintz, Sidney W. "American Eating Habits and Food Choices: A Preliminary Essay." *The Journal of Gastronomy* 2, 3 (1986): 15–22.

Mirsky, Richard M. "Perspectives in the Study of Food Habits." *Western Folklore* 40, 1 (January 1981): 125–33.

Monniger, Joseph. "Fast Food." *American Heritage* 39, 3 (April 1988): 68–75.

Montano, Mario. "The History of Mexican Folk Foodways of South Texas: Street

Vendors, Offal Foods, and Barbacoa de Cabeza." Ph.D. diss., University of Pennsylvania, 1992.

Moore, Willard B. "Metaphor and Changing Reality: The Foodways and Beliefs of the Russian Molokans in the United States." In *Ethnic and Regional Foodways in the United States: The Performance of Group Identity*, edited by Linda Keller Brown and Kay Mussell, 91–112. Knoxville: University of Tennessee Press, 1984.

Mueller, William, and Brad Edmondson. "From Farmer to Table." *American Demographics* 10, 6 (June 1988): 41–44.

Narayan, Uma. "Eating Cultures: Incorporation, Identity and Indian Food." *Social Identities: Journal for the Study of Race, Nation and Culture* 1, 1 (1995): 63–86.

Nathan, Joan. *American Folklife Cookbook*. New York: Schocken Books, 1984.

National Research Council. *What Is America Eating?* Washington, D.C.: National Academy Press, 1986.

Neustadt, Kathy. *Clambake: A History and Celebration of an American Tradition*. Amherst: University of Massachusetts Press, 1992.

———. " 'Born among the Shells': The Quakers of Allen's Neck and Their Clambake." In *"We Gather Together": Food and Festival in American Life*, edited by Theodore C. Humphrey and Lin T. Humphrey, 89–109. Logan: Utah State University Press, 1991.

Newman, Jacqueline M. *Melting Pot: An Annotated Bibliography and Guide to Food and Nutrition Information for Ethnic Groups in America*. Second edition. New York: Garland Publishing Company, 1993.

Newton, Milton E. "Sliced Tomatoes for Breakfast." *Pioneer America* 9, 1 (July 1977): 11.

Newton, Sarah E. " 'The Jell-O Syndrome': Investigating Popular Culture/Foodways." *Western Folklore* 51, 3–4 (July–October 1992): 249–67.

Nichols, Nell B. *Good Home Cooking across the U.S.A.: A Source Book of American Foods*. Ames: Iowa State College Press, 1952.

Oliver, Sandra Louise. *Saltwater Foodways: New Englanders and Their Food, at Sea and Ashore, in the Nineteenth Century*. Mystic, Connecticut: Mystic Seaport Museum, Inc., 1995.

Ostmann, Barbara Gibbs, and Jane Baker. *Food Editors' Hometown Favorites Cookbook: American Regional and Local Specialties*. Maplewood, New Jersey: Hammond, 1984.

Page, Linda Garland, and Eliot Wigginton, editors. *The Foxfire Book of Appalachian Cookery*. Chapel Hill: The University of North Carolina Press, 1992.

Page, Louise, and Berta Friend. "The Changing United States Diet." *BioScience* 28, 3 (March 1978): 192–97.

Pangborn, Rose Marie, and Christine M. Bruhn. "Concepts of Food Habits of 'Other' Ethnic Groups." *Journal of Nutrition Education* 2, 3 (Winter 1971): 106–10.

Park, Edwards. "Around the Mall and Beyond: Smithsonian's Third Annual Conference on Stuff." *Smithsonian* 25, 4 (July 1994): 12–15.

Passariello, Phyllis. "Anomalies, Analogies, and Sacred Profanities: Mary Douglas on Food and Culture, 1957–1989." *Food and Foodways* 4, 1 (1990): 53–71.

Penka, Allison M., Dennis A. Ferris, Michelle J. Pickert, and Rebecca A. Gould. "A Survey of Student Food Preferences at a Midwestern High School." *School Food Service Research Review* 20, 1 (1996): 7–12.

Perdue, Charles L., Jr., editor. *Pigsfoot Jelly and Persimmon Beer: Foodways from the Virginia Writers' Project.* Santa Fe, New Mexico: Ancient City Press, 1992.

Perrin, Patricia. "Louisiana French Foodways: The Perpetuation of Ethnicity in the Lafourche Area." *North American Culture* 2, 1 (1985): 3–9.

Pillsbury, Richard. *From Boarding House to Bistro: The American Restaurant Then and Now.* Boston: Unwin Hyman, 1990.

———. *No Foreign Food: The American Diet in Time and Place.* Boulder: Westview Press, 1998.

———. "From Hamburger Alley to Hedgerose Heights: Toward a Model of Restaurant Location Dynamics." *Professional Geographer* 39, 3 (August 1987): 326–44.

Pillsbury, Richard, and John W. Florin. *Atlas of American Agriculture: The American Cornucopia.* New York: Macmillan, 1996.

Pollan, Michael. *Second Nature: A Gardener's Education.* New York: Laurel, 1992.

Powers, Jo Marie, and Anita Stewart, editors. *Northern Bounty: A Celebration of Canadian Cuisine.* Mississauga, Ontario: Random House of Canada Ltd., 1995.

Powers, William K., and Marla N. Powers. "Metaphysical Aspects of an Oglala Food System." In *Food in the Social Order: Studies of Food and Festivities in Three American Communities*, edited by Mary Douglas, 40–96. New York: Russell Sage Foundation, 1984.

Pritchett, James. "Amish Cuisine: Pennsylvania Dutch Cooking at Its Best." *Revue Française D'Études Américaines* 11, 27–28 (February 1986): 67–75.

Prosterman, Leslie. "Food and Alliance at the County Fair." *Western Folklore* 40, 1 (January 1981): 81–90.

———. "Food and Celebration: A Kosher Caterer as Mediatior of Communal Traditions." In *Ethnic and Regional Foodways in the United States: The Performance of Group Identity*, edited by Linda Keller Brown and Kay Mussell, 127–42. Knoxville: University of Tennessee Press, 1984.

Pyle, Jane. "Farmers' Markets in the United States: Functional Anachronisms." *Geographical Review* 61, 2 (April 1971): 167–97.

Quandt, Sara A., Joan B. Popyach, and Kathleen M. DeWalt. "Home Gardening and Food Preservation Practices of the Elderly in Rural Kentucky." *Ecology of Food and Nutrition* 31, 3–4 (1994): 183–99.

Randall, Elizabeth, and Diva Sanjur. "Food Preferences—Their Conceptualization and Relationship to Consumption." *Ecology of Food and Nutrition* 11, 3 (1981): 151–61.

Raspa, Richard. "Exotic Foods among Italian-Americans in Mormon Utah: Food as Nostalgic Enactment of Identity." In *Ethnic and Regional Foodways in the United States: The Performance of Group Identity*, edited by Linda Keller Brown and Kay Mussell, 185–94. Knoxville: University of Tennessee Press, 1984.

Ratcheson, Peggy Steiner. "Food and Fashion in United States Society: The Mass-Culturalization of Gourmet Cookery." Ph.D. diss., Washington University, 1986.

Rauche, Anthony T. "*Festa Italiana* in Hartford, Connecticut: The Pastries, the Pizza, and the People Who 'Parla Italiano'." In *"We Gather Together": Food and Festival in American Life*, edited by Theodore C. Humphrey and Lin T. Humphrey, 205–17. Logan: Utah State University Press, 1991.

Reinecke, George F. "The New Orleans Twelfth Night Cake," *Louisiana Folklore Miscellany* 2, 2 (1965): 45–54.

Rikoon, J. Sanford. "Ethnic Food Traditions: A Review and Preview of Folklore Scholarship." *Kentucky Folklore Record* 28, 1–2 (January–June 1982): 12–25.

Ritzer, George. "The 'McDonaldization' of Society." *Journal of American Culture* 6, 1 (Spring 1983): 100–107.

Roark, Michael. "Fast Foods: American Food Regions." *North American Culture* 2, 1 (1985): 24–36.

Rooney, John F., Jr., and Paul L. Butt. "Beer, Bourbon and Boone's Farm: A Geographical Examination of Alcoholic Drink in the United States." *Journal of Popular Culture* 11, 4 (Spring 1978): 832–56.

Root, Waverly. *Food: An Authoritative and Visual History and Dictionary of the Foods of the World.* New York: Simon and Schuster, 1980.

Root, Waverly, and Richard de Rochemont. *Eating in America: A History.* New York: Wm. Morrow, 1976.

Rorabaugh, W. J. "Beer, Lemonade, and Propriety in the Gilded Age." In *Dining in America 1850–1900*, edited by Kathryn Grover, 24–46. Amherst: University of Massachusetts Press, 1987.

Ross, Alice. "Corn: Stone-Age and Iron-Age Confrontations in North American Colonies." In *Food in Motion: The Migration of Foodstuffs and Cookery Techniques.* Proceedings of the Oxford Symposium of Food and Cookery, 1983. Edited by Alan Davidson, 23–37. Leeds: Prospect Books, Ltd., 1983.

Rozin, Elisabeth, and Paul Rozin. "Some Surprising Unique Characteristics of Human Food Preferences." In *Food in Perspective.* Proceedings of the Third International Conference on Ethnological Food Research, 1977. Edited by Alexander Fenton and Trefor M. Owen, 243–52. Edinburgh: John Donald, 1981.

Sackett, Marjorie. "Folk Recipes as a Measure of Intercultural Penetration." *Journal of American Folklore* 85, 335 (January–March 1972): 77–81.

———. "Recipes." In *Kansas Folklore*, edited by S. J. Sackett and William E. Koch, 226–38. Lincoln: University of Nebraska Press, 1961.

Sacks, Maurie. "Computing Community at Purim." *Journal of American Folklore* 102, 405 (July–September 1989): 275–91.

Sanjur, Diva. *Hispanic Foodways, Nutrition, and Health.* Boston: Allyn and Bacon, 1995.

———. *Social and Cultural Perspectives in Nutrition.* Englewood Cliffs, New Jersey: Prentice-Hall, 1982.

Sauder, Robert A. "Municipal Markets in New Orleans." *Journal of Cultural Geography* 2, 1 (Fall–Winter 1981): 82–95.

Schinto, Jeanne. "The Art of Eating Words." *Yale Review* 79, 3 (Spring 1990): 489–500.

Schofield, Mary Anne, editor. *Cooking by the Book: Food in Literature and Culture.* Bowling Green, Ohio: Bowling Green State University Popular Press, 1989.

Schoonover, David, editor. *The Cincinnati Cookbook.* Iowa City: University of Iowa Press, 1994.

————. *P.E.O. Cook Book.* Iowa City: University of Iowa Press, 1992.

Schrock, Earl F. Jr. "Traditional Arkansas Foodways." In *An Arkansas Folklore Sourcebook,* edited by W. K. McNeil and William M. Clements, 172–211. Fayetteville: University of Arkansas Press, 1992.

Schroedl, Alan. "The Dish Ran Away with the Spoon: Ethnography of Kitchen Culture." In *The Cultural Experience: Ethnography in a Complex Society,* edited by James Spradley and David W. McCurdy, 177–89. Chicago: Science Research Associates, 1972.

Schul, David E. "A State-Fair View of Midwestern Food." Master's thesis, University of Kansas, 1997.

Seaton, Beverly. " 'Making the Best of Circumstances': The American Woman's Back Yard Garden." In *Making the American Home: Middle-Class Women and Domestic Material Culture 1840–1940,* edited by Marilyn Ferris Motz and Pat Browne, 90–104. Bowling Green, Ohio: Bowling Green State University Popular Press, 1988.

Shakow, Don. "The Municipal Farmer's Market as an Urban Service." *Economic Geography* 57, 1 (January 1981): 68–77.

Shapiro, Anna. *A Feast of Words: For Lovers of Food and Fiction.* New York: W. W. Norton, 1996.

Shapiro, Laura. *Perfection Salad: Women and Cooking at the Turn of the Century.* New York: Farrar, Straus and Giroux, 1986.

————. "Do Women Like to Cook?" *Granta* 52 (Winter 1995): 153–62.

Sherman, Sharon R. "The Passover Seder: Ritual Dynamics, Foodways, and Family Folklore." In *"We Gather Together": Food and Festival in American Life,* edited by Theodore C. Humphrey and Lin T. Humphrey, 27–42. Logan: Utah State University Press, 1991.

Shifflett, Peggy A. "Folklore and Food Habits." *Journal of the American Dietetic Association* 68, 4 (April 1976): 347–50.

Shortridge, Barbara G., and James R. Shortridge. "Consumption of Fresh Produce in the Metropolitan United States." *Geographical Review* 79, 1 (January 1989): 79–98.

————. "Cultural Geography of American Foodways: An Annotated Bibliography." *Journal of Cultural Geography* 15, 2 (Spring–Summer 1995): 79–108.

Shortridge, James R., and Barbara G. Shortridge. "Patterns of American Rice Consumption 1955 and 1980." *Geographical Review* 73, 4 (October 1983): 417–29.

Silverman, Deborah Anders. "Folklore's Contribution to the Development of Ethnicity among Polish-Americans in Western New York." Ph.D. diss., State University of New York at Buffalo, 1996.

Simoons, Frederick J. *Eat Not This Flesh: Food Avoidances from Prehistory to the Present.* Second edition. Madison: The University of Wisconsin Press, 1994.

Sims, Martha Caroline. "An Analysis of Food and Foodways in Contemporary Women's Fiction." Master's thesis, Ohio State University, 1989.

Singer, Eliot A. "Conversion through Foodways Enculturation: The Meaning of

Eating in an American Hindu Sect." In *Ethnic and Regional Foodways in the United States: The Performance of Group Identity*, edited by Linda Keller Brown and Kay Mussell, 195–214. Knoxville: University of Tennessee Press, 1984.

Skillman, Amy E. "No Smoke? No Fire: Contemporary Hamming the Ol' Fashioned Way." In *"We Gather Together": Food and Festival in American Life*, edited by Theodore C. Humphrey and Lin T. Humphrey, 125–36. Logan: Utah State University Press, 1991.

Smith, Stephen A. "Food for Thought: Comestible Communication and Contemporary Southern Culture." In *American Material Culture: The Shape of Things around Us*, edited by Edith Mayo, 208–17. Bowling Green, Ohio: Bowling Green State University Popular Press, 1984.

Sobal, Jeffery, William Alex McIntosh, and William Whit. "Teaching the Sociology of Food, Eating, and Nutrition." *Teaching Sociology* 21,1 (January 1993): 50–59.

Sokolov, Raymond. *Fading Feast: A Compendium of Disappearing American Regional Foods*. New York: Farrar, Straus and Giroux, 1981.

———. *Why We Eat What We Eat: How the Encounter between the New World and the Old Changed the Way Everyone on the Planet Eats*. New York: Summit Books, 1991.

———. "Everyman's Muffins." *Natural History* 94, 6 (June 1985): 82–85.

———. "Shades of Carolina Rice." *Natural History* 102, 2 (February 1993): 70–72.

Sommer, Robert. *Farmers' Markets of America: A Renaissance*. Santa Barbara, California: Capra Press, 1980.

Sommer, Robert, John Herrick, and Ted R. Sommer. "The Behavioral Ecology of Supermarkets and Farmers' Markets." *Journal of Environmental Psychology* 1,1 (March 1981): 13–19.

Sommer, Robert, Margot Stumpf, and Henry Bennett. "Quality of Farmers' Market Produce: Flavor and Pesticide Residues." *Journal of Consumer Affairs* 16, 1 (Summer 1982): 130–35.

Sommer, Robert, Margaret Wing, and Susan Aitkins. "Price Savings to Consumers at Farmers' Markets." *Journal of Consumer Affairs* 14, 2 (Winter 1980): 452–62.

Spindler, Audrey A., and Janice D. Schultz. "Comparison of Dietary Variety and Ethnic Food Consumption among Chinese, Chinese-American, and White American Women." *Agriculture and Human Values* 13, 3 (Summer 1996): 64–73.

Starr, Kathy. *The Soul of Southern Cooking*. Jackson: University Press of Mississippi, 1989.

Stedman, Jane W. "Edna Ferber and Menus with Meanings." *Journal of American Culture* 2, 3 (Fall 1979): 454–62.

Steelman, Virginia Purtle. "Socio-cultural Factors Related to Food Habits and Attitudes in Selected Louisiana Communities." Ph.D. diss., The Louisiana State University and Agricultural and Mechanical College, 1972.

Steiner, Rodney. "Drinking-Place Names in the Central United States." *Journal of Cultural Geography* 6, 2 (Spring–Summer 1986): 19–34.

Stern, Jane, and Michael Stern. *Eat Your Way across the U.S.A.* New York: Broadway Books, 1997.

————. *Goodfood.* New York: Alfred A. Knopf, 1983.

————. *Roadfood.* Revised edition. New York: HarperCollins Publishers, 1992.

————. *Roadfood and Goodfood.* New York: Alfred A. Knopf, 1986.

————. *A Taste of America.* Kansas City: Andrews and McMeel, 1988.

————. "America's Vernacular Cuisine: The Food That Dare Not Speak Its Name." In *A Conference on Current Research in Culinary History: Sources, Topics, and Methods.* Proceedings, 1985. Edited by Jillian Strang, Bonnie Brown, and Patricia Kelly, 162–63. Hingham, Massachusetts: Culinary Historians of Boston, 1986.

Stewart, George R. *American Ways of Life.* New York: Doubleday & Company, 1954.

Story, Richard David. "Boutique Farmers: The New Age of Agrarians." *New York* 26, 38 (September 27, 1993): 42–48.

Summers, Bill. "Wild Spring Greens." *Missouri Folklore Society Journal* 10 (1988): 51–60.

Szathmary, Louis. "How Festive Foods of the Old World Became Commonplace in the New, or the American Perception of Hungarian Goulash." In *Food in Motion: The Migration of Foodstuffs and Cookery Techniques.* Proceedings of the Oxford Symposium on Food and Cookery, 1983. Edited by Alan Davidson, 137–43. Leeds: Prospect Books, Ltd., 1983.

Tangires, Helen. "American Lunch Wagons." *Journal of American Culture* 13, 2 (Summer 1990): 91–108.

————. "Contested Space: The Life and Death of Center Market." *Washington History* 7, 1 (Spring–Summer 1995): 46–67.

Taylor, Joe Gray. *Eating, Drinking, and Visiting in the South: An Informal History.* Baton Rouge: Louisiana State University Press, 1982.

Tebbetts, Diane. "Food as an Ethnic Marker." *Pioneer America Society, Transactions* 7 (1984): 81–88.

Terry, Rhonda D., and Mary A. Bass. "Food Practices of Families in an Eastern Cherokee Township." *Ecology of Food and Nutrition* 14, 1 (1984): 63–70.

Teufel, Nicolette I., and Lisa K. Staten, editors. *S.N.A.C.* (A Collection of Syllabi for Nutritional Anthropology Courses). Washington, D.C.: The Council on Nutritional Anthropology, 1991.

Theodoratus, Robert J. "The Changing Patterns of Greek Foodways in America." In *Food in Motion: The Migration of Foodstuffs and Cookery Techniques.* Proceedings of the Oxford Symposium on Food and Cookery, 1983. Edited by Alan Davidson, 87–104. Leeds: Prospect Books, Ltd., 1983.

————. "Greek Immigrant Cuisine in America: Continuity and Change." In *Food in Perspective.* Proceedings of the Third International Conference on Ethnological Food Research, 1977. Edited by Alexander Fenton and Trefor M. Owen, 313–23. Edinburgh: John Donald, 1981.

————. "Rags to Riches: Salmon's Rise from Poor Man's Food to Gourmand's Delicacy." In *Food Conservation: Ethnological Studies.* Proceedings of the Seventh International Ethnological Food Research Conference, 1987. Edited by Astri Riddervold and Andreas Ropeid, 169–76. London: Prospect Books, Ltd. 1988.

Theophano, Janet. "It's Really Tomato Sauce But We Call It Gravy: A Study of Food and Women's Work among Italian-American Families." Ph.D. diss., University of Pennsylvania, 1982.

————. "A Life's Work: Women Writing from the Kitchen." In *Fields of Folklore: Essays in Honor of Kenneth S. Goldstein*, edited by Roger D. Abrahams, 287–99. Bloomington, Indiana: Trickster Press, 1995.

Tice, Patricia M. "Gardens of Change." In *American Home Life, 1880–1930: A Social History of Spaces and Services*, edited by Jessica H. Foy and Thomas J. Schlereth, 190–208. Knoxville: University of Tennessee Press, 1992.

Time-Life Editors. *The Time-Life American Regional Cookbook*. Boston: Little, Brown and Company, 1978.

Trillin, Calvin. *Alice, Let's Eat: Further Adventures of a Happy Eater*. New York: Random House, 1978.

————. *American Fried: Adventures of a Happy Eater*. Garden City, New York: Doubleday & Company, 1974.

————. *Third Helpings*. New Haven, Connecticut: Ticknor & Fields, 1983.

Trulson, Martha. "The American Diet: Past and Present." *American Journal of Clinical Nutrition* 7, 1 (January–February 1959): 91–97.

Tuchman, Gaye, and Harry Gene Levine. "New York Jews and Chinese Food: The Social Construction of an Ethnic Pattern." *Journal of Contemporary Ethnography* 22, 3 (October 1993): 382–407.

Underhill, Linda, and Jeanne Nakjavani. "Food for Fiction: Lessons from Ernest Hemingway's Writing." *Journal of American Culture* 15, 2 (Summer 1992): 87–90.

van den Berghe, Pierre L. "Ethnic Cuisine: Culture in Nature." *Ethnic and Racial Studies* 7, 3 (July 1984): 387–97.

Van Esterik, Penny. "Celebrating Ethnicity: Ethnic Flavor in an Urban Festival." *Ethnic Groups* 4, 4 (1982): 207–27.

Vance, Rupert. "Climate, Diet, and Human Adequacy." In *Human Geography of the South: A Study in Regional Resources and Human Adequacy*, by Rupert Vance, 411–41. Chapel Hill: University of North Carolina Press, 1932.

Verano, Luis F. "A Fruit for All Seasons: The Pear's Long Journey West." *Journal of the West* 17, 2 (April 1978): 94–104.

Vietmeyer, Noel. "Exotic Edibles Are Altering America's Diet and Agriculture." *Smithsonian* 16, 9 (December 1985): 34–43.

Villas, James. *American Taste: A Celebration of Gastronomy Coast-to-Coast*. New York: Arbor House, 1982.

Visser, Margaret. *Much Depends on Dinner: The Extraordinary History and Mythology, Allure and Obsession, Perils and Taboos of an Ordinary Meal*. New York: Grove Press, 1986.

————. *The Rituals of Dinner: The Origins, Evolution, Eccentricities, and Meaning of Table Manners*. New York: Grove Press, 1991.

Wachs, Eleanor. " 'To Toast the Bake': The Johnston Family Clambake." In *"We Gather Together": Food and Festival in American Life*, edited by Theodore C. Humphrey and Lin T. Humphrey, 75–87. Logan: Utah State University Press, 1991.

Wallendorf, Melanie, and Michael D. Reilly. "Ethnic Migration, Assimilation, and Consumption." *Journal of Consumer Research* 10, 3 (December 1983): 292–302.

Waters, Alice. "The Farm-Restaurant Connection." *Antaeus* 68 (Spring 1992): 96–104.

Weaver, William Woys. *America Eats: Forms of Edible Folk Art.* New York: Harper & Row, 1989

———. *Sauerkraut Yankees: Pennsylvania-German Foods and Foodways.* Philadelphia: University of Pennsylvania Press, 1983.

———. "From Turtle to Tripe: Philadelphia Pepperpot, a Street Food from the West Indies." In *Public Eating.* Proceedings of the Oxford Symposium on Food and Cookery, 1991. Edited by Harlan Walker, 287–94. London: Prospect Books, Ltd., 1992.

———. "*Die Geschickte Hausfrau:* The First Ethnic Cookbook in the United States." In *Food in Perspective.* Proceedings of the Third International Conference on Ethnological Food Research, 1977. Edited by Alexander Fenton and Trefor M. Owen, 343–63. Edinburgh: John Donald, 1981.

———. "White Gravies in American Popular Diet." In *Food in Change: Eating Habits from the Middle Ages to the Present Day.* Proceedings of the Fifth International Conference on Ethnological Food Research, 1983. Edited by Alexander Fenton and Eszter Kisbán, 41–52. Edinburgh: John Donald, 1986.

Weiner, Mark. "Consumer Culture and Participatory Democracy: The Story of Coca-Cola during World War II." *Food and Foodways* 6, 2 (1996): 109–29.

Weintraub, Linda, editor. *Art What Thou Eat: Images of Food in American Art.* Mount Kisco, New York: Moyer Bell Ltd, 1991.

Welsch, Roger L. "American Pie." *Natural History* 104, 10 (October 1995): 30–31.

———. "American Plains Indian Ethnogastronomy." In *Ethnologische Nahrungsforschung: Ethnological Food Research.* Reports from the Second International Symposium for Ethnological Food Research, 1973. Edited by Nilo Valonen and Juhani Lehtonen, 319–26. Helsinki, Finland, 1975.

———. "An Interdependence of Foodways and Architecture: A Foodways Context on the American Plains." In *Food in Perspective.* Proceedings of the Third International Conference on Ethnological Food Research, 1977. Edited by Alexander Fenton and Trefor M. Owen, 365–76. Edinburgh: John Donald, 1981.

———. "We Are What We Eat: Omaha Food as Symbol." *Keystone Folklore Quarterly* 16 (Winter 1971): 165–70.

Welsch, Roger L., and Linda K. Welsch. *Cather's Kitchens: Foodways in Literature and Life.* Lincoln: University of Nebraska Press, 1987.

Wenkam, Nao S., and Robert J. Wolff. "A Half Century of Changing Food Habits among Japanese in Hawaii." *Journal of the American Dietetic Association* 57, 6 (July 1970): 29–32.

Western, John. *A Passage to England.* Minneapolis: University of Minnesota Press, 1992.

Wheaton, Barbara Ketchum. *A Bibliography for Culinary Historians: Using the Harvard University Libraries and the Arthur and Elizabeth Schlesinger Library on the History of Women in America.* Cambridge, Massachusetts: n.p., 1985.

Wheaton, Barbara, and Patricia Kelly, compilers. *Bibliography of Culinary History: Food Resources in Eastern Massachusetts.* Boston: G. K. Hall, 1988.

Whelan, James Patrick, Jr. "From Forest, Stream, and Sea: Aspects of Self-Sufficiency in the Nineteenth-Century Louisiana Diet." Ph.D. diss., Louisiana State University, 1989.

Whit, William C. *Food and Society: A Sociological Approach.* Dix Hills, New York: General Hall, Inc., 1995.

Whit, William C., and Yvonne Lockwood, editors. *Teaching Food and Society: A Collection of Syllabi and Instructional Materials.* College Station, Texas: Association for the Study of Food and Society, 1990.

Whitaker, Jan. "Catering to Romantic Hunger: Roadside Tearooms, 1909–1930." *Journal of American Culture* 15, 4 (Winter 1992): 17–25.

Whitehead, Tony. "Sociocultural Dynamics and Food Habits in a Southern Community." In *Food in the Social Order: Studies of Food and Festivities in Three American Communities,* edited by Mary Douglas, 97–142. New York: Russell Sage Foundation, 1984.

Whorten, J. C. "Eating to Win: Popular Concepts of Diet, Strength, and Energy in the Early Twentieth Century." In *Fitness in American Culture,* edited by Kathryn Grover, 86–122. Amherst: University of Massachusetts Press, 1989.

Williams, Brett. "Why Migrant Woman Feed Their Husbands Tamales: Foodways as a Basis for a Revisionist View of Tejano Family Life." In *Ethnic and Regional Foodways in the United States: The Performance of Group Identity,* edited by Linda Keller Brown and Kay Mussell, 113–26. Knoxville: University of Tennessee Press, 1984.

Williams, Jacqueline B. *The Way We Ate: Pacific Northwest Cooking, 1843–1900.* Pullman: Washington State University Press, 1996.

———. *Wagon Wheel Kitchens: Food on the Oregon Trail.* Lawrence: University Press of Kansas, 1993.

Williams, John Alexander. "From Backyard Garden to Agribusiness: Italian-American Foodways in the West." *Folklife Center News* 11, 2 (Spring 1989): 4–6.

Wilson, Christine S. "Food—Custom and Nurture: An Annotated Bibliography on Sociocultural and Biocultural Aspects of Nutrition." *Journal of Nutrition Education* 11, 4 (October–December 1979) Supplement 1: 213–63.

Wolf, Thomas H. "Once upon a Time a Cookbook Was a Recipe for Excess." *Smithsonian* 22, 8 (November 1991): 118–31.

Wolfe, Wendy S., Charles W. Weber, and Katherine Dahozy Arviso. "Use and Nutrient Composition of Traditional Navajo Foods." *Ecology of Food and Nutrition* 17, 4 (1985): 323–44.

Yang, Grace I-Ping and Hazel M. Fox. "Food Habit Changes of Chinese Persons Living in Lincoln, Nebraska." *Journal of American Dietetic Association* 75, 4 (October 1979): 420–24.

Yergin, Marc. "The Demographics of Gardening." *American Demographics* 7, 4 (April 1985): 34–37.

Yoder, Don. "Folk Cookery." In *Folklore and Folklife: An Introduction,* edited by Richard M. Dorson, 325–50. Chicago: University of Chicago Press, 1972.

———. "Historical Sources for American Traditional Cookery." In *Discovering American Folklife,* by Don Yoder, 115–41. Ann Arbor: UMI Research Press, 1990.

————. "Pennsylvanians Call It Mush." *Pennsylvania Folklife* 13, 2 (Winter 1962–1963): 44–53.

————. "Sauerkraut in Pennsylvania Folk-Culture." *Pennsylvania Folklife* 12, 2 (Summer 1961): 56–69.

————. "The Sausage Culture of the Pennsylvania Germans." In *Food in Perspective*. Proceedings of the Third International Conference on Ethnological Food Research, 1977. Edited by Alexander Fenton and Trefor M. Owen, 409–25. Edinburgh: John Donald, 1981.

————. "Schnitz in the Pennsylvania Folk-Culture." *Pennsylvania Folklife* 12, 3 (Fall 1961): 44–53.

Zanger, Jules. "Food and Beer in an Immigrant Society." *Society* 33, 5 (July–August 1996): 61–63.

Zelinsky, Wilbur. "The Roving Palate: North America's Ethnic Restaurant Cuisines." *Geoforum* 16, 1 (1985): 51–72.

————. "You Are Where You Eat." *American Demographics* 9, 7 (July 1987): 30–33.

Zwicky, Ann D., and Arnold M. Zwicky. "America's National Dish: The Style of Restaurant Menus." *American Speech: A Quarterly of Linguistic Usage* 55, 2 (Summer 1980): 83–92.

Index

About the Contributors

CARY W. DE WIT recently received a Ph.D. in geography from the University of Kansas. His dissertation on sense of place in the American High Plains explores ways in which a landscape can affect the mood and character of people. Currently he is an instructor at the University of Alaska at Fairbanks.

STEPHEN FRENKEL, a native of the Pacific Northwest, is a visiting assistant professor of geography at the University of Washington. Beyond his interest in coffee, he studies the commodification of culture in modern America and the landscapes of colonialism in Africa and Latin America.

C. PAIGE GUTIERREZ holds a doctorate in anthropology from the University of North Carolina. Her interests in Southern folk culture are reflected in a book, *Cajun Foodways* (University Press of Mississippi, 1992), and an appointment by the Mississippi Committee for the Humanities as scholar-in-residence for Biloxi.

MARJORIE A. HOOVER is retired in Duluth, Minnesota. After studying at Washington State University, she worked as a home economist in several west-coast cities and in the Duluth area. She also has undertaken free-lance writing assignments for the Minnesota Historical Society and other studies about local and regional history.

JAMES F. HOY, a professor of English at Emporia State University, is an authority on ranching in Kansas. He is the author of *The Cattle Guard: Its History and Lore* (University Press of Kansas, 1982), and was the compiler/editor for *Prairie Poetry: Cowboy Verse of Kansas* (Wichita Eagle and Beacon Publishing Co., 1995).

LYNNE IRELAND is associate director of the Nebraska State Historical Society in charge of museums and historic sites. She holds a M.A. in American folk culture from the Cooperstown Graduate Program (University College at Oneonta/New York State Historical Society) and, besides traditional foodways, has an interest in undergarments as a reflection of cultural attitudes toward women. She currently is producing a television history of Nebraska.

THOMAS D. ISERN is a professor of history at North Dakota State University. His interests, at the interface of folklore and history, are demonstrated in *Custom Combining on the Great Plains: A History* (University of Oklahoma Press, 1981) and in *Bull Threshers and Bindlestiffs: Harvesting and Threshing on the North American Plains* (University Press of Kansas, 1990).

ANNE R. KAPLAN serves as editor of *Minnesota History* and of the Minnesota Historical Society Press. Her doctoral dissertation at the University of Pennsylvania examined ethnic foodways in Minnesota. She also has written a history of the Folk Arts Foundation of America.

JAMES L. KELLY, a professor of geography at the University of Hawaii at Hilo, has interests in both American and Asian culture. He has written about the history of land grants in Hawaii, the images of Paris in the 1920s, and the characteristics of places where novelists elect to live.

CHARLES F. KOVACIK, a professor of geography at the University of South Carolina, is an authority on Southern culture. He is the coauthor, with John Winberry, of *South Carolina: A Geography* (Westview Press, 1987) and has studied land-use changes on former plantations and the role of health conditions and images in the growth of cities.

HARRY GENE LEVINE is a professor of sociology at City University of New York-Queens College. When not eating Chinese food, he writes about issues of alcohol and drug abuse and about the general process of social disorganization. Another interest is the history of sociology.

GEORGE H. LEWIS was born in Maine but has spent his professional career in California where he is a professor of sociology at the University of the Pacific. His publications include *Side-Saddle on the Golden Calf: Social Structure and Popular Culture in America* (Goodyear Publishing Co., 1972) and *All That Glitters: Country Music in America* (Bowling Green State University Popular Press, 1993).

TIMOTHY C. LLOYD is the director of folklife programs at Cityfolk in Dayton, Ohio. While working at the American Folklife Center in Washington, D.C., he coauthored *Folklife Resources in the Library of Congress* (American Folklife Center, 1994). He also has written *Lake Erie Fisherman: Work, Identity, and Tradition* with Patrick Mullen (University of Illinois Press, 1990).

WILLIAM G. LOCKWOOD is an associate professor of anthropology at the University of Michigan. His book *European Moslems: Economy and Ethnicity in Western Bosnia* (Academic Press, 1975) reflects an ongoing interest in ethnic theory and the ethnology of peasant cultures. He also is a former coeditor of *The Digest: A Newsletter for the Interdisciplinary Study of Food.*

YVONNE R. LOCKWOOD is the Folklife Extension Specialist at the Michigan State University Museum at East Lansing. She is coeditor of the *Michigan Folklore Reader* (Michigan State University Press, 1987) and the author of *Text and Context: Folksong in a Bosnian Muslim Village* (Slavica Publishers, 1983).

SABINA MAGLIOCCO is a folklorist and an assistant professor of anthropology at California State University-Northridge. She has written *The Two Madonnas: The Politics of Festival in a Sardinian Community* (Peter Lang, 1993) and was named a 1996 Guggenheim Fellow to study ritual among American neopagans.

JOSEPH T. MANZO, a professor of geography at Concord College in West Virginia, grew up in the diner country of northeastern Pennsylvania. He has wide-ranging interests that include Islamic culture, sports geography, and ethnicity. He also has written extensively about attitudes of nineteenth-century Native Americans toward the process of removal.

JOHN A. MILBAUER is an associate professor in the Department of Geography and Sociology at Northeastern State University in Tahlequah, Oklahoma. Although a New Yorker by birth, his interests are in the cultural geography of the West, including the landscapes of mining.

WILLARD B. MOORE holds a doctorate in folklore from Indiana University. He has interests in folk art, material culture, and festivals, and has served on the staffs of the Minnesota Historical Society and the University of Minnesota Art Museum. He is editor of *Circles of Tradition: Folk Arts in Minnesota* (University of Minnesota Art Museum, 1989).

MICHAEL O. ROARK teaches in the Department of Earth Sciences at Southeast Missouri State University. With an interest in culture regions, he has studied French, German, and mining settlements in Missouri and the early migration patterns into Indian Territory and Oklahoma.

GAYE TUCHMAN is a professor of sociology at the University of Connecticut. Her interests in gender and the media are suggested by the titles of two of her books: *The TV Establishment: Programming for Power and Profit* (Prentice-Hall, 1974) and *Hearth and Home: Images of Women in the Mass Media* (Oxford University Press, 1978), the latter with Arlene Daniels and James Benet.

WILBUR ZELINSKY is a professor emeritus at the Pennsylvania State University. He has been a pioneer in many areas of cultural and population geography including material culture, place names, and religion. His books include *The Cultural Geography of the United States* (Prentice-Hall, 1973) and *Exploring the Beloved Country* (University of Iowa Press, 1994).

About the Editors

BARBARA G. SHORTRIDGE is an assistant professor in the department of geography at the University of Kansas. She was born in the bratwurst and dairy land of southern Wisconsin and became interested in map design while an undergraduate at the University of Wisconsin. After working at Rand McNally in Chicago, she earned a doctorate at the University of Kansas. Marriage and the births of two daughters led to time away from academia and to stints of organizing nursery-school boards and teaching English to wives of international students. She published a series of articles on map symbolization in the late 1970s and early 1980s, but gradually became more interested in cultural geography, especially in issues of gender and everyday life in the United States. Her *Atlas of American Women* was published by Macmillan in 1987, and this has been followed by three studies about food. More foodways research is in the planning stage along with an article on the spread of household modernization across the Great Plains. A large perennial garden is her principal avocation.

JAMES R. SHORTRIDGE is a professor of geography at the University of Kansas. He was raised on fried chicken, bacon-seasoned green beans, and peach cobbler in Pleasant Hill, Missouri, and became a geographer by trying to figure out whether his home state was part of the West, South, or Midwest. He graduated from Dartmouth College and earned advanced degrees from the University of Kansas. After studying general agricultural issues in the early 1970s, he began to focus more on the cultural aspects of rural life. He has written about American religion and material culture but now concentrates on historical, perceptual issues. The growth of regional consciousness in the Great Plains is one ongoing concern. He has published three books, all with the University Press of Kansas: *Kaw Valley Landscapes: A Traveler's Guide to Northeastern*

Kansas (1988), *The Middle West: Its Meaning in American Culture* (1989), and *Peopling the Plains: Who Settled Where in Frontier Kansas* (1995). The Middle West book was supported by a Guggenheim Fellowship in 1979–1980. He recently retired from a long career in slow-pitch softball.